Copyright ©2010 by Mark Knight
Published by Cacti Knights
All Rights Reserved.

This book is for individual use only. The unauthorized reproduction, distribution, or sale of this material, including electronic reproductions is strictly prohibited. Please contact the publisher at for information regarding possible exceptions to this provision.

ISBN 978-0-9826533-2-6
Third edition: June 2015

www.waykiwayki.com

For Riley, Laine, Luke, Jagan

With special thanks to C & M, who separately presented the esoteric tools that once mastered gracefully peeled away the veil of Isis.

Preface
Where Are We Now?
    The Year 2010 .... - 2 -
    The True System Model .... - 3 -
    Cogs in the Wheel .... - 6 -
    Sheeople .... - 8 -
    Evolution & Change – Part 1 .... - 15 -

Spirituality
    Simply Explained .... - 28 -
    We have fallen as far as we can .... - 32 -
    Primary ways to raise vibration .... - 42 -
    Axioms .... - 54 -
    Manifestation .... - 55 -
    Reincarnation .... - 58 -
    Purpose .... - 60 -

Towards a Higher Vibration
    Chakras .... - 64 -
    Ingestion .... - 68 -
    Yogic Practice .... - 69 -
    Raja Yoga (Meditation) .... - 72 -
    Pineal Gland or Third eye .... - 78 -
    Techniques .... - 82 -
    Sexual energy .... - 85 -
    Synchronicities .... - 86 -
    DMT & Shamanism .... - 90 -
    The Journey is to the Self .... - 95 -

PART II – PROGRESSIVE KNOWLEDGE
    Glitches in the Matrix .... - 102 -
    Reality is an illusion? .... - 105 -
    Consciousness .... - 106 -
    Sacred Geometry .... - 109 -
    Times Past .... - 113 -

- Ancient Egypt Snippets .... - 113 -
- Religious Cult Snippets... - 117 -
- Christian Snippets .... - 127 -
- Hermetic Snippets .... - 138 -

Hermetic Laws
- The Law of Mentalism.. - 152 -
- The Law of Correspondence .... - 153 -
- The Law of Vibration.. - 154 -
- The Law of Polarity .... - 154 -
- The Law of Rhythm .... - 155 -
- The Law of Cause and Effect .... - 155 -
- The Law of Gender... - 156 -

Hermetic Qabalah Introduction

El Arbol De La Vida
- The Lightning Strike, Pillars, & Triads .... - 166 -
- Negative Existence... - 168 -
- The Four Worlds .... - 170 -
- The Veils... - 176 -
- The Temples of the Sephiroth .... - 178 -
- 1, Kether, The Crown. .... - 181 -
- 2, Chokmah, Wisdom.. - 183 -
- 3, Binah, Understanding. .... - 185 -
- 4, Chesed, Mercy. .... - 190 -
- 5, Geburah, Severity. .... - 192 -
- 6, Tipareth, Beauty.. - 195 -
- 7, Netzach, Victory.. - 198 -
- 8, Hod, Splendour .... - 200 -
- 10, Malkuth, Kingdom... - 205 -
- The Qlippoth .... - 208 -
- Paths Reference .... - 209 -

Numbers & Gematria
- Esoteric Numerical Symbols .... - 211 -

- Hebrew and Gematria .... - 214 -
- Qabalistic Numbers .... - 217 -

Elements & Astrology
- The Four Elements .... - 220 -
- The Zodiac & Planetary Bodies .... - 224 -

Tarot
- Major Arcana .... - 231 -
- Minor Arcana .... - 239 -
- Court Cards .... - 240 -
- Divination .... - 240 -

Dreams & Astral
- The Astral Plane .... - 243 -
- Mental Travelling .... - 250 -
- Astral Travelling .... - 251 -

Pathworking & Skrying
- Introduction .... - 256 -
- How to Skry upon the Tree .... - 258 -
- The Paths and Spheres .... - 262 -
- Entry to Tipareth .... - 272 -
- Deity Yoga .... - 281 -

The Unwritten Qabalah
- Introduction .... - 284 -
- Spiral Rocket Fuel .... - 285 -
- Diagrams .... - 287 -

Alchemy & The Philosophers' Stone
- Introduction .... - 298 -
- Alchemical Art .... - 306 -
- The Philosophers Stone .... - 312 -
- Conclusion .... - 315 -

Emerald Tablet Merkaba Ascension
- Introduction .... - 319 -

The Emerald Tablet	- 322 -
Prerequisites	- 324 -
The Merkaba Motors	- 327 -
Life Trajectory	- 329 -
Self Alignment	- 331 -
Dreams and Yesod	- 334 -
Daytime Work	- 338 -
Merkaba Rising	- 340 -
Descent	- 360 -

"Curious people are the ones who expose."

Preface

After the research undertaken to complete my first book, *Wayki Wayki*, it became crystal clear that the real wisdom within our realm lies with the adepts who have carried forth the knowledge from the ancient mystery schools, and also within the shamanic lineages from various ancient cultures. It became apparent that there is a secret history full of secret teachings, and that the history and reality we're fed by the absurd, corrupt, greedy world elite in the early 21st century is just a small fraction of what we actually are, and what actually is.

Through following synchronicities and signpost experiences I ended up at a self-initiatic temple of the mysteries in the Maya highlands. There I lived in a pyramid for a hundred days studying the esoteric unwritten Hermetic Qabalah and Hermetic Alchemy. My process included a 55 day silent meditative fast that allowed me to go deep enough into the Qabalistic archetypal world to push my consciousness and core being across an archetypal veil. Once there, I was able to glean how this ancient philosophy and science has held truth and wisdom that has stood fast throughout millennia, a truth that is wholly related to the authentic self.

After this experience, there was little rest, I was offered an adventurous quest high up a volcano to be guided one on one by a master of quantum physics, astrophysics and Hermetic Philosophy. This more recent hundred day process was mostly based around the Hermetic Emerald Table from ancient Egypt, along with Merkaba mysticism.

From both of these practical experiences it became indisputable that the esoteric traditions are based more on science than theology or myth, and that the occult, alchemical, esoteric, and yogic schools from various traditions can all take one to a very similar place. From this sacred place the world can be viewed how it really is, and not how one has learned it to be.

The very root of Hermetic Alchemy and the esoteric traditions has always been concerned with techniques that manipulate the human physiology, in turn creating altered states of consciousness that can then be nurtured. These states are then able to provide a supernatural intelligence, or state that *can* be used for practical purposes. Many leaps in evolution have come from the use of related mysticism and the associated altered states; in science, art, medicine, astronomy, and philosophy. With these leaps coming from a whole host of well known adepts and alchemists such as Pythagoras, Plato, Newton, Leonardo da Vinci, Alexander the great, Leibniz, Freud, Jung, Kepler, Gurdjieff, Steiner, plus many others.

Three main streams have helped to destroy much of the true wisdom that is inherent within our realm; the bigotry and repression within mainstream religions, the tyranny within the world elite, and group think within societies and cultures. For one example amongst the hundreds available; the Vatican holds most of the world's esoteric doctrines and scrolls from sources such as the library of Alexandria, the Essenes, and the Maya, but the Cardinals and Popes (that are themselves adepts of occult teachings) paradoxically throw at the people a man made exoteric, dogmatic, Egyptian based Catholicism. This example does not even take much objective neutral research or detective work to fully understand for oneself.

***

This book's main aim is to preserve some of the true ancient wisdom and to create a bridge to ones true self, and for us to see, feel and remember just how powerful our minds actually are. The techniques and archetypal handles explained in the latter chapters have stood up for millennia, and much symbolism around us in the modern world commemorates the ancient philosophy and science of Hermetics.

Many thousands of years ago the initiatic knowledge which evolved into that of the current Tibetan, Sufi, Yogic and Qabalistic streams were held in one type of schooling and priesthood. It is the ancient flood and the following fragmentation of race, language and culture that created the current diversity, but each path still has its roots still in full view. While we will look at Hermetic Qabalah and Alchemy, we are really just using these as tools to achieve a desired aim; the aim of taking core consciousness to a very special, sacred and practical place.

"Fruits from the past need to bear seeds again so that there are ripe fruits in the future"

In modern times, the words Hermetics, Qabalah, and Alchemy are rarely understood or even known by the masses. This book will explain it nice and easy from a more rational, physiological, psychological and scientific view, and certainly not from a Jewish, theological or new age view. Truth is really the only real religion there is, it is the only tangible thing to be worshiped, and truth can be explained without too much fluff.

The first few chapters will set up the necessary foundations because we cannot explain the inner workings of Hermetics before explaining some things about people, society, spirituality, science, history, and reality beforehand.

Before we continue, we should make it very clear that I am not a part of any of the secret societies which have carried forth the occult knowledge from the ancient mystery schools of Egypt, Persia, Greece and Rome. I am just another person amongst many searching for truth amidst a modern world full of beauty, love, colour, falsity, ego, fear, madness and folly.

The divulging of much of this information is taboo in many circles and is something I have recently contemplated many times, but I feel this book is a must due to the current time our species finds itself. The overriding factor in this internal debate is that no one owns truth, truth is available to anyone, it is self sufficient and doesn't need or seek followers. It just is. Truth has nothing to prove to anyone nor has any rules or dogma attached. It just is, and the mystics, adepts, and alchemists of the past, present and future will always speak the same truth.

"Sit down before fact like a child, and be prepared to give up every preconceived notion, follow humbly wherever and to whatever abysses nature leads, or you shall learn nothing."
Thomas Henry Huxley

PART I BELIEFS

"People's beliefs and convictions are in almost every case gotten at second-hand, and without examination, from authorities who have not themselves examined the questions at issue but have taken them at second-hand from oters."
Mark Twain

Where Are We Now?

The Year 2010

This book is really aimed to be read in future years, and before we look into anything like Merkaba mysticism we need to start at the start by recording some key truths of where our species currently finds itself in 2010. Some may look at some of this section as negative, but truth is truth, and ignorance, plus turning a blind eye to certain facts and issues evident in our world does not make them go away. Focusing purely on the countless positives and beauty of this realm also does not make facts go away either. A man may stroll out of his house and walk down the path under a blue sky to meet his beloved and feel the world is a jewel of unspeakable beauty, and in its purest essence this is completely true, but it does not disguise the fact there are some damaging and harmful agendas currently being carried out. Many of these are snowballing and they affect every single living organism on the planet plus all those soon to be born into life. Too many people think they are on this planet to admire the scenery and ensure that there are enough enjoyable distractions to create a wall of ignorance towards the authentic self, and the major imbalances of the world.

We should instead look at this section as a springboard for wanting ones personal power back, and to start thinking about balance and polarity. It is better to not view anything as positive or negative, it is clearer and of more truth to look at things as balance and imbalance. Too much of any energy slips into imbalance, for example, too much strength turns into anger, too much cold turns to freezing, and too much mercy turns into weakness. We will elaborate on this later.

Our species as a whole is currently imbalanced with self gain, greed, apathy, group think, nationalism, egoism, and materialism dominant.

Too many have no concern of others, of the ancient civilizations, or of the future generations to come. The saving grace is that the current status quo is not sustainable and the planet cannot and will not take the current norms much longer. A shift of consciousness is taking place and is currently gathering momentum. Post world war two, stability, normality, and a solid system was sold to the wanting defeated battered human, but this system of globalisation is now an out of control parasite upon the planet. But rest easy and do not fret because the current imbalance is necessary to create the friction for change. It is always darkest before dawn. As a fractal individual people do not like change, a person usually needs something inbalanced to happen before desiring change, before being ready to dare to change.

The True System Model

People are sold a false view of the model of power and how agendas and world policy are created and furthered. At present, and for recent decades, the large corporations, large banking cartels (also effectively corporations) and elements of secret societies have controlled media, governments, regulatory bodies, think tanks, energy, utilities, pharmaceuticals, food, military decisions, and therefore, the nations and the people.

Faster and faster we are seeing fewer corporations as they are being aggressively gobbled up and merged into the increasingly growing larger corporations.

The money turned over by of these massive corporations is much larger than that of most countries. Due to this, plus the facts that governments borrow money from banks at interest and receive funds from corporations, why is it we believe that governments hold the power? We think this due to the repeated official line booming out of the corporate controlled mainstream media. It's quite an ingenious system, and the true model looks like the following:

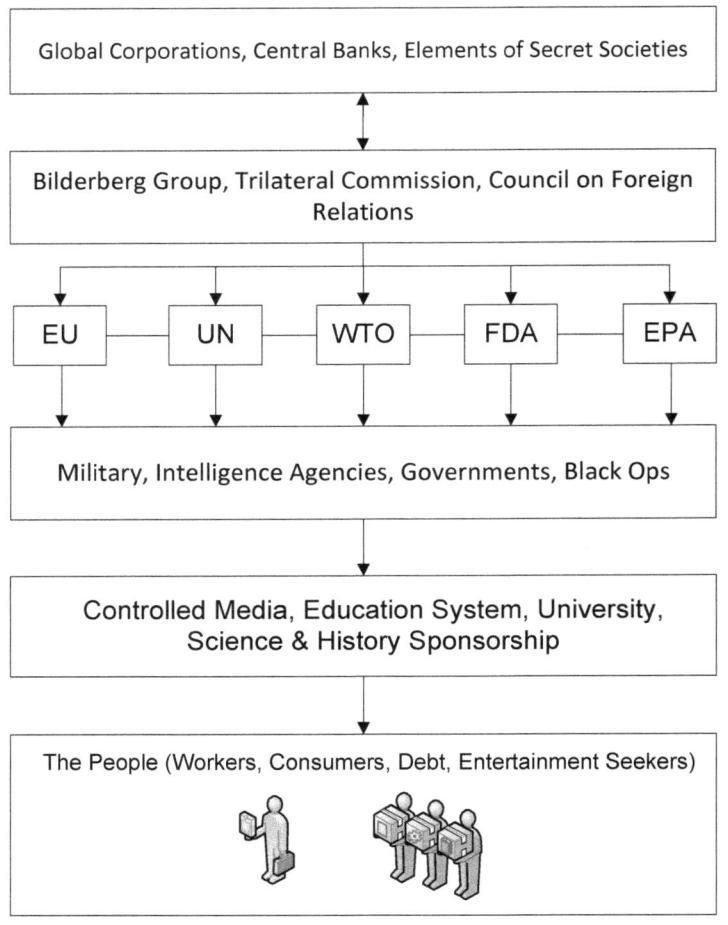

Note: European Union, United Nations, World Trade Organisation, Food & Drug Administration, Environment Protection Agency

The most important thing to know about this system is what is known as the revolving door, this is where the same unelected and relatively unknown people flitter between many parts of this system. For instance, one could sit on the Bilderberg meetings, be a finance minister and also be a consultant for a private black operations (unaccountable and illegally funded) military corporation, or, a government senator will sit on the FDA and also be a director of two large bio-tech food corporations.

What holds this whole system up is that the masses are groomed to fit into and support it via the educational and debt cogs. The people are perpetually fed the illusions of electoral democratic governments via the media. Those who stand for these illusory elections are groomed by the think tanks below the corporations and banks, and these electorates are really nothing more than public relations frontmen and spokespeople to further the agenda of the corporations and banks above. This has been going on for more than a hundred years and some elements of secret societies such as the Jesuits and the Freemasons (who were hijacked by the Illuminati) have been involved in creating and sustaining this model for even longer.

If you're interested in this subject matter, or you dispute it, start your research at the truths behind 9/11, the history of the French and US revolutions, or the rise of Knights Templar in the twelve hundreds. These three threads all take you to the same place and same set of truths. In the early 21st century this research was named "the conspiracy movement," and came about due to unfiltered direct access to information plus the mainstream media providing very little *real* journalism. Einstein said condemnation without investigation was the highest form of ignorance, alas, this is abundant in 2010.

In 2010 there are over 13,000 lodges and over seven million Freemasons worldwide. It must be stated that most members are oblivious to the esoteric lore and Rosicrucianism held at the highest levels of their order. The Freemasons are not bad per se, not by a long way, they have actually kept true spirituality alive amidst the age of materialism; keeping alight the symbolism and beliefs going back to Osiris and beyond. Masons swear oaths to study the hidden secrets of nature and science in order to better know ones maker, and many often do community and charity work. The films Avatar and The Matrix have strong Masonic and Gnostic links and both contained a wealth of beauty and positivity amongst deeper symbolism. But there is a point to make, and the notable change occurred in the late 18th century when Adam Weishaupt and his Bavarian Illuminati order infiltrated and effectively took over the Freemasons. Weishaupt's writings included that the final aim of the secret society was nothing less than to win power and riches to obtain mastery of the world. He drew diagrams showing how easy it was for one clear mind to direct hundreds of thousands of other minds. Freemasonry changed in this time for the worse, and medium and low level Masons are still oblivious to much of their true history, and to what goes on in the higher degrees.

Cogs in the Wheel

So what is the core problem with this current power model the worlds populous lives within? It is all based on the misuse of money and nature. Money in principle is an ideal system, in its raw essence it is a gauge of human energy exerted, an exchange system, but this system has evolved into a controlled beast that is greedy for only one thing, profit, and profit at any cost; forcing honesty to become naivety. It is this greed and desire for power that has fuelled the current unsustainable growth-oriented trajectory. Another factor being that money was delinked from limited precious metals to generate unlimited amounts of credit, and credit creates debt which creates profit.

> *"Only after the last tree has been cut down, only after the last river has been poisoned, only after the last fish has been caught, only then will you find that money cannot be eaten."*

With extreme profit and control being primary goals there leaves little or no care for pollution, resources, nature, or people. Instead there is the emphasis on the corrupt buying of legislation, people and poorer countries. The whole system is constantly promoting and delivering fear and a low vibration in many guises, none more evident than the current lie streams of world terror, manmade global warming, and pandemics. It is this manipulation and attack on the average person's energetic vibration with fear that is the biggest cause for concern at the time of writing.

The human organism should be in growth mode, and only sometimes have the need to be in protection mode when it is essentially required.

The human organism certainly cannot be in both at the same time. Due to the fear being peddled by this system we are forced into protection mode, we are on guard, ready to fight, focusing on surviving. Therefore, as most of our energy is spent on protection on an individual level, as a species we have not been growing.

Much could be written about the worst culprits heading up this corporatocracy we live under, but I urge you to research for yourself what the following really get up to: Monsanto, DuPont, Enron, WorldCom, Exxon, Chevron, BP, Shell, Halliburton, KPMG, Bechtel, AIG, Cargill, GE, Philip Morris, Wal-Mart, Coca Cola, Pfizer, Nestle, Carlisle Group, Procter & Gamble, and the Rothschild and Rockefeller dynasties. Just one hour of objective research could start to impede on a whole belief system.

The system is out of control and amongst scores of issues there are currently patented genetically modified unhealthy foods sold in mass through corporate supermarkets, the suppression of free energy, absurd rules, the non-stop manipulation to consume, and technology designed for profit instead of sustainability, efficiency or abundance.

At present another planned economic crash is gathering momentum and if this was not planned it would be the exception in history. The system has always created a problem so then it can implement the pre-planned solution once the reaction has been gleaned (problem, reaction, solution). In the case of the economic crisis the solution is that the large central banks will eat up the smaller banks and even nations, and the people will be groomed to accept a new world currency or a new electronic based currency held on a chip (along with personal information and history).

The western education system also fits snug into the model, it does little more than prepare children to be tax-paying workers to feed the system. The teachers are often young 'robots' who have never left the education system themselves, trained to deliver a curriculum they have no say in. The most outrageous thing is that most teachers don't even question the curriculum, a curriculum which has little regarding emotional or inner work, how to grow food, how to build a house, natural cycles, creativity, expression, community, nature, real substantial important history, or the mathematics behind mortgage repayments. Any of these teachings would give self power to people, but at the level of curriculum, the system strategically creates guards against such information and growth.

The best thing is not to fight or attack this system because anger and negativity feeds it. If you protest your heart is not at peace, and you only verify the enslavers. The best thing is to ignore it, and to live consciously with a small pure footprint that does nothing to support the system. Living consciously could mean asking yourself what bank you use, where your groceries are grown and by whom, what chemicals are in your deodorant, or carefully choosing your source of media for knowledge on what is going on in the world. The list of conscious living and conscious consuming is endless but it really does make a difference because you are one cell in the complete organism. Each affects the whole.

The problem with ignoring the system it is that it makes you feel bad to not be infected by cultural illusion because it's called alienation. The reason we feel alienated is because the society is infantile, trivial and stupid. So the cost of sanity in this society is a certain level of alienation.

None of these cogs are 'bad,' they embody, and are the manifestation of the human collective consciousness, and for a while longer many will continue to feed the causes without knowing it, and others will also attempt to heal at the symptom level, ignorant that things can only change at their root. The cogs are seemingly negative, but certain events create an awakening of the madness that resides within the repressed self. The more the madness, the more realisation, equating in more change brewing. This is always the way.

> "This moment is as it is, as it cannot be otherwise."
> Eckhart Tolle

Sheeople

> "People are machines governed by external influences, but each human can cease to be a Machine."

All people have goodness within them, and nearly everyone on the planet if given the choice or chance would spend their life helping the planet and the species with something that they loved doing. Most people with a natural (organic) upbringing seem to spend their lives in this mode anyway.

The system forces people to be locked in survival mode (the lowest circuit, Sephirah and chakra as we will see) needing money, which in this model is currently little more than biosurvival chips. The effect of this is that many people take a career or job purely to survive regardless of the jobs ethics, product, effect, or contribution to the future of the species or planet. In many cases the job that is performed helps to keep the whole system and status quo ticking along. With hundreds of millions of people living daily within the painful harmful effects of this system, there are hundreds of millions more spending their lives holding up and feeding this system via their careers and ego based consuming traits.

At present there are millions of people in costumes (uniforms) that enforce rules that keep this whole system model hanging together at its edges. They never question their rules and don't even know why their rules exist. They enforce them simply to "have a job" and to "earn biosurvival chips." Their souls have been bought, their minds have been neutralised, and they hinder the species. They are toxic.

Someone steals food, the system provides police, judges, courts, and cages (prisons), and then gives the person free food. Why not just give the person some food in the first place and cut the rest out?

As so many people are forced into this survival mode they are naturally forced to think of themselves first. For instance, an electricity bill rising twenty five percent (decided by a large corporation) is worse than half a million children dying in Iraq due to sanctions (also effectively decided by large corporations). It is worse because it only affects the 'me,' but it is this care for the 'me' over others that will invert collectively in the coming years...because it will need to.

We should be aware that this system knows just how malleable the human mind is, we are like sponges waiting for imprints and this is well known behind the curtain. Any person can learn Japanese, Arabic, or any other language, and can hold and recite whatever has been ingested. Even a girl in the nineties was barking on all fours in her teens after being raised in isolation as a dog! We can only know and be what we have fed and induced into our consciousness, therefore, the more inputs we have put into our minds from reading, mentors, experiences, history and cultures, the more we have to reference from to form our opinions and decisions. There is no human nature. There is only human behavior indicative to environments. These environments are both physical and psychological. Our minds are in essence not what we believe, but are simply storage containers, saying that, our minds also place a veil across our true essence.

What are beliefs anyway? They are not reality if we have not consciously chosen them. They create structures and limitations upon our reality. They reflect the conditioning of our environment, and we often possess conflicting beliefs that stop us from accomplishing our innermost desires.

Language and words are often looked at by the mind incorrectly too. Everyone uses a language, and for practical matters this is not a problem, but when a conversation enters a complex or abstract arena, people are rarely fully understood as they wish to be understood. Words just don't do the job well enough. People often argue when they soon realize that they are thinking the same thing, or vice versa. If we pick almost any word at random, for example, "earth," or "sensation," or " feeling," with just a little thought it soon becomes apparent that these words mean different things and conjure different images, conceptions, and associations in every single human mind on the planet. Words are used to condition humans, the list is endless, but a few are; program, consumer, should, surcharge, license, and weekday.

Opinions, perceptions, associations, (and even money) all help to fray truth, and this helps to keep truth more occult. But truth will always stand tall for those seriously wishing to seek and hunt it down. It seems wherever money is insufficient to bury truth, ignorance, propaganda, and short memories finish the job.

People need to find a word, a name, or a label for things, especially for things they don't understand or that they fear. Many think that if they have found a name for something then they understand it, but if one really thinks upon actual words themselves, one sees they often provide wrong associations, wrong clarifications and that the whole realm of language is completely subjective and vague.

The words I will use in this very book are written using a flawed language system that lacks a perfect ability to convey the complete truth. Therefore by default I'm fighting an uphill battle.

The true concepts behind words and language allow the people behind the mainstream media to attach images and shapes to words to continuously drive mind control grenades into the audience psyche to caveat against free thinking or curiosity. This sounds extreme, but in years to come this will be common knowledge and even possibly taught as history.

The aggressive delivery of entertainment, adverts and group think opinions via the controlled media molds literally hundreds of millions of people's perception of the world. It gives these people (maybe more appropriate to say 'biological media receivers') their self esteem and cultural standing gauges because for many it is the only source of input. The media keeps people in blindness and away from thinking about any real issues by selling people a trivial illusory world of fear, celebrity, fashion and gossip. It is quite ingenious but is now starting to fray at the seams. We are being sold a lie, but less and less people are now buying it.

The crowd generally does not want, or seek knowledge (even with nearly every text and book ever written accessible within their homes via the internet), and as the leaders of the crowd cleverly increase fear and a dislike of anything new, unknown, or mystical, the "group think giant" stands high and grows taller and taller.

To witness how the current slavery of mankind is based on fear, just look at what people spend their money on and where the biggest crowds are. These observations clearly show how people are in fear; looking for entertainment, observers, self-esteem, herds, and lovers, all to divert themselves from what is real, worldly important and deep within themselves.

> "Happy slaves are the most grim enemies of freedom."
> Marie von Ebner-Eschenbach

> "Humans are controlled to defend the madness that enslaves them."

> "When man becomes a willing slave he no longer needs chains, he becomes fond of his slavery, attached to it, fearing any different….this is the most damaging state the species can find itself."

> "Why keep slaves in a cage if you can make them pay everywhere they go."

The essence of many people died in childhood, they are often just imitations of others and a result of inputs from the surrounding culture. Apathy reigns supreme, apathy is the new religion, the new worship. People arrive home and close and lock the doors, they sigh in relief as they fall into a cosy armchair in a docile, passive mood, ready to receive more preconceived inputs from the TV. As well as closing the door, people close themselves too; closing feelings, closing their souls and true essence, running from expression within a closed society. It really is mass madness, and our children are going to laugh at this generation, or more probably, shake their heads in dismay.

If someone told you before you came to earth about its colour, natural beauty and vegetation and what a human being can feel, express, create, and do, what would you picture? Now think about what was actually going on in 2010, do you think this is the way we were meant to live, or can potentially live? If everyone on the planet stopped for one hour and meditated or contemplated on whether their life here benefited humanity or the planet, a shift would occur right now for sure. Alas, if I went into the street and asked random people, "What are you doing and why are you doing it?" I would be looked at as crazy.

We can still turn to the decades old eight-circuit brain system created by "consciousness map maker" Dr. Timothy Leary. In a simplified adaptation, we can see how our consciousness can be locked into a low vibration. This is archetypal and should be looked at as an educator for when we later introduce Qabalistic archetypal thought.

The Four Survival Circuits: Their Fixations and Anchors:

Each of the first four 'survival brain circuits' below are driven by variations on the primary will to survive. Each circuit has a fixation that refers to a concentration of consciousness in specific experiences which activate the circuit. Fixation also demonstrates how consciousness can become fixed, or 'stuck,' in one circuit over another.

The linked 'anchors' below refer to how we know a circuit has been earned, integrated, and ready to serve as a stabilising influence for absorbing and integrating the shock from its higher circuit (1 is linked to 5, 2 to 6, 3 to 7 and 4 to 8).

C-1 Physio-Biological Intelligence; the will to survive fixations: food, shelter, self-preservation, material goods, safety and security.

Anchor: degree of confidence earned and maintained to assure physical survial.

C-2 Emotional-Territorial Intelligence; the will to power fixations: self-defense, territoriality, status, ego-strength, emotional honesty.

Anchor: degree of emotional confidence earned and maintained to assure personal worth.

C-3 Symbolic-Conceptual Intelligence; the will to sanity fixations: thinking, problem solving, analysis, semantics, system theories.

Anchor: degree of mental confidence earned and maintained to assure peace of mind.

C-4 Social-Moral Intelligence; the will to socialize fixations: friendship, domestication, sexual rites and tribal identity, ethical codes, religions.

Anchor: degree of social confidence earned and maintained to assure sense of belonging.

The Four Post-Survival Circuits: Their Catalysts and Shocks:

Catalysts refer to whatever triggers and stimulates the specific energy, or current, within the circuit.

Shocks refer to the specific impact these currents and energies have to stimulate growth and evolution in their corresponding survival circuits, i.e. 5 and 1, 6 and 2, 7 and 3, and 8 and 4.

C-5 Somatic Intelligence of Body Wisdom and Five Senses.

Catalysts: whatever triggers the experience of rapture, communion with nature, Tantra (yoga, meditation, ritual), charisma, second wind, falling in love (endorphins) and the expanding presence of being here now. The Shocks of Ecstasy and Bliss (absence of suffering).

C-6 Intuitive-Psychic Intelligence of the Brain, Spine, & CNS.

Catalysts: whatever triggers the experience of the energetic body or aura, the second attention, intuition, clairvoyance and other psychic abilities, ritual magik, reality selection, direct perception of a relative nature of reality. The Shocks of Uncertainty and Freedom (absence of falsely assumed certitudes and dogmas).

C-7 Mytho-Poetic Genetic Intelligence of DNA and the Planetary Entity.

Catalysts: whatever triggers the experience of ancestral and past life memories, autonomous archetypes, synchronicity, planetary (Gaia) mind, cosmic consciousness. The Shocks of Indivisibility and Cosmic Unity (absence of dualistic consciousness).

C-8 Quantum-Nonlocal Intelligence of Subatomic interactions.

Catalysts: whatever triggers near death experience, out of body experiences, the dreambody/dreamtime continuum, communion with Void and the mysterious singularity at the heart of subatomic activity. The Shocks of Death and Impermanence (absence of ego-identification and release from physical body).

The eight circuits (obviously derived from the eastern philosophy of the chakras) are not to be thought of as a fixed hierarchy as such, and the complex relationships between each are extremely well put in Robert Anthony Wilson's 1983 book, Prometheus Rising (which is now past a twelfth printing).

It is safe to say that most humans live within the first four circuits, but it is equally safe to say that there are ways of activating and achieving the higher circuits. Alignment and attunement with universal truths is one sure fire way to get the motor running warm in the Tarot Trump VIII Chariot.

***

A man that is in fear, apathy and hatred sets up a society to reflect it, therefore the wars and the corporate and banking monsters that create them are actually at one with the people, at one with the collective mind. So what we are seeing in the world today is just a manifest symptom of a long and complex plan, with the real root issues and causes lying in consciousness, individually and collectively. The wicked and weak cannot fall lower than the lowest in each person, it is all a reflection, a barometer. People need to stop blaming and being angry, the world is telling us what is wrong, and it is with the self.

Many people are waking up to the agenda of the world elite, the levels of manipulation, and the need to look within themselves. In recent years through the spread of awareness and information, many more are waking up each day. It is like popcorn, pop, pop, pop, pop, and this leads us to only one place, evolution and change.

Evolution & Change – Part 1

On a simple level it does not take genius to work out that change is on its way regarding the human species and the way we live on the planet. The forests are being cut down, animals are becoming extinct, sea life only has a forty year or so expectancy, natural eco-systems are being destroyed, pollution and waste is on the increase, the one world government is not too far away, and technology is moving unbelievably fast. On the opposite track, individual's awareness, consciousness and self realisation is on the rise. It is a powder keg, a time bomb. We also know that if the population level of mankind continues to increase at its current rate (the rate of which has increased in a major way since the start of the 20th century) we will all be standing shoulder to shoulder by around the 27th century (according to scientist Stephen Hawkins).

Something has to give, and that something will mark a significant point in our species evolution.

***

After a pilgrimage through the ancient Maya sites and villages I came away with some niggling questions. Even though there are still some Maya daykeepers keeping alive knowledge from this ancient Mesoamerican culture, it is arguable whether the current Maya tribes are actually the descendants of the builders and inhabitants of the great ancient pyramid cities. The question of whether the current Maya tribes are just descendants from those that worked the land around these ancient cities needs to be asked, and the mystery as to why the ancient cities were deserted when the Spanish discovered them in the 17th century has never been truly solved.

The Yugas from the ancient civilization that lived in the Indus Valley (North India) also looked at time and epochs as being a link of celestial motion to mankind's mental and spiritual development. The complex Yuga system melts into the vast sea of Hindu mythology and presents on one level a repeating cycle of 24,000 years; an ascending and descending of 12,000 years. The Yugas state that mankind has recently had 12,000 years of declining mental development that reached its nadir in 500AD, and that man had reached a high peak around the year 11,500BC (where we find evidence of an advanced civilization all around the planet).

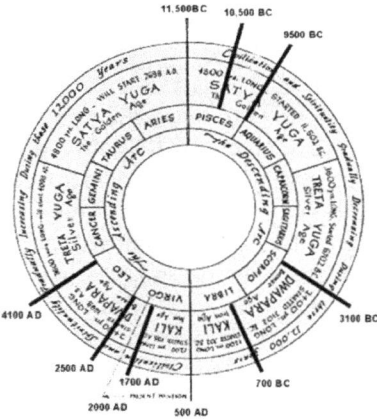

The recent low vibrating Kali Yuga fits with the time of the dark ages, and the start of the Dwapara Yuga fits well with the Renaissance period. The Yuga system states we are still in a period of darkness and materialism but are back on the way up to a higher vibration.

***

Recently in isolation I conglomerated a large historic timeline of the human species from 10,500BC to present day covering two walls of my volcanic shack. It became apparent that empires, civilizations, and power regimes rise and fall and come and go just as naturally as the seasons and the tides. It became clear that centuries and baktuns (Mayan) often destroy or progress what the prior one created, and that only the most harmonious empires stand up to any test of time. The Ancient civilizations in Egypt, Mexico, Guatemala, Peru, Greece and Rome were empires that stood firm, and the common factor in these was that they had prophets, kings and priests, possibly in turn providing for the people's minds, bodies and souls.

Our consciousness at an individual level usually has awareness and focus placed in the events and emotions of the current day, or week, but if we alchemically raise our awareness regarding time we can see that things are speeding up, evolving, curving in, just like a golden phi spiral (which we will look into in depth much later).

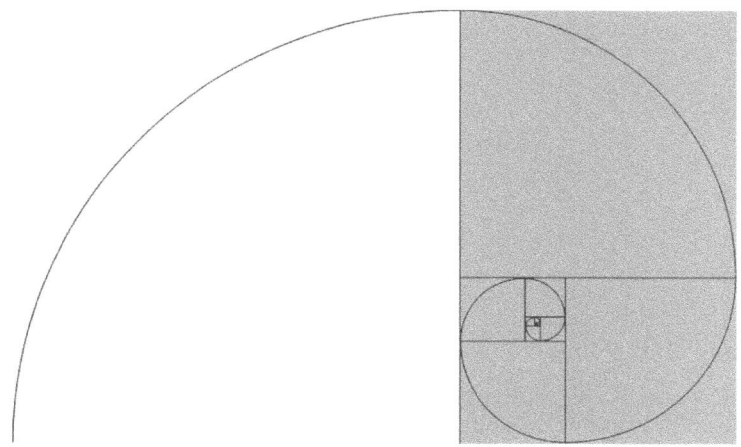

Just to paint a picture, if we cut our planets precession of the equinox in half and place the year 2012 at the end of one half of the precession, we then see the start at 10,988BC (pretty much when the Sphinx was built). With the knowledge that the 26,000 year processional cycle is 360 degrees, and 72 years is 1 degree, we can find a fractal. The fractal being that the average life of man is about 72 years, and man breathes approximately 26,000 times a day.

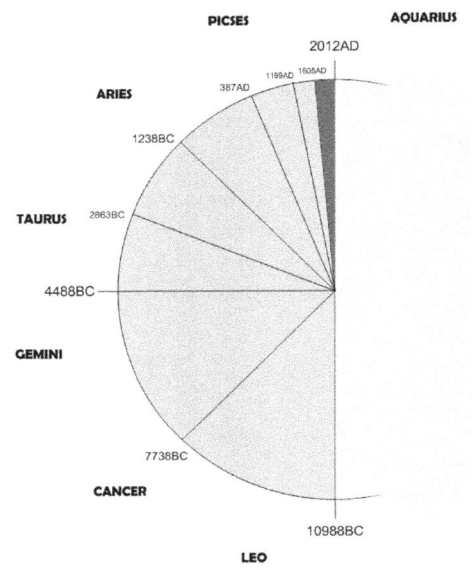

This gets a little more curious when we acknowledge that the sphinx has a body of a lion and the head of a man, I believe this may signify the current half cycle from Leo (symbolised as a lion) to Aquarius (symbolised as a man). The Sphinx faced Leo on the sunrise of the vernal Equinox in 10,988BC and is soon to face Aquarius. Is this by chance, or is it to tell us this period of time from Leo to Aquarius is an age known to the ancients?

This is theorising and not the reason for this line of thought, what I want to show is that the evolution of consciousness is speeding up. Almost everything of note in our species evolution has happened in the most recent section (1/32 as a fraction of half of a precession). When our species entered this most recent section (shown in the darker shade) we only just knew the world was round, but we knew not of gravity, printing books, the laws of motion, or telescopes. Only in the tiniest recent slither have we seen the coming of electricity, telephones, cars, world wars, nuclear fusion, television, space travel, internet, DNA cloning, and cell phones. It is also only in this tiny slither when Freud and Jung started to study and break down the anatomy of the sub conscious and the ego. If one watched a movie from ten years ago, then twenty and forty years ago, one would realise just how quick things are speeding up, and how more dense and complex consciousness is becoming.

One could elaborate on this, but just a little thought and contemplation shows we are heading towards a centre, a more complex and dense section of a golden phi spiral. This is completely natural and actually how much of the fractal nature of the Universe works.

We can even micro manage, and looking loosely at the last hundred years or so we can see friction increasing. This is not precise and is only a snap shot of a thought stream, and again, it is only to share the concept.

1900
Plank
Photography
Einstein
Radio   Hubble
Television
Helicopter
Computer

Big banks and Corps.

Federal Reserve
                 WW1
Tesla technology hidden
Sugar, and alcohol spread
Great depression, gold seizure

WW2
UN Israel   FBI CIA
Post war consumerism

1950
LSD   Carl Jung
DNA
Space travel

        Hydrogen bomb
Bar codes
       Mcdonalds
Bilderberg
JFK murdered

Big bang proved
Hippies
More sex equality
More festivals
Yoga comes west
Berlin wall down
New Age
Cell phones
Internet boom
       More choice

TV in most homes
Globalisation in full swing
Vietnam creation by banks
Media and Hollywood controlled
AIDS created
              Diana
Oil, food, and energy controlled
Rise of celebrity
GM and Aspratame

2000

Organic and holistic living
Alternative media
awareness on rise

9/11 staged
Non elected EU   Swine flu
Less freedoms
Staged economy crash

The diagram is just to encourage some thought. It's conceptual and subjective, and beginning to think conceptually and subjectively now will help for later on. Thinking of the species as a whole and thinking of large time spans is something the alchemists did, and something one can use geometrically.

From the diagram it does not take a genius to realize something has to give and that time for change is coming very soon. The diagram could be looked at in many ways, but really it shows the rise of control by a world elite co-existing with a rise of awareness in the individual. This is the aforementioned powder keg that is going to create a change.

We hold as a species, the misconception that evolution is linear and has always been gradual over thousands of years, whereas in truth evolution comes in spurts and fits and comes about when there is a tremendous need for an organism to survive.

But what *is* evolution?

The evolving part of this planet is only the organic life, it's the only way it can be. If organic life does not evolve, the planet does not evolve, and if ever that were the case then the ray of creation would have stopped flowing through the species marking the end of all we know. Evolution is how creation reveals itself. It is the actualisation of potentiality. It happens when conditions are appropriate just like a seed having to wait for the right rainfall and sunlight for it to happen.

Evolution is linked to life, therefore, evolution always has been and always will be linked to consciousness, this again is the only way it can be.

Teachers (repeater robots) indoctrinate children to believe evolution is all natural selection and that we are just animals. Darwin's theory was nothing more than a theory and this is covered in depth in my other writings. This stops people asking who they are, where they come from, and the meaning of life. It stops spirituality at a young age.

If children grew up and always did and thought what their elders did and thought there would never be any evolution, Einstein agreed with this and said that doing the same thing and expecting the world to change was insanity.

It is *only* through a new awareness, a new consciousness, a new thought, or a new visualisation that manifested change *can* occur. It is an evolution of the "will," the "will" inherent within conscious and subconscious mind that opens the doors of manifest change. Manifested physical change is the *symptom* of evolution and not the *cause*. If we fractal this down to a single man, he visualises himself being free of alcohol and having a new job helping wildlife, and this is the main criteria for this change to commence; from a visualisation fueled with will.

Moving further into the fractal, one wakes up in bed and visualises getting up and drinking some water, and then one does this. As this is done so many times over and over, the visualisation has turned into an impulse, a feeling, an urge, an energy reservoir signature in astral.

A visual thought form is a symbol that represents a concept or thought in someone, it stays within the realm of concept until the thought form manifests into reality. All things created with the mind have the ability to manifest outside the mind because the human mind is a microcosm of the universal mind. Mind is the only thing that changes our world.

The evolution of consciousness is a natural and divine phenomena, it is in essence the oneness absolute wishing to experience itself with more depth, complexity and choice; to seek new, to seek more, with no knowledge of good or bad.

Within this realm we have observed this rise in depth and complexity over millions of years as mineral, to vegetable, to animal, to human, or really, as matter to flesh, to mind, to consciousness. But is this statement the full picture? Science drums into us that matter came before mind but that is only a theory, whereas the adepts of Hermetic Philosophy *know* that mind came before matter.

Consciousness and awareness have always been on the rise in line with linear time, with spurts and fits of ascended awareness.

Humanity evolves by a few looking at the world differently, and a new world can only come from a new world view, and only from a new world view that has the potential to be shared by the many. It only takes a few people to visualise a new world view concept for the domino effect within collective consciousness to kick in. Everything works like this, it is always just one person, or a small group of people that evolve first and just like a cell in your body changing it affects the whole. But for the oneness spirit rushing through the species to really clasp onto a new world view, the world view must be the "easiest way" and "like to like." The properties in the plane of causality must be amassing. Those with the world view and vision must have the clearest of minds and purest of souls; a clear channel so to speak or random forces come into play.

> *"There is one thing stronger than all the armies of the world, and that is an idea whose time has come."*
> Victor Hugo, 19th century author

The physical world is little more than a mirror of the collective consciousness on an individual level and on a collective level, a complex giant mirror. Again, the current issues in the world are the mirror for the current low collective consciousness, but these issues are actually the required friction for the new consciousness to wake up and change. Knowing this, we need not fear, attach or desire as we can each help the flow of evolution with our thoughts and imagination alone.

We are connected via our souls to the source of creation, and we can transform the flow of creation. People who have changed history have not been the greatest generals or politicians, but the artists and thinkers. An individual sitting alone in a room, giving birth to an idea can do more to change the course of history than a general who commands thousands on a field of battle or a political leader who commands the loyalty of millions.

> *"It is in unconscious involuntary manifestation that all evil lies."*
> *Gurdjieff*

"The destructive mentality we face today initially arises from the notion that the substance of the universe is matter; however, quantum physics and ancient mysticism both reveal this is not the case. At the most fundamental basis of our universe is consciousness from which everything emerges. A sea of infinite consciousness is the source of all there is. All matter originates and exists only by virtue of a force... We must assume behind this force the existence of a conscious and intelligent Mind. This Mind is the matrix of all matter."

When habits need to be broken to ensure the survival of the organism, we see this event in nature and call it evolution. In 1988 an experiment was conducted were a few lactose intolerant cells were placed in an environment with only lactose for food. Each lactose intolerant cell should have died but they understood they faced a problem of survival. They replaced their defective lactose enzyme with a functioning one to utilise lactose for food. These and other stem cell experiments show that the environment alters the fate of the cell, even when a group of cells in different environments are genetically identical. So genes respond to life! Therefore, if a cell knows how and when to evolve when it is facing extinction then all organisms do.

The human construct is made up of around fifty trillion cells but it is still a single cell organism. The cells in a human are all individually conscious because they all feed, communicate and seek to survive. An octave higher, all humans are cells within the earth's collective consciousness. The human has meridian energy channels, and the Earth has energy lines known as leylines where many ancient Pagan sites were built upon. We can go up another octave and see that the planets are cells in the solar system, and then that our sun is just one cell in our galaxy, and our galaxy is a cell amongst the millions of other galaxies that make up the single cell universe. Each affects the whole but this truth is ridiculed by the blind. The word organism literally means "any living thing capable of response to stimuli, reproduction, growth, and development, and maintenance of a homeostasis as a stable whole." Our cells *and* our universe do this. For us humans, the Earth is the higher organism governed by consciousness.

The world is a living being, this was understood by the ancient philosophical alchemists who referred to the spiritual essence of the world as The Anima Mundi (the soul of the world). Text will never make you believe this fully, you need to go there to feel it and know it and that's what this book is a vehicle for.

The large evolutionary change about to occur has already started but it's so subtle most do not notice it. Most people have their consciousness in the 'I' and in the surroundings of their own visual space and don't look above, behind or beyond. But a new breed of person is here and this new flow of spirit within the human species is one of the main factors towards knowledge of the coming shift in consciousness. More people are giving up the continually media delivered goal of being financially wealthy surrounded by material luxury, people are instead putting focused energy into creating joy, freedom, improvements, community and peace of mind.

The notion of money being the root of all evil is dying out too as people are realising that blaming the money is simply an escape, a way out. Most don't admit that it is our dependency on the money that is flawed so they blame the money even though there is no law that says we must use the notes in circulation. We go looking for the enemy in everything else other than ourselves and because of this we will never find, or conquer the real adversary that disconnects us from the reality of our realm.

The old ethos' of dog eat dog, every man for himself, and survival of the fittest are also dying out, there are more people living in freedom, there are more people raising their awareness and consciousness, more people aware of this absurd profit based self gain system we are told to live in. The old comments of "it doesn't matter as long as I am happy" are falling and there are more people knowing that truth and integrity are the only foundations for prolonged happiness. There are more people working on themselves and their personal power, more people seeking truth and asking questions.

This can only go one way, and it is for the better. These are exciting times.

This flux of a new flavour of spirit flowing through our species is the catalyst for the coming changes, whether the source of this is natural, divine or galactic is open to much debate, and this book does not wish to get lost within theories. The children in 2009 seem more compassionate, more empathic, and less likely to abide to authority or follow rules blindly. Many teenagers are looking at the big corporations as out of control monsters to be avoided, more are looking at how to share positive expressions of themselves via music, various forms of art and sharing communities.

The artificial inauthentic lives of glamour, fashion, mass entertainment and city trends are soon to be left behind. It is becoming collectively known that inauthentic egoistic living is not progress for a species that finds itself on its knees. Young people are now refusing to feed a system that does nothing for the progress of the planet.

There are still far too many floaters in the river's flow and not enough swimmers, but soon we are going to see many more swimmers, and the swimmers will reach out and help the floaters that deep down also want to swim – then we can all swim together.

Many know and feel that change is coming, that the changes coming are needed for the future of the planet. But most important to know is that destiny is never yet written, we are writing it every single day, and writing it within every single "now" moment. We live in a free-will realm but still obey the higher flow of spirit experiencing itself. It is akin to not being able to stop the flood of water down the mountain but having the free will on where to place the sandbags and pebbles to make things better.

"You cannot stop the waves but you can learn to surf."

The changes that are coming are likely to be large ones, therefore they are sure to bring noise and confusion before things settle for the better. One will need inner peace, inner stillness and to realise ones true self power and potential to be a beacon in this time, and this is where much of the ancient knowledge can, and will help.

Those caught thinking that the replenishing of ATM cash machines and the rolling wheels of supermarket delivery lorries are infinite may get caught out in the coming time. But maybe this is karmic? Some people do not wish to open their eyes no matter what is presented before them and karma can be the only answer for such ignorance prevalent in the early twenty 1st century.

"Growth of knowledge goes against ignorance, and growth of ignorance goes against knowledge."

"Virtue out of knowledge will always be superior to innocence out of ignorance."

Esoterically, and held within most secret societies is the belief that we have fallen from spirit and are currently on a small island of matter, fallen from the demi-Gods which were celebrated and re-imagined by the ancient Greeks. It is written in hidden doctrine that man used to have unhindered access to the spirit world and then as matter slowly hardened, the skull at the third eye became completely solid in recent centuries. It is the cataclysm that took place between 12,000BC and 9,500BC that probably caused the trauma that gave birth to a collective stronger ego, and in turn more separation and duality.

The ancients saw nature as an equal, in Egypt they personified each God as an animal, and shamanic tribes have always had etheric bonds to animals and natural forces. It is only now where our disconnection is so large that we are not only disconnected from nature, we are destroying it.

The Qabalistic Tree of life along with the Yugas looks at this descent from spirit to material and the return journey back up, and the archetypal, meditative, subjective, and objective Tree of Life will be the key to our study later.

Regardless of esoteric belief at this junctia, for humanity to evolve into the manifestation of one of the species highest potentials, scientific non-dogmatic spirituality must be embraced or it could well be game over. Until that time when we learn the operational laws of the spiritual world, until we admit that the spiritual world is an eternal part of our normal waking reality we will continue to be blinded to the powers and abilities the world elite wield against an ignorant populace. A populace separated from its heritage of spiritual divinity. The solution is in the self.

'Evolution & Change Part II' will be presented after our journey is completed.

Spirituality

"Place wisdom before scepters and thrones because what use are material riches when one is in constant fear of material lack and death? Man was born to learn, a natural curiosity proves this. Stagnation, idleness and ignorance are all characteristics degrading to humanity."

"He's a fool who wants a proof of what he cannot perceive; and a blockhead who tries to make such a one believe."
William Blake

Simply Explained

The problem with spirituality is that many people in the west think it is either a case of worshiping one of the thousands of forms of Christianity (so much for oneness and monotheism) and attending church on a Sunday, or cuddling new age fluffy hippies amongst some painted trees. If these really were the only choices I think I might run and hide amidst the irrational safe fluffy clouds of atheism too. Spirituality is not about worshipping this or that, or following a system of beliefs, or pretending to practice unconditional love. It is simply about understanding who and what you are, and this means observing impartially the workings of your mind in relation to the world of things.

Here are some of simple concepts many don't realise; Jesus wasn't a Christian and Buddha wasn't a Buddhist - these institutions are both manmade. Also, the word spirit comes from the Latin Spiritus, whose root meaning is "breath." Other close nouns such as the Sanskrit Prana and the Hebrew Ruach also mean "breath" or "life."

Atheism is one of the best examples of labeling something so one does not have to think about or face something. Many "atheists" deep down recognise infinite awareness and therefore are not really atheists, the word means different things to different people, and the word does not describe well enough the concepts in people's minds.

> *"Atheism is rather in the lip, than in the heart of man....*
> *The contemplative atheist is rare."*
> Francis Bacon, 1625

It is of little wonder that spirituality is mocked. The religions have created dogma and rules, the ancient myths have turned into lies, the lies have turned into rules, and adherence to these rules has replaced the personal experience of the myths. But this is the way it has been ever since Rome, and even before; every organisation, be it religious or political always devolves into self interest and corruption, and wherever there are groups of authority, there are always people wanting to be in charge.

Religion wields the double bladed axe of guilt and fear, and trauma through guilt and fear is the basic hypnotic control mechanism; instill fear through trauma and you automatically instill control. This is effectively hypnosis, and living with any form of fear is living in a hypnotic state, be it the indoctrinated fear of hell, death, or whatever, any form of fear inflicted upon oneself is hypnosis, period.

In the west even spiritual discussions have become taboo. Many people's defenses and barriers are immediately raised, but when actually pressed, many people do state that at their core they actually believe in something, or at least would like to entertain the notion of something.

Spirituality is actually something very simple, no rules, no religion, no codes or oaths, and certainly no parting with any money. It is primarily and basically whether your mind set, inner feeling and inner knowing is in concept X or Y.

Concept X:

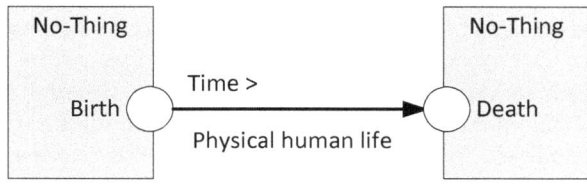

Concept Y:

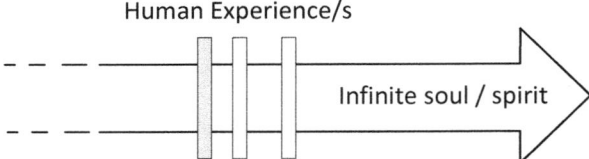

Even though various ancient sacred texts far predating Christ, plus shaman from around the world firmly sit in the Y concept, most people in the western world are currently happily fixed in the X camp. In many parts of the western world, conformed society and the media stay well away from even the notion of Y being believed, a picture is painted to make it look weird, wavy and far out.

But X is a little nonsensical if we break it down and look at it rationally.

People say all the time, "You only live once," but how do they really know? When we show no-thing in X, and when we mention no-thing in this section, I am meaning no form of any kind; no matter, no consciousness, no realm, no intelligence, no emptiness, no dimension and not even a concept of potential in any way.

Remember, X people believe that they will cease to exist when they die, therefore it would be quite absurd of them to believe that before they were born they were alive in any way. Furthermore, before they were born there exists the same conditions; non-conditions since no-thing (ceasing to exist) has no properties.

In other words, the no-thingness before their birth and after their death are exactly the same thing. How could 'they' be different when they don't have properties?

So if, after their death they are in the same situation of so-called no-thingness as before their birth, then the absolute truth is that they will be reborn again. Why? Because they were born out of that no-thingness already! Here they are, they are alive! Out of the same no-thing they will return to, they have come out of, for no reason at all. Therefore, that implies they will live forever as one form or another or as pure consciousness does it not?

How can something that doesn't exist, exist? How can no-thing exist? It is a contradiction. No-thing doesn't exist because it isn't, it hasn't, and it won't. But the X camp have a mental concept about no-thing, like it is blackness, or sleep or similar, but this is false as there is no-thing to think about. In fact that's a false statement, there IS NOT no-thing to think about.

Therefore, the diagram X above is wrong. There should be no properties before and after death.

Believing in the ceasing to exist implies consciousness and time, "here I am, I am ceasing to exist for a time." Where does this time come from? If there is a thing to be found what-so-ever, then there is consciousness, because any-thing (or some-thing) can only exist if there's a witness or observer.

To further dampen the X concept, we each have a brand new human body every seven years, every single cell replaces itself, some every day, but most take longer. All proteins are turned over in body every six months, as are all the molecules within the face. During these replacements where does our soul, memory and consciousness (core awareness) go? Those who look at this life as a physical X journey need to realise that the physical does not even last seven years and that the inner core awareness cannot be located in the physical vessel.

So really we need to re-evaluate the X concept, as what these believers are really stating is that the core awareness stays for the period of the human life and the physical matter associated is subject to complete overhauls (cell-replacement). One must ask the X camp, where does this consciousness come from, live, and go to during the cell replacements? Where is consciousness?

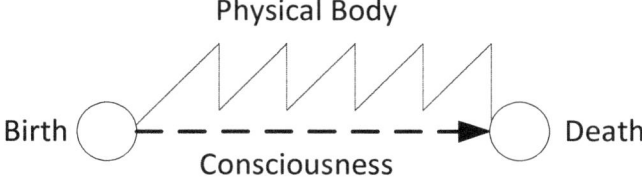

Now this looks diagram looks very silly, but this is what hundreds of millions of people believe and live by.

Even a top surgeon with all his technology cannot locate ones soul, memory or core awareness. One can see electrical pulses neurologically in the brain but one cannot locate core elements of soul, memory and consciousness even though every one of us knows and can feel that they exist. These three logically must be non-local, it is the only rational explanation, and this in turn lends itself to the realms and concepts such as astral, akasha, collective consciousness and the cosmic mind. Even scientists such as Dutch cardiologist Pim van Lommel found it was impossible for the brain to store even a fraction of our thoughts and experiences.

> *"Of course we are spiritual beings in a vessel, look how long it takes us to get used to using it, about ten years!"*

We have fallen as far as we can

We have become spiritual morons, spiritually impaired, locked into the materialistic egotistical plane. The main culprit of blame for this mess is the incorrect and absurd way success is measured and presented; spiritual attainment, inner peace and how one helps and contributes to others does not even have a place on the scales of success. These scales are mostly taken up by materialistic and self created status defining yard sticks.

This section is going to go pretty deep and be hard hitting for some, if you are after a fluffy spiritual book this is not the one for you, but if you are seeking light, the latter sections of this book will shine the core essence of the sun directly into the core essence of your being for days on end, but you can't have one without the other. Look at this as a lesson in polarity as my research covers truths that cross many boundaries.

The root of humanities fall is that people define themselves by their stories, for example someone may introduce himself as a Married Doctor who likes golf but in reality he is none of these things. His name is a label given to him upon birth, his status of marriage is not fixed, his wife could leave him or they could grow apart, and his fondness for golf could dwindle due to his putting game collapsing. These are only stories and labels and are all subject to change, but we define ourselves again and again by status, by what we do, by cultural standing and by what we possess. We have become human doings and not human beings.

People project out an identity and as others agree with it, it comes back to the individual and helps to further cement it. The people who are constantly projecting these masks out to others are often the ones who really need some time for true self discovery and inner blockage removal. Often these are the people who struggle to be alone in quiet time and are always seeking distractions.

The false personality is given to a person from influences, it's not his own, it is not him or her. It can change from others, it can change from one's own will, but we define the 'I' with the personality, we link them as though they are bonded forever, but all is impermanent, especially the personality.

So what does actually define you? Your ideas, thoughts, imagination, intent, will, and nothing else whatsoever. This is pure truth as it is only these things that can create any energy towards anything that you can actually perceive. These things all happen well before physical manifestation and this is what Hermetists look at in a controlled way;

>	Idea > Imagination > Thought > Fuel > Manifest

>	*"Ideas are seeds of action."*

To not run away with Hermetics at this early stage we need to get back to the subject at hand and elaborate. For our view of ourselves we use the word 'I' daily, but it is our concept and view of the 'I' that is incorrect. The 'I' changes so much, minute to minute, "I am hot," or "I am cold," but the 'I' is none of these things as these are impermanent feelings, sensations, and states of various 'now' situations. If we close our eyes and try and locate the 'I' we cannot do it, we cannot find it. We associate the 'I' with the physical body; "I am this body," "this is me," and we create a view of ourselves that is rarely shared by others. We self define and build up an image of ourselves; an illusory personality that only exists in our own heads. It's such a waste of energy. This is the mask of the ego, and we use it as a veil to hide what we really are deep down. Some do this consciously, some sub consciously, and this is what keeps our soul, our innermost desires, feelings and blockages hidden. This manifests in the world as broken toxic people that in turn can only create a broken, toxic world. This is where we are in the year 2010.

But we do need our ego, or "individualism" onside. To have our individuality as a strong flexible ego is necessary to manifest our innermost dreams in the external world at large. If we had no ego at all we would float into the void and cease to experience the illusion of separation and duality, so beware the new-agers cashing in on the premise of destroying the ego. The game is really about integrating our ego and keeping it tamed, thinking of it as a child. The ego gives us our determination, will, intent and strength, the problem only arises when one does not have an integrated ego; a will to receive ego, an ego that needs to be seen to be above and better than others, the ego that seeks observers. This type of ego is dominant in the world today; just contemplate how many conversations we hear of people talking in the mode of self gain and self cherishing.

The imbalanced ego is caused by believing and buying fully into the illusion of separation, and thinking that the five sense arena is all there is to the human experience. This causes the perpetual wish to please these senses with as many earthly material pleasures as possible. But it is like drinking salt water when one is thirsty, one will never be satisfied and will always be striving and chasing. Strangely, the western world deems this 'success' but this is from manipulation by the elite who know the truths of reality. The only real winners within this framework are the elite making the big decisions with their interwoven corporations and banks raking in the cash from toxic ego.

Success is supposedly the man with a big house, big car, a career with subordinates, and surrounded in his spare time by expensive sense feeders (e.g. food, physical comforts, and admirers). Success is deemed intellect and being knowledgeable, but this is really little more than being a hard disk for literature. People are defining themselves by the amount of information they have poured into themselves. "Look at me, I am clever and successful because I read fifty books on the 19th century cotton industry, I am an expert." It's nonsense. "Expert" is just a title and is not fact for no one is ever the ultimate example or authority on any matter.

Many of the financially wealthy business men and experts leading these "successful" lives do not seem happy. Just walk around a motorway service station one morning on the M25 that circumnavigates around London and feel the atmosphere. It is a grey vibration of impatience, lack, striving, pressure and stress. The luxury holiday for two weeks when one has lived in this pressure and stress for the rest of the year is not a fluid way to live either. It is gluttony and lordliness crammed in to a gap, it's too much of a contrast; a short term procured happy spike with nothing for the soul to actually keep or learn. This is unnatural and unhealthy, but what this seems to do is keep the souls desire for a 'true authentic life of purpose' covered, appeased, and silenced.

The West has fallen for the temptation of possession; lovers, things, stuff, mine, want, vanity, which all really means lack. There is little room for humility, humbleness or reducing ones footprint, and rare thoughts for those without basic necessities. The big corporations push this mind set onto the people via a torrent of different angles, and the people, like sheep, follow the lab rat style maze like sheep without a sheep dog, we are in a mess.

We feel incomplete, insecure and unfulfilled, so we look outside to people and things to fill this gap. Then when we find a person or object to possess, we idolise, overestimate, strive, crave, and grasp. We then achieve the possession only to realise it is impermanent, incomplete, and can only make the 'I' happy sometimes. Then we start the cycle again in a dream like state of ignorance.

It's okay to enjoy the senses and what pleasures the world can give us. It's the putting of these pleasures before problems of the self, before devotion to creation that is the problem. It is the attachment to these pleasures, the craving for them, striving for them, and using them as an escape from the world's real issues that is toxic. All of which is a created manipulation that the world has fallen for.

We push our death under the carpet, we fear it and can't face it. We lie to ourselves about our choices, and look at ourselves as passive victims of some outside force. We look back in guilt and forward in anxiety, hiding in the herd mentality with unbelievable unhealthy seriousness.

Life plans and decisions are often based and made upon the foundations of worry, irritability, doubt, and most commonly, the fear of not having enough money (bio survival chips). These decisions always start a cycle of a repeating pattern that takes one to a similar predicament to allow the person the chance to actually make a life decision based upon soul and heart. We are here to learn and evolve, not look for comfort or to feed an illusory ego.

Good souls and amazingly talented creatives have sold out to live in the cycle of debt and luxury, they feed the advertising and corporate worlds and their inner poetry and expression has been sold. In 2010 the big corporations exploit the genius mind for advertising, it is madness. Artists are natural explorers of the interior psychological spaces, but in our mass market culture many of them are forced to either pander to the outside, surface world of fashion and appearance, or languish in dark caves themselves. When an artist expresses psychological truths, they commonly seem to fall on deaf ears with an audience so obsessed with plot, action, and everything else external.

The creatives, geniuses, and other skilled minds are avoiding stillness by replacing it with fun, chitchat, and neurotic attention. Living like a robot in a life-mold reservoir, piloting it from the fear cockpit; fear of looking within, fear of stepping out of the herd, fear of their status not being as it should. Living in an artificial city life with the slick apartment, the TV shows, the packet food, the ipod (i-disconnect), the car, the soulless fucking, the booze, the fads, and the fashion. It is all a million miles from nature and anything that can actually connect a human. Would the renaissance creatives have sold out so readily? No, but then again, they did not have a noose around their neck as tight as the beast system that exists in 2010.

The people working within the political system and global village are all party to the crime, hanging around low vibrating people, around low energies, and having their own sanity affected so that they continue to apply the insane status quo. It is worker ants who are building the walls of the global village for a global government.

Can we actually call a civilization that needs governing a civilization? Surely any man that seeks or has such power over other men is inherently weak?

Our society brushes old people under the carpet, there is little respect for them, and only a very few people visit elders to seek wisdom or hear their tales. No wonder many old people are bitter, they have no say in their local community or in how the young ones are brought up. In natural environments and tribes all around the world throughout history, this is all in harmony.

People's thinking is not their own, but they are sold a lie to make them think their life is a choice of their own and not one that is delivered. Our society tells us what to repress consciously and subconsciously, often subliminally and via the societal norms, so therefore we are not individually seeing the world directly or authentically because we have had a thick wall of a veil placed upon us. As we are not being our complete whole selves, and as we are not even aware of this, gaskets of repression open up and blast our individual blockages into the giant mirror of the collective unconscious. It is a feedback loop; the deranged world creates deranged people, then that is mirrored back to make the world more deranged.

As the world effects mind and the mind effects world, we can see that the only break in the loop is in the self, there is no other link in the chain to actually have any real tangible affect upon. The way of selfhood, looking at and finding out what and who you are is the main criteria for enabling a massive difference on a global scale. It is hard to comprehend at first, but it is true if you think about it deeply enough.

The problems in the individual are also emotional, many people place an unhealthy large portion of the source of their happiness into lovers and spouses (often two different things). Behind this the elite controlled popular music, magazines, and various media angles push us towards this behavior. Love is not something to be found or lost. Love is an energy that we can tap into at any time, and is something we can share and direct.

Attaching a level of happiness to a barometer of how someone else is being and acting towards us promotes and creates nothing but insecurity, emotional imbalance and low self esteem. Admittedly this is not easy to transmute above in every instance because love is full of the fire element, but the point here is that true happiness comes from one person, you, and unhappiness also comes from one person too, you again. In relationships often the words "I love you" can translate to, "I want you to say this to me, I'm confused and lost, you are my emotional refuge and that's why I cling to you. Guide me, possess me never abandon me, admire me more than anyone else and become my audience." People get married and for many they sign away their individual lives, they think that is what they are supposed to do and then get resentful along the way. The shadow of this kind of partnership leads to codependency, possessiveness, power/control dynamics, and imbalanced partnership equations in which one person plays the savior, teacher, parent, and provider, and the other plays the victim, student, child, and beneficiary.

Attaching blame to someone or something is another way of labeling externally so we don't have to look within the self, and harsh as it may sound, playing the victim is always about control and attention, every time, no matter what the circumstance.

You are responsible for your own emotions, period.

Our moods and feelings are more based upon energy and the invisible than things we can see and touch; how do you feel when you are with someone? Family, friends, and lovers all have different energy signatures, the restaurant there is expensive but the cheaper one down the road feels better, the house is a mansion and luxurious but feels cold and bitter, he looks scruffy and dirty but his honest smile is pure and heart-warming. We have these feelings and sensations but we rarely actually listen to them or uncover and process them. They are often covered up by layer upon layer of imprints and labels.

***

Killing us, controlling us, and owning us is what it's all about. Slowly, methodically, lucratively, every corporate advertisement is fashioned to suck dry our wealth, our health, and our wisdom. This is achieved through hypnosis via the language and number messages directing us subliminally. Eventually this leads to stress on our body, an inability to focus mentally, and in desperation we grab any form of seductive pleasure in an attempt to re-energize. Humanity is not born corrupt. We are taught corruption and we've had our five senses bombarded and trained to succumb to corrupt notions.

The world elite and their minions enjoy the certain knowledge that the spiritual realm not only exists and at all times interpenetrates our phenomenal world; they also know how to manipulate elements of these spiritual dimensions to make things occur at a given place and time according to their wishes. On the more mundane level, they know how, through the manipulation of words, sounds, and symbols to change people and the flow of events of the world in which we all move. If magik can be defined as, "The art and science of causing change (in our world) to occur in conformity with will", then the world elite (who know with a certainty that the spiritual realm exists as a part of our "ordinary" sensory reality) have also learned how to bend, shape and manipulate that reality and the people within it to affect change which will benefit them.

Emotional energy is spiritual energy, and this is extracted and harvested on mass scale, the depths of this is not in the scope of this book but you can research it for yourself.

As we sleepwalk through our daily lives most of us rarely think how the spiritual world always interpenetrates our own. We rarely question what may be happening in the world of pre-manifestation, the spiritual world, where what is to become real begins to form and take shape before it actually appears in our phenomenal world of physical reality.

None of the world elite's manipulations enjoy a foregone conclusion of success; they only become successful because they brook no strong, knowledgeable resistance in our world to their operations on the planes of manifestation which interlock with our planes of physical reality. It is not simply the ignorance of the laws of the world of the spirit which preclude us from challenging the elite at their own game; it is the fact that our feeble, rational mind, (which bears as much relationship to full spectrum reality as our puny egos bear to the power and capacity of our total mind), cannot bear to admit that it does not have all the answers, or all the knowledge of all things in the universe and the surrounding dimensions.

And it is from this arrogance of rational ego that the elite will continue to be able to manipulate those who refuse to grasp the knowledge and use of the laws of the realm of spirit. We will continue to provide them with an unassailable advantage until we too fine tune our spiritual perceptions and learn to reverse the forces they have unleashed upon us and our world.

One way or another, the world elite intend to preside over a micromanaged global system. The collapse project is now well underway, and the 'surround your enemy' project seems to be more or less completed. From a strategic perspective, there will be some trigger point, some stage in the economic collapse scenario when geopolitical confrontation is judged to be most advantageous. It's a multi-dimensional chess board, and with the stakes so high you can rest assured that the timing of the various moves will be carefully coordinated along with mythical, Qabalistic, and sun God symbolism.

There is a kind of spiritual law that says that in order to do something, you need the consent of the victims, so to create a world government with a microchipped population the illuminati need the consent of the population. This consent will come from thought forms in people that have been created by fear, duality, and separation from oneness. It is a holographic construct, a pure illusion that keeps us separated from our own infinite consciousness.

> *"We wrestle not against flesh and blood, but against principalities, against powers, against rulers of darkness of this world, against spiritual wickedness in high places."*
> Ephesians 6:12

***

The paradox is that many of the spiritually impaired we have just described do actually have spiritual yearnings. They do not even know it because the source of these yearnings is covered up by external illusions in a society where humans are enticed by the five sense reality.

The builder who wolf-whistles passing girls is actually spiritual, he is looking to be in oneness unity with that girl, he is imagining sexual union and admiring natural beauty.

The youths up all night dancing at illegal parties on drugs are seeking freedom and union, they are entering an abstract state of consciousness and sharing it in a tribal shamanic manner. They are escaping this crazy system.

The football fan who snorts cocaine and drinks lager before the match is seeking bliss from his team winning a game that is a great spectacle. He is participating in a grandioso male atmosphere in a game of poetry, and he seeks union by hugging his friends when a goal is scored. He is looking for bliss, to belong, and to feel unity.

The formula one racing car driver is alchemically pushing his human physiology to its peak so he can control his fear and heartbeat whilst performing a harmonious overtaking maneuver of pure perfection. Even though he has sold out and is really nothing more than a revolving advertising board for greedy money men, this is his core desire and the experience he is working towards.

People take time off work to be near the sun and the sea, to be near light, near warmth, near the calming water element. They cannot even look at the sun but naturally just want to feel its radiance. They seek the light, just like all flowers and trees do, but this is never mentioned.

People take photos of their children and carry the photo at all times in a much opened wallet. One glimpse at this simple smile from unconditional love changes a whole mood.

People are also meditating without even knowing it, those in traffic jams or long road journey switch onto autopilot and contemplate, reflect and observe their life and thoughts. Those sunbathing too, they enter a "zone," and also those who after reading a novel let the images in their minds float across the field of awareness observing what feelings they stimulate.

We are seeking love, light and unity all the time, this is very spiritual, and it is a part of our core essence, part of where we came from and where we will end up. All humans want love in their lives, but many misperceive it, people don't surrender to love so they fill the void with sex, alcohol, drugs, and the quest for fortune all an attempt to bridge the illusory gap of separation.

***

How do you know you 'are'? You only know you 'are' due to awareness of consciousness. Too many people don't experience that they 'are,' they don't experience their own existence, they just
"experience the experience." With no awareness that they are valuable by virtue of their existence, they cannot really value others.

Conditioning, delusions and the artificial limits we place on ourselves prevent us from finding our authentic selves, our divine hidden nature.

Facing our true inner selves is relatively unknown in today's world, "sorry I am not coming to the pub tonight, I'm getting in touch with my authentic self in nature."

People In 2010 know complex machines very well, but not the most important one, themselves. They can work planes, computers, satellites and robots but not their own machinery to its optimum state. It's crazy, hours are spent tweaking the home computer or car to make it run perfectly but nowhere near the same care and attention is applied to the self. Houses are cleaned in military style by those with obsessive compulsive disorders but never a thought for cleaning their inner selves.

But who are we deep down inside? When we hear an answer we don't like we deny it, and project it onto someone else and judge them for it. It is repression on an individual level, but the collective consciousness does this and this is extremely cancerous. If we face inner demons and work on them we don't project them into the physical world.

We hate and insult people who remind us of what is missing in our selves, or wish we had more of. We harm the people that remind us of what we don't like about ourselves because we are scared of solving internal problems. Asking or getting help for deep blockages is seen as a weakness, something a real man would never do, but it is arguably the males that have the most problems when it comes to expression. This all can lead to deep self hatred, and this sort of self destruction in the self leads to all the acts of hate and destruction apparent in the world.

But again and again, it is a mirror, the masses not accepting and hiding their true self on an individual level and running to vanity and materialism is reflected in the way the world is run and the way that nature is treated. It is a fractal of the cancer disease; cancer is created by cells not communicating properly with the conscious signal of the whole, they grow out of control and spread. It's the same within a single human, if not communicating properly to the self (internal world) it then appears within the earth (the external world).

*"Each of us is something of a schizophrenic personality,
tragically divided against ourselves."*
M. L. King Jr.

*"People will do anything, no matter how absurd,
in order to avoid facing their own soul."*
Carl Jung.

Primary ways to raise vibration

I'm not going to write too much because text can only do so much. Later we are going to use Hermetic Alchemical Qabalah to actually go there because the best book to read is the one within you, within your own life, within your own spark of true essence. This book also won't tell you to just go and love life and all creation, this book is going to take you to the place where you can see and feel it all for yourself, through the great work, the operation of the sun, the work of the Philosopher. However, I do want to talk about some basic simple things, especially from those moving from the X camp to the Y camp, or even those still in the X camp.

Every living organism in this realm has an electromagnetic field and a vibrating frequency and this is proven by quantum science. The vibrating frequency within a human can be measured, and David Hawkins plus his team of scientists did thousands of clinical tests and measurements using Kinesiology. They found the obvious, that fear and hate is a low vibration and that love and acceptance is a high vibration. An encapsulating look at their results shows the scale.

20 - Hate, shame, depression, suicide, misery.

30 - Evil, blame, demonizing.

50 - Hopelessness, apathy.

60 - Regret, despondency.

100 - Grief, fear, anxiety. This is where Christianity vibrates.

125 – Desire, craving, wanting, addictions. This is societal normality.

175 - Anger, pride, arrogance.

180 - Narcissistic ego.

200 - Integrity; responsibility for actions. Caring for the welfare of the planet and mankind. A new energy comes in here, physiological changes occur in neurons and hormones, new thought pathways emerge.

250 - Letting go; an okay if it happens, okay if it doesn't attitude.

350 > 500 - Integral genius; amazing thought, great for research, science and medicine, alchemy.

450 - Strong new energy arrives, Kundalini in eastern philosophy.

500 - Love transformation.

500 - upwards new subjective spiritual realities emerge.

540 - Non duality, unconditional love, a way of being.

It was estimated by the scientists that only 15% of humans are over 200 and that the human nervous system holds up until 800.

A raised vibration effects the world in many ways, when you touch a door handle your energy is left there for a long time, when you walk down the isle of a supermarket your vibration affects others by just walking past them, and when you enter a room full of strangers your vibration effects the energy of the room, and so on.

So how does one raise vibration, or attain spiritually even if one is still in the X-camp from the previous sections?

Well, there is nothing to really do or to attain. Spirituality is not something to be searched for, it is not external, it isn't a thing, and hunting around different gurus and retreats in India and reading tons of books is not the full answer either. The holistic types who cash in large profits in their swanky chakra healing parlours by patching up bankers and corporate hounds are to be avoided too, they miss the point completely, as do those with the wavy clothes hugging everyone and being sickeningly extroverted and externally open beyond what is comfortable to others. It is more about being *internally* open, and having a firm grounding in science and the natural laws our universe and 3D-reality comply to. It is a spiritual minefield out there, and most mines are easily spotted, they are labeled with a $ sign.

Spirituality is really at essence just a knowing and feeling that you have a permanent unchangeable I, the I that is awareness as consciousness. In most western people there are many 'I's all quarrelling, hence there is no unity within.

This concept could take just a second, ping, there we go, full spiritual attainment because there is nothing to look and search for and nothing to be realised. Just stopping and relaxing into that core awareness in short spurts as much as one can, will enable one to then realise and feel that there is so much more space everywhere. Soon the short spurts will become automatic and then it becomes obvious and apparent that all is perfect, that points of views are not needed, and that all thought forms, perceptions, projections and emotions all come from, and goto this field of pure awareness.

Attaching to labels and group think prevents being in the permanent unchangeable I awareness, all this has to go or at least be turned down. We only require to just be in our awareness each 'now' moment.

But we should elaborate a little more on what tangible easily implemented information can help us raise our vibrating frequency.

The best things to do are already done by millions who tell themselves they are not spiritual, many will argue these are not spiritual but I can assure you they are the most spiritual things one can do;

- Swapping mainstream media news for nature.
- Having our consciousness and attention in the present moment, in the now.
- Using, feeling and being in the intuition / inner knowing.
- Being curious and inquisitive about life, creation and everything.
- Transmutation above judgment.

Let us look into these five a little more.

Mainstream media bypasses much of the conscious mind and goes straight for the sub conscious using studied methods. Those that cease the input from this beast and spend more time in nature will notice a change in vibration probably more than anything else that is shared in this whole book! Nature is a high frequency and when one is in nature it simply raises the frequency of your being.

***

Being in the now sounds easier than it actually is, because as we mentioned earlier, most people have their consciousness in the past few days and the coming days. Being in the now is not against planning, making strategic decisions about the future, or looking back and contemplating. What being in the now alleviates is scattered energy, scattered energy that is anywhere but the present moment. Millions of people are always looking back and thinking "what if...," and "I should have done..." instead of looking back and grabbing the lessons and integrating them for the now. Millions of people are also looking forward, living in multiple maybes and drifting within them. We need to be warriors, project to the future, make the best decisions we can based on all the related information and feelings we have, and then get back to the present moment. When new information or feelings come, we project again and re-evaluate.

Unless we are in the present moment, we are not really living, because the past has gone and is never to return and the future never comes. Tomorrow does not exist, it's an incorrect label for conceptual communication reasons. Even when we look back at history we look at it incorrectly, what we call the past is really a series of "now" moments.

When we eat we are already diving our fork and consciousness into the next mouthful instead of concentrating our awareness on the mouthful we are currently chewing. All we can ever actually have is the current mouthful so we should focus upon it and enjoy it.

Once we experiment and play with the now, we realise that all fear is a fear of what might happen in the future. Fear is never actually present when a real issue is currently being carried out, it is a projection into the future. This goes for anger and a whole bag full of other traits that do nothing to serve the human experience.

Surrendering confidently to the present moment with our minds adapting to the circumstances which we find ourselves in is true mastery.

> *"The moment you enter the NOW with your attention, you realise that life is sacred. There is a sacredness to everything you perceive when you are present. The more you live in the now, the more you sense the simple yet profound joy of being and all the sacredness of all life."*
> *E Tolle.*

***

We all have intuition, the same amount, it is just a case of whether it is either developed or underdeveloped. Many would say it is more within a female, and esoterically, intuition is a more female left brain attribute, but this does not mean it is only within women physically. Women tend to use it more as they generally are more in tune with their inner world than men, who place their consciousness more in the outer world.

So what is the intuition and how do we develop it?

All we do in life is accept and reject, attract and repel, and within this folly of harmonious chaos we are constantly making decisions. Usually we make these decisions based on intellect and parameters that are firmly external in the material physical world but intuition is all about getting out of the physical, out of the intellect, out of the mind, and into that inner knowing and inner feeling. If we have a decision to make, instead of weighing up via the intellectual and looking at the physical logistics and outcomes we can go inside ourselves, open up internally and observe how it feels. We can listen closely to what is going on in there by visualising one outcome and seeing how it feels just behind our solar plexus. We can feel what is going on there and listen calmly to what emotions and feelings arise. We can visualise a multitude of potential outcomes of a single decision and collect a selection of comparable feelings.

We can also use our intuition when listening to someone, listening to someone is an art only few are really masters in. When we listen to someone we should give our full attention and focus, and even if we know masses about the subject matter or have grander stories, we still should listen attentively, and more importantly, to open up and feel. This gives us much more information than just the just words we ingest. This takes some practice and dedication but is worth it, in this practice have to overcome the fact that many people talk at people and not actually to them.

The best example of intuition is when we're just about to close the door when leaving the house and we have a feeling we have forgotten something. What is this experience? What is actually happening? The subconscious mind and inner knowing are trying to communicate with the conscious mind you, the intellectual you, and the more we disregard this voice or sensation, the more it shrinks and goes away; tired from being ignored. The more we listen to this inner sensation, the more it grows and becomes the best ally in life we could ever wish for.

Have you ever gone to view a house with a person who uses their intuition a lot? They will feel the house, they will sink into their intuition. Oftentimes the house could tick all the logistical boxes but the intuition says no, it doesn't feel right.

Other examples of the intuition and inner knowing are:

- Feeling / knowing someone is lying.
- Feeling / knowing someone is watching you.
- Feeling / knowing something is missing.
- Feeling / knowing there is more to a story.
- Feeling / knowing it's the right person or job.
- Feeling / knowing danger is close.
- Feeling / knowing someone is upset or has a problem.

The more we live in the intuition, the more we bridge the gap between the subconscious and conscious minds, and when these fuse (as we will show and discuss later) some amazing things can occur. But even in the early stages of living more in the intuition we realize we have an inner guidance, an internal compass in life, making sure we go where we need to, and to attract and repel who we need to. Listening and acting upon the intuitive sensations in my opinion can save a few carnations as we are making sure we are going down the correct fork in the road to learn the lessons we need to learn. When we don't face the lessons we need to learn they keep repeating and don't move on; the plane of causality waits for the correct causal ingredients to emerge for the lesson to present itself again until one gets it right. This wait can take years, decades or even life times.

Intuition places ones consciousness in a universal flow, whereas mind likes to place ones consciousness within rigid routines based on logical decisions. The flow that intuition steers one towards is open to everyone.

It is amazing in 2010 how some people are so in the intellect, and some people would even shun or dispute the idea of intuition even existing. A surgeon cannot find it, so where is it? The game of true selfhood is not to gain more knowledge, it is actually to go in reverse, not to add but to subtract, to be made nothing, and the best vehicle for this is the Qabalistic Tree of life.

For academia to overcome ignorance in any way, one needs to have curiosity and wondering, and with what is coming in our species evolution we will need fewer people who are purely concerned with academic concerns.

***

The fourth item is to be curious and inquisitive, this is an important dormant faculty that raises consciousness. Free thinking and contemplating the world around you from your core being, and not from group think can lead one to certain doors.

Many millions of humans go through their whole life without asking any real questions, the conveyor belt of school, work, television, and shopping gets in the way. Well these peoples will only have to come back again, probably with a harder local culture and local environment, in (as Buddhists would say) a lower rebirth. This will keep happening until they get it somewhat right.

We all ask questions every day, but I am talking about real questions. The ones that many never ask until they have a real scare, or lose a close relative, or have a serious illness, or plainly just enter their natural curiosity without holding onto group think that results from local cultural imprints.

What sort of questions are these? Well there are hundreds that cover poetic philosophical metaphysical science, but a small diverse cluster are:

- Why am I here?
- What am I?
- Who am I?
- What is my purpose?
- What is the purpose of life?
- Creation; What is it? How did it initialise? How does it appear?
- What is consciousness?
- What are thoughts?
- What am I doing and why am I doing it?
- Why is natural drinking water not available to all?
- Why do people really believe that they own parts of the earth?
- There are well over a million million people on the earth and only a small profit based elite control the rules, is this natural?
- Why is food contaminated with sugar and toxins for the reason of profit?
- Why do "authorities" ask for passports and papers to prevent a human to travel and move freely?
- Why do many of the financially rich live in closed fear with alarms, walls, and security in their lives?
- How come, with the issues in the world today, a chocolate company recently had an attempted buy-out amounting to ten billion Euros and this was accepted as normal?
- Why do I have to treat another person as an unquestionable authority just because he wears a costume (uniform)?
- Where is anti-gravity?
- What is the other side of a singularity in a black hole?

Asking questions, real free-thinking questions, no matter how absurd they may first appear is a very spiritual concept, it enables one to think as a core entity, as a unique part of creation. In this mode you realize you are an essence, and that rules, authority and dogma are just folly and have no place in your unique life force consciousness.

It's absurd is it not? We are spinning and spiralling through space stuck to a planet solely because of its large mass, in an existence based on illusory linear time which in itself is really just a bendy dimension. We are strange, beautiful, complex creatures, and some real inner questions need asking, and these lead to a higher more exuberant vibration.

We are so lucky at the moment, we have so much information at our disposal, so many places we can travel to, there is so much beauty to revel in, but also, and above possibly all else, we are about to witness the whole species entering into a massive spike in its evolution. Living a life like a conforming robot solidly within the cultural and societal imprints is a waste, a pure waste. We should be clambering for ring side seats, not in the parking lot clamping cars.

Through history, the people who have been concerned with the question, "Why am I here" have helped us evolve in theology, science and philosophy, but millions never even ask this or only give it a fleeting thought.

All humans have a strong inbuilt curiosity and this is proven in childhood. We all know that between the ages of five and eight children often spend all day asking why, only to have the annoyed parents lie or create dead ends to force them to be quiet. In schools the indoctrination of children via poor right brain arithmetic and rigid robot-like discipline soon nullifies and tames this natural curiosity.

But go and try It for yourself, spend all of tomorrow asking why, to the train conductor, to the parking attendant, to the postman, to your boss, ask why all day and you will soon see that people like to stay within the nice warm comfort blanket that the local culture and media weaves.

I was in Dallas recently passing through on my way back to Europe and this really was the land of the organic human robot, I was scared and nearly got shot for accidentally smuggling a banana in from Mexico. Before escaping to the ego zoo (though not without its creative enclosures) of New York I was told my newly procured unopened water bottles were not allowed on my flight even though they were purchased from a machine not five metres from the flight gate. I asked the man in costume why not and he replied that he did not know the reason but that it was just the rules and his job was just to impose them. Now this is the crux, and also what millions of others are doing today; he is spending his life doing something for reasons unknown to him just so he can earn bio survival tickets. He questions nothing. The system has bought people who would otherwise possibly question it and placed them into a uniform. These costumes seem to have a special fabric that kills any curiosity or ability to question anything within the wearer, they have become guardians of the matrix.

The motivation behind these big free thinking real questions is a big force, it also helps to start the engine of the chariot tarot trump and this line of curiosity can be directed towards some deeper questions in other archetypal areas that we will delve into later.

***

Refrain from judging is the final item on the list that pushes us towards a higher vibration, and within this we could also place labeling, categorising and status defining. This is all a complete waste of energy but all of us do this and it is real work to cease any sort of judging. Instead of judging we can understand, learn and accept, because whenever we are judging there is always a chance for these growth opportunities. If we judge we will be judged, and usually when we judge it's out of not being able to accept or understand fully.

But this also means not judging ourselves. Many of us fear the judgment of others, usually parents, peers and lovers, and this ends up with us judging ourselves to preempt the coming judgers. This is a serious waste of energy and the answer to this trait is to just be, just be yourself and relax into the space that is awareness. The fear of being judged is folly, and so is harsh self judgment, it equates to a low vibration and needless energy loss; it only hinders the self, no one else.

We judge without thinking, we justify our judgments by our subconscious cross referencing to past imprints, we also hide and bury many of our judgments, and this all ends up in blockages in the physical body, it just does not serve us in any way and has to go.

So in situations where we normally judge, we need to get into a habit of catching ourselves, and then asking ourselves, what is there to understand? What are the lessons? What am I to learn? These are the only things that matter and they help us evolve and vibrate higher.

Acceptance, it is what it is, enter the space. This is true non-judging.

***

We waste energy on so many things; unnecessary and unpleasant emotions, bad moods, unnecessary haste, and interest and attention on aimless things happening around us. We can use this surplus energy for repair and clarity, resulting in a higher vibration.

After implementing these four main things into your life, your vibration will raise, and to be honest there will probably be no notable change for 21 days. But sooner or later your vibration will increase and this could lead to an experience of self realisation.

***

Gurdjieff spent many years in a Sufi mystery school and later became one of the most admired mystics and philosophers our species has witnessed. He mentioned quintessential strivings that characterised a person who is working to awaken their consciousness, (when Gurdjieff spoke of 'awakening' it was almost always connected with consciousness). From his book, "Beelzebub's Tales to His Grandson" he listed and grouped these strivings:

First Striving: "To have in their ordinary being-existence everything satisfying and really necessary for their planetary body."

Second Striving: "To have a constant and unflagging instinctive need for self-perfection in the sense of being."

Third Striving: "The conscious striving to know ever more and more concerning the laws of world-creation and world-maintenance."

Fourth Striving: "The striving from the beginning of their existence to pay for their arising and their individuality as quickly as possible, in order afterwards to be free to lighten as much as possible the Sorrow of our common father."

Fifth Striving: "The striving always to assist the most rapid perfecting of other beings, both those similar to oneself and those of other forms, up to the degree of the sacred Martfotai, that is, up to the degree of self-individuality."

> *"Only the one who fully comprehends the difficulties of awakening can understand that long and arduous work is needed to wake up."*
> *Gurdjieff*

Awakening is not a goal or a concept, it is an inner metamorphosis.

***

So even though there is nothing to do, there are things one can do. Truth is just a line of text, but to go and feel truth, and to really know truth we need to take consciousness there via the vehicle of a raised vibration.

Axioms

Living with rules and rigidness day to day is not the way, but the following axioms really serve my experience of this realm, and each help to raise vibration.

- Everyone is a learning gift, as are all experiences and events.
- Giving aligns to higher energies because the human condition is currently very dense and mostly within the will to receive.
- Freedom is to love without asking for anything in return.
- The simplicity of it all dawns on you that you can give up what doesn't serve you and attract what does.
- Only shock and experiences change man.
- We are *all* looking for inner and emotional peace.
- Be there for others but don't let your energy be drained by sympathy hunters and victims.
- We become what we think, life is shaped by mind.
- Allow pain, feel pain, do not be free from pain, but accept pain with an untroubled mind.
- Say what you mean, and be careful to mean what you say.
- You only need your own approval.
- Everything you need to know is within you.
- You can often accomplish more by doing less.
- Fear is natural, but does not need to be cowardice.
- The world desires my existence.
- Spend time alone each day.
- Accept you cannot be everything to your lover.
- Face fears as they often signal towards camouflaged desires.
- You cannot suffer a loss of something that is not yourself.
- Regard what doesn't belong to you as though it does belong to you.
- Develop imagination, will and stillness.
- Don't define yourself by your appearance.
- Don't keep useless objects. Throw anything away that's not been used for six months.
- Don't forget the dead but don't allow them to invade your life.
- Never visit anyone just to pass time.
- Ensure where you live is sacred, especially sleep space.

- Conquer pride then no one can humiliate you.
- No one ever actually owns anything, items we can see with our eyes are only ever on loan.
- No thing or person is a possession.
- Choose locations from three criteria: How can I help? How can I evolve? What can I create?
- The only permanence is impermanence.
- Don't take up too much space.
- Problems and challenges are tests with gifts within.
- Don't stay in the same place for too long, it creates stagnant energy. If you do, move items around, freshen things up, see different people and alter routines.
- Make strategic decisions and then wait knowingly, but be fluid and flexible to allow for signs and synchronicities to alter plans.
- Don't be too impressed upon by strong personalities.
- He who grasps for too much, holds on to little.
- All balance and imbalance is dependent on the state of mind of the individual and not actually within the issue or person one is projecting onto. In other words, all projections from our mind are subjective and no actual thing or person has any-thing inherently attached to it/him/her.

Manifestation

Many fluffy new age books preach that one can manifest their whole life, but if this was the case we would each never ever be surprised would we? Above the levels of manifestation, (or plane of thought, visualisation and attention), are the laws of karma and causality, so therefore manifestation can only occur if the karmic balance is congruent and the environmental causal attributes are close by.

Some people are in life paths with a more set trajectory than others for sure, but we ALL have free will, not just of actions but of thoughts. It is these thoughts that are really more important than actions because they are the seeds for all actions.

What actually creates a thought? Each thought construct comes from the sea of conscious awareness that sits behind the mind and ego. We can create a thought construct by ourselves due to our motivations and desires, or from encounters with the external world. After we have a conversation with someone we then play movies in our mind that elaborate and play with the constructs and images we received and shared during that conversation. Often we will have some desired outcomes and we then direct more energy into these images, and it is these images, or visualisations that create physical manifestation.

Example 1. Julie meets Janet, and they talk about what to wear on Friday night, afterwards, and fleetingly, Julie plays in her mind what the environment will be like Friday night and what she could wear. She finds an image in her mind she likes the most, it fits, it feels good, and she goes into her mind and looks at this image many times and this gives focus, attention, and therefore energy toward this thought construct and visualisation. Now, unless the planes of karma and causality disagree or do not permit, she will end up Friday night in the outfit she has visualised.

This is simple stuff and pretty much how life works, but what Julie is doing is only semi-unconscious manifestation, and we can make this work for us consciously.

Example 2. Dan has an interview for a job he really wants and has been working towards for years. Dan can visualise the interview going well with him being calm, collected and confident. The more energy he puts into this visualisation the more energy for this manifestation will be present at the time of the actual interview. It really is this simple.

Once I was forty days into a meditative isolated silent fast, when a friend came in, "Mark, I know you are in silence, but all I wanted to say was I have a place you can stay when you are finished, good luck, bye." That was it, but for hours images came into my mind, what is the place like? Will we get on? When will I go there? Does she need a reply? And I dreamt about it that very night. This interrupted my state for about thirty hours, and this is how normal life works; we have all these inputs and outputs and it creates a sea of harmonious chaos in the mind, amidst the 40,000 or so thoughts each day.

The mind creates, it gives birth, and hence the world changes. Mind can go to the past, the future, a location, and can change, choose, and reason. It is always (normally) in motion, looking to solve. Scientists think we are just bipedal animals without feathers, but we are the only living organism on this planet that can build an empire, wonder where we came from and look at stars and plan to conquer them. We really are magnificent.

Manifestation is inherent in every intention and desire, and intent and will are the mechanics for its fulfillment. Intention and desire in the field of pure potentiality have infinite organising power, and when we introduce an intention in the fertile ground of pure potentiality, we put this infinite organising power to work for us.

Visualising gives energy to a potential in the quantum field, but there are some rules; never visualise a negation, e.g. "I won't ……", and don't come from a place of self desire and self wanting which would equate to coming from a place of "I'm not that, I don't have that." Just hold in mind the highest ideal.

You can always think and visualise yourself into the best You that you can possibly be, into your full potential, but you can also think and visualise yourself into a disaster by believing any bad press you put out about yourself. If you want to be something, start believing you can be that, and visualise.

Manifestation could be looked at as a self organising agent within the vacuum, a feedback loop so to speak. With focused intention feeding into the vacuum it is easier for it to come back, but the feedback is modified by all the others feeders (people) too.

Quantum science backs up manifestation too where subatomic particles wait for "intention" to be placed upon them before manifesting into actuality.

Life is a mental projection, as is the universe, as is the tree, as is the insect. We live within our minds, as does intellect, emotions, likes, points of views, stories, and projections. Our thoughts are so important, especially those that have our intention fueled desires. Once we make a decision, the universe conspires to make it happen.

The magus uses will and imagination with heartfelt desire to direct consciousness to achieve a goal. It is the aligning of will with universal will. This works all the time for all of us, we are all magicians really, but we don't use this much and we create counter images in our minds which cancel out our desires. It is deep in the subconscious mind where these counter images rise from, therefore we need to be pure, balanced, and cleansed mentally if using this seriously for specific goals. If manifesting seriously, then do not impeach upon the free will of other people or you are abusing karmic laws, and always remember that energy flows where attention goes, and that the fast your energy, the quicker things manifest.

> *"In the beginning there was desire, which was the first mind; Sages, having meditated in their hearts, have discovered by their wisdom the connection of the existence with the non-existent."*
> The Hymn of creation, The Rig Veda.

Reincarnation

Every major culture in the world has believed in rebirth at one time or another, from the Druids to the Greeks, to the great philosophers. Plato, Kant, and Schopenhaur were three of many philosophers that believed in rebirth, and to the Eleusinian philosophers birth into the physical world was a literal death and true birth was when the soul rose from the flesh. Reincarnation and transmigration has always been taught in the mystery schools and shamanic tribes but most think that the concept of reincarnation is just a Buddhist concept. The Vatican in a meeting in the year 1235 did a good job of changing their stance and hiding reincarnation from their doctrines. The much misunderstood Bible has many statements linking to reincarnation, and here are just a few of them:

- And many of them that sleep in the dust of the earth shall awake. Daniel 12:2
- Turn thou us unto thee, O Lord; and we shall be turned; renew our days as old. Lamentations 5:21
- For I have no pleasure in the death of him that dieth, saith the Lord God; wherefore turn yourselves and live ye. Ezekiel 18:32
- Though they dig into grave (seol), thence mine hand take them; though they climb up to heaven, thence will I bring them down. Amos 9:2
- When I have opened your graves, O my people, and brought you up out of your graves, and shall put my spirit in you, and ye shall live, and I shall place you in your own land. Ezekiel 37:13,14
- The story of John being a reincarnation of Elijah. Matthew 11

Mystics and yogis are often said to see many of their past lives, and a regression or hypnosis session performed by a skilled practitioner can bring up past experiences on earth from within a different vessel.

Professor Ian Stevenson from the University of Virginia has published over twenty cases of people who have recalled their past lives and then found real-world proof to back up their visions.

There are some examples that help to back up the claims of reincarnation:

- When we take to something new with such skill and ease it is like we have done it before.
- When we meet someone and there is an unbelievable compatibility, shared with strong emotions and feelings.
- When someone for no catalyst reason in this lifetime really does not like something such as water, or heights.
- Going to a country or place, and really feeling like you have been there before.

Buddhist and other doctrines state that this is the only realm where we can affect and rebalance our karma, and it is this karma that dictates what sort of rebirth we are going to have next if we come back.

Many attained Lamas in Tibet have claimed to have chosen their next rebirth, and the way the next Dalai Lama is chosen is based upon the child remembering objects from his past life.

Buddhism and other doctrines give examples on ways to transmute across the veil, and to be honest, not preparing in any way to pass over in a calm meditative state with no bitterness or resentment would be foolish.

Literal Qabalah looks at man's auric egg always being in the AIN SOPH, and that carnations take place within the same auric egg until one is liberated from the wheel of necessity. The doctrines state that human souls dwell in an upper hall, where the decision is made as to which body is entered.

There are mentions in Hermeticism about reincarnation too. As Hermes states, "O son, how many bodies we have to pass through, how many bands of demons, through how many series of repetitions and cycles of the stars, before we hasten to the One alone?"

Many people state that they would rather not come back to this realm, but it is what one doesn't like that will bring one back – one needs to understand the lessons.

Reincarnation makes too much sense to shun, and it appears we arrive here with three things; our past lives karma, our astrological birth traits, and free will. The karma and astrological traits can be transmuted above, but for this we need to raise our vibration even higher.

Purpose

Purpose, -n: 1. something set up as an object or end to be attained, 2. the reason for which something exists or is done.

As we keep coming back and it's all a bit of a spiritual joke (to some it appears to be far too serious), we might as well do something half useful whilst we are lugging these dense vessels about. To do something useful is to define some sort of purpose.

What is my purpose in life? So many people never even ask the question and this creates a world full of boats without rudders crashing into one another. Many people blunder their way through life bouncing off random events akin to a pinball, generating and living in misery.

Life should have plan and purpose, to use ones faculties to their highest ideals. Aims we come here with are to create peace, freedom and happiness, but because people end up swayed by moods and small problems, they lose sight of any real purpose. The fact is that each and every human has dormant natural talents and gifts just ready-waiting to be shared.

The Hermetic adept does not allow his life to be determined by the exterior world but manipulates the world to create lives of peace, freedom and happiness, but only a positive, highly achieved concentrated mind can do this.

What about a life of real purpose? A life of real purpose and value is for sure linked to the following:

- To create and innovate using faculties to help others.
- To become master of the self.
- To help and protect the future of the planet.
- To help those oppressed or less fortunate at the root cause.
- To create self expression (art, work, love) so others can enjoy and/or grow.
- To create more truth and freedom for humanity.
- To be obtain a warrior like inner peace.

Many who wish to help others soon realise they are themselves are in no state to help others, people jump into voluntary, charity and humanitarian work (often symptoms weed pruners) only to see that their energy is not ready. One needs to help the self first. Even a high adept, highly attained lama or yogi all still work on themselves daily, so how is it the ego driven emotionally crazed westerner thinks they don't need to?

To find purpose, don't look at yourself through the eyes of the world or be influenced by thoughts of criticism from others. Know that everyone has a purpose in life; a unique gift or special talent to give to others. When we blend this unique talent with service to others, we experience the ecstasy and exultation of our own spirit, which is the ultimate goal of all goals. When you work on your purpose you are a flute through whose heart the whispering of the hours turn to music.

But how do we find and align with our highest purpose? It is not that hard as we are constantly in the act of creating ourselves by our choices by what we feel passionate about. We just need to look up and out of our own lives, and into the bigger picture.

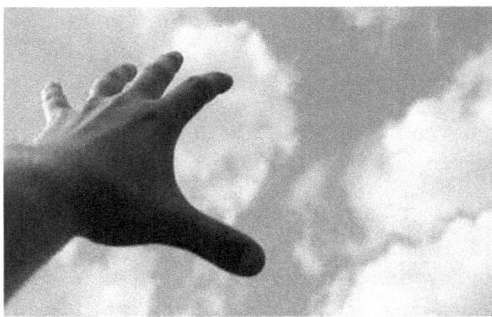

A good way is to go within and ask the following questions in meditation:

- What are my highest ideals in my life?
- Where am I now?
- What are the obstacles in my life stopping me from getting where I am now to my highest ideals?
- How do I overcome the obstacles?
- What is my true purpose?

When is the last time you spent a solid twenty four hours away from all people and all media? How is one supposed to find a true purpose or any real clarity without going deep within the self without distractions from external energy inputs?

A true integral purpose must have other souls and the improvement or preservation of the planet within its cockpit. Instead of looking outside for a purpose, or joining others ideas, one can simply go and create for oneself. This may sound idealistic but what else is there to do but do what you love? We have so little time and making a living doing what you don't love doing is not a living, it's a dying. How do you make a living? By making a life that makes a difference is the only integral and worthwhile answer.

Go for direct experience and trust yourself. Go with the flow and everything will fall into place. Think of everything you have control of and think of it from an artist's perspective; "How in some sense can I better this?" When we strive to become better, everything around us becomes better too.

When life is your work, and your work has swapped from being a dent in your time to a flow in your life, you are on your purpose. Then people, ideas, synchronicities and abundance all flow towards it, it just needs some courage to make the initial jump, and to turn down the voice of fear that creates reasons not to make that jump.

> *"The way of cowardice is to immerse ourselves in a cocoon in which we perpetuate our habitual patterns. When we are constantly recreating our basic patterns of behavior and thought, we never have to leap into fresh air or onto fresh ground."*
> *Shambala*

> *"What we do for ourselves dies with us. What we do for others and the world remains and is immortal."*
> *Albert Pine.*

Imagine a world full of so much diversity that each individual's enthusiasm became the driving force behind one's life work, where one's life work was as distinctive as one's own fingerprint. A world where every job and every service had its own caretaker that performed its tasks with so much love and care they freely wanted to giveaway these services. A world of harmony and service where all needs are met and provided by someone that was just as equally grateful to give as well as they were ready to receive. Idealistic it may seem now, but in coming years this may look much more real.

> *"However unhappy a man may be, the moment he knows the purpose of his life a switch is turned and the light is on. If he has to strive after that purpose all his life, he does not mind so long as he knows what the purpose is. Ten such people have much greater power than a thousand people working from morning till evening not even knowing the purpose of their life."*
> *Sufi master Hazrat Inayat Khan*

> *"Work is to discover your work, then with all your heart give yourself to it."*
> *Buddha*

> *"Don't bend; don't water it down; don't try to make it logical; don't edit your own Soul according to the fashion. Rather, follow your most intense obsessions mercilessly."*
> *Franz Kafka*

Towards a Higher Vibration

Why would one wish to have a higher vibration? To raise awareness, to attain to more core wisdom that exists inside the self, to be able to see more, feel more, to have more clarity, to sharpen the intuition, and to develop a warrior-like serenity in the face of any even or situation. Being more connected to all that is, allows one to really experience the human experience and to really fully live.

Our left and right brain are firewalled off, and humanity is generally locked into the left brain. Working towards a higher vibration will help synchronise and balance both sides of the brain and open up a much bigger range of reality

To make ourselves as fine-tuned a system as possible opens up a new heightened awareness which will become a basis for levels of self realisations and some glorious gifts from higher spheres. We are aiming to invite more life force energy into us, and through us in clear, unblocked energy channels. This force is known as Prana, Chi, life force, and many other names.

When looking to raise our vibration we must cover some basics in Eastern philosophy to help lay the foundations for later on. All Hermetic adepts have knowledge of the core eastern philosophy that is currently being evolved into a fluffy cash-in for much of the new-age arena. The Hermetist and the yogi are essentially both mystics, both looking for an ecstatic relationship to the universe, a more comprehensive consciousness. Yoga is ultimately a science of emptying the mind and raising one's vibration, and Hermetics is ultimately a science of will, imagination and intent.

Chakras

The ages old system of the Chakras is being adhered to daily by more and more people, why? Simply because they exist, and modern science from Dr Hiroshi Motoyama and others has proved that we each have an aura and energy meridians linking to the chakras.

Various esoteric groups, mystics and philosophers explain the chakra system a little differently but the essence is always the same.

The ancient yoga of the chakra system aims at trans-substantiating consciousness through the energy centers of the body's spinal column and brain. From the coarsest, densest, and slowest vibrational frequencies of the Muladhara root chakra at the coccyx to the most refined, subtle, and fastest vibrations of the Sahasrara crown chakra at the skullcap. A vertical pathway has been thoroughly and meticulously mapped out centuries ago infusing a priori status on the crown chakra as a final resting place for the attained. This has been known as adepthood, shiva-shakti consciousness, enlightenment or sammadhi.

Chakra is a Sanskrit word literally translating to vortex or whirlpool, and the seven chakras span upwards from the dense to the subtle signifying our ascent away from the material plane and the ego.

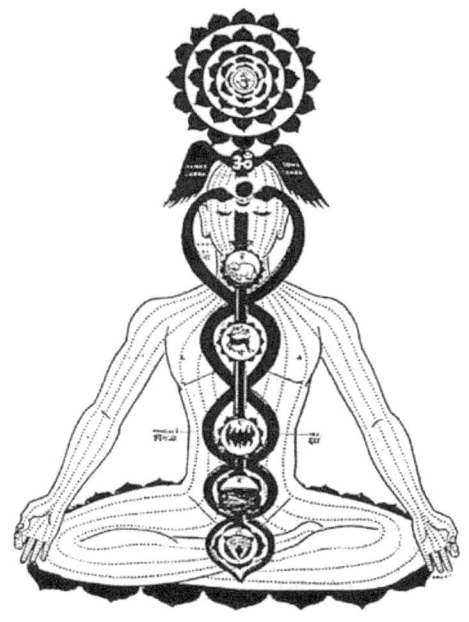

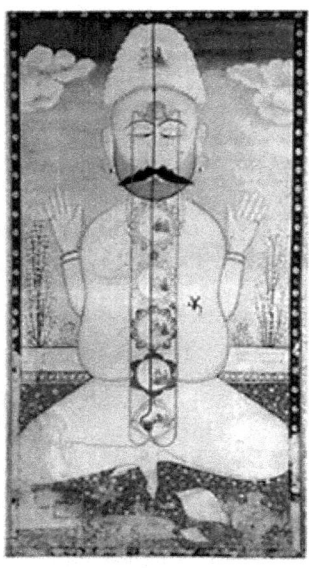

Many healers and shaman can locate which chakras are blocked, over active, or under active using a variety of methods. Once a specific chakra is re-balanced, the related symptoms manifesting in the physical world improve. Alternatively we can work on our chakras simple by visualising them, vibrating a corresponding resonance into them, or looking at what in our life relatively needs addressing. Every fibre of our being, and every ailment, emotional hang up, trauma or baggage from the past can be linked to one of the chakras, and when a chakra is activated or healed, our mind and consciousness undergo changes that have a significant relevance to our lives.

So in a brief summary what is linked to each chakra?

First Chakra, Muladhara, 4 petaled red lotus.
Physical body support, coccyx, safety, grounding, providing.

Second Chakra, Svadisthana, 6 petaled orange lotus.
Sexual organs, pelvis, duality, creativity, sex, desire, relationships.

Third Chakra, Manipura, 10 petaled yellow lotus.

Stomach, spleen, gallbladder, action, self esteem, decisions, honour, connect, belonging.

Fourth Chakra, Anahata, 12 petaled green lotus.
Heart, circulation, love, forgiveness, compassion, hope, trust.
Fifth Chakra, Vishudda, 16 petaled blue lotus.
Throat, thyroid, choice, strength of will, expression, communication.

Sixth Chakra, Ajna, 2 petaled violet lotus.
Pineal and pituitary glands, intuition, truth, mind, insight, wisdom.

Seventh Chakra, Sahasrara, 1000 petaled white lotus.
Muscular system, skin, selflessness, ethics, spirituality, mysticism, devotion, clairvoyance.

Most of humanity is stuck firmly in the lower three chakras. High Tantra talks of the five Pancha Tattvas; meat, fish, grain, wine and sex. As many societal traditions today are based around unethical ingestion of all of these, it keeps the populous deep in the lower chakras.

Each of us arrives into this realm with just the base chakra activated, the spirit arrives and sees the world as a baby with only the constant need for survival. As we get older, we start to notice duality and separation more, and it is this new view of separation that decreases the fearless feats we partake upon as a child. As we get a bit older still, we then start to desire physical intimacy and move higher into the second chakra. Most humans only rise up to the third chakra, the ego, and the strong decisions and actions to support it. Staying here is living a life only fractional to what is possible within the complex human organism.

The raising of vibration helps to raise the Kundalini energy up through the chakras, traveling up the psychic passage in the centre of the spinal cord. Kundalini is also referred to as Devi, Kali, Saraswati, Lakshmi, Shakti, the path of the initiate, and the stairway to heaven. Kundalini energy is illustrated in Eastern Philosophy as a sleeping serpent coiled three and a half times around the base chakra and in western art this energy is symbolised often as a ladder or caduceus rod. The seven seals in the book of revelation also refer to the Chakras and the Freemasonic thirty three degrees that members seek to climb are representative of the thirty three segments in the spinal column.

Raising Kundalini can be done with a guru or guide but it is really self-initiatic. No-one knows the self better than the self and one will know which chakras are in what state after just a short time of serious focus and work. But there is a warning; if too much energy is directed to this channel when ones physiology (or life) is not ready for it, some harsh effects can ensue.

Itzhak Bentov performed some experiments on people rising through the chakras and he found bio-magnetic field changes and transmutation of the body's biorhythms. In his conclusions he stated he found large physiological changes that led to altered consciousness, "This magnetic field radiated by the head acting as an antenna interacts with the electrical and magnetic fields already in the environment."

When the Kundalini energy rises, there is a physiological change, a metamorphosis, priorities and attachments change, self expression and creativity is enhanced, and the transformation of cells takes place at a higher rate than normal.

The three pillars of the Qabalistic Tree of life are the three paths of ascent that correspond with the Ida, Pingala, and Sushumna pathways in the Vedic (Aryan) system of yoga, all the systems have links from their common ancient source.

> "Everybody must remember that awakening Kundalini is the prime purpose of human carnation."
> Swami Satyananda

Ingestion

Diet is really important, with just eleven days with no meat, no processed foods, and no refined sugar, one will really feel a tangible difference. Meat takes over ten hours to digest whereas fruit and vegetables take less than an hour, and as up to thirty percent of our energy is used for digestion, we can free this energy up by what we eat. When we eat animals we are also ingesting the energy of the life the animal led. Conscious eating and cooking helps too, focusing good energy and gratitude onto what is being prepared and placing awareness towards each mouthful both have an effect upon physiology. Ingesting food is a big energy change and one that we can pilot.

In the west we mistake lightness for hunger, many think that feeling full and heavy means being well fed. This is just not true and many times we are light and empty but full of all the energy we need.

Drinking three litres of pure fresh mineral water for eleven days will also really make a big difference. This will detoxify the whole system and enable us to realise that often when we think we are hungry we are really just in need of water.

Ingestion also means excluding toxic people, toxic information and toxic aesthetics; these all affect our vibration. We need to use the virtue of discrimination towards what comes into our electromagnetic field if we are trying to seriously raise our vibration.

"Don't invest yourself where you do not wish to find yourself."

Yogic Practice

Yoga really means unity and can be done washing up, walking around a shop, in a physical posture, or in a four year solitary retreat in a cave, there are so many different levels. It is really a level of awareness, the level of unity, but in the west it has turned into a large business with quick "fast food aerobic style" yoga clubs with bright lights, ego, and the selling of mats at thirty dollars. This is not yoga I am afraid to say. Within Yoga, what can raise our vibration is a sample from pranayama, asana, and even mudra, bandha and bhakti yoga. Breathing is pretty important, stop doing it for four minutes and you should get the idea why, but we don't put much emphasis on the importance of breath nor its related science. Paranayama itself is not only breathing work, it is a means of increasing prana in the body.

Those that breath slow and more into the belly instead of the chest (children do this automatically) live longer healthier lives, and when one takes some deep breaths time seems to slow down whereas in fast breathing, time seems to speed up. Just placing our awareness into our breath during the day in any situation gives amazing results. Breathing large amounts of oxygen and prana effects endocrine glands, the will is strengthened and the person is flooded with creative positive energy.

Most yogic breathing is through the nose but during this we should attempt to breathe through the front of our throat at the same time using soft attention. Just deep breathing like this every day for a short while will relax the whole system. Performing seven seconds of breathing in, then three seconds of holding, then seven seconds of out breathing, followed by a further three seconds of holding also does so much for our biorhythms too. This is known as seven three seven breathing and should be done for at least a few minutes. Pore breathing is powerful, just lie down and breathe in through every pore in your skin, not just in through the nose to the lungs, feel yourself filling up with energy from the bottom of the belly up the chest and shoulders, and then filling up the head. When you feel comfortable with this you can inwardly pore breath affirmations or energy to different areas and breathe out stagnant energy. With pranayama, practice of focused attention and visualising will increase the effects tenfold.

Asana is posture work and one does not have to go to a yoga school or share space with too many fluffies to do this. One can just simply do some stretching each day. Some yoga schools and attendees suffer from ego, and it is best to avoid those ones, along with schools that are not teaching you to go away and perform your own yoga practice. Asanas are a way of manipulating and getting to know your body. Asana is really the training of the mind to communicate to the body.

It is probably better to learn some asanas and then do yoga on your own in your own space and to check back in with a teacher from time to time to ensure bad habits have not formed. The Sivananda group of asanas and many of the other Hatha flavours that have a strong emphasis on the spine are a sure way to raise ones vibration and flexibility. Flexibility is very important when we are looking to increase vibration as it releases blockages. With asanas, they are best done first thing in the morning before any food is ingested, and the most important asana is savasana performed at the end of a session. This is like a dead body state and here one can use visualisation techniques to activate the chakras with extra fuel in the tank.

If one is using pranayama and asana techniques, one can add in mudras and bandhas, these are postures and locks that manipulate, block, and seal the movement of energy around the body. Adding some devotional spiritual music or chants in ones yoga practice can also open the way towards bhakti yoga if one so desires.

With yoga, don't read too many books or listen to too many rules, yes there are things we should not do with our bodies but if we are stretching whilst controlling deep yogic breaths with a relaxed mind we are raising our vibration and clearing blockages guaranteed.

> *"Yoga tells us to awaken our minds, to develop the energy within ourselves so that we can attain a much greater, fuller and more total existence. Evidence is piling up to show that there is a psychic side to our lives, that the mental and intangible is far from imaginary, but is powered by an energy."*
> *Swami Satyananda Saraswati, Kundalini Tantra*

Raja Yoga (Meditation)

Meditation is absolute core to raising vibration and this was known to the ancients in Egypt, Mesoamerica and the Indus Valley. Even mainstream religions have many spiritual practices that are actually some form of disguised meditation.

To many meditation seems boring, but it is the core foundation for some later techniques that will pave the way to experiences that are about as far from boredom as one could possibly imagine. Most humans clear away unused items but rarely ever consider clearing away the "thinking mind." When this is cleared away one realizes that consciousness goes far beyond thoughts.

> "Sitting in meditation you can travel further than Columbus ever traveled and to lordlier worlds than his eyes rested upon. Come with me and we will bathe in the fountain of youth."
>
> Israel Regardie, The Magic of The Tree of Life

So what are the initial benefits of meditation before we explain how it actually works?

- Gain insight to the nature of mind.
- Control and feel emotions instead of suppressing them.
- Relieve stress and tame the constant thought chatter.
- Renew energy, increase health and ones length of life.
- Produce clarity of mind, insight, and increased creativity.
- Eliminate habits and character traits that don't serve the self.

We live in our heads mentally, so what is more beneficial than gaining insight to the nature of mind?

The brain is an electromagnetic organ and all electrical activity within the brain emanates four categories of brain waves.

- Beta 13-30 cycles per second; Alert, awake, concentrating, speaking, thinking logically.
- Alpha 7-13 cycles per second; Relaxed, reflecting, meditating.
- Theta 4-7 cycles per second; Drowsy, day dreaming, meditating, dreaming, astral traveling, lucid dreaming, shamanic journeys, REM sleep.
- Delta; 1.5-4 cycles per second; Deep dreamless sleep.

At certain brain wave frequencies, a sense of "ego boundary" vanishes. In the "theta" state we are resting deeply and still conscious, at the threshold of drifting away from or back into conscious awareness. As the brain enters these deeper states, our consciousness is less concerned with the physical state and the border of separation plus new vibrations can be realised.

Someone who has attained to a decent level at meditation can induce the alpha and even theta states whenever they wish, and this is what will open up the doors we will be knocking on later.

Dr Newburg and his science team studied a group of Tibetan monks in meditation for an hour and afterwards stated that, "During meditation, people have a loss of the sense of self and frequently experience a sense of no space and time and that was exactly what we saw." Other scientific study of meditation has shown activity in the left prefrontal cortex which is associated with concentration, planning, meta-cognition (thinking about thinking), and positive affect (good feelings). There are similar studies linking depression and anxiety with decreased activity in the same region, or with dominant activity in the right prefrontal cortex.

So, how does one meditate?

There are endless books, teachers and classes from many different disciplines, if you pick this route you may soon get swamped and lost. The best way to learn meditation, like anything in life, is to practice it alone. It's easy as there actually isn't much to actually do.

- Create some time preferably early morning or at sunset.
- Find space clear of energy and clutter, a candle or stick of incense can help as they work to clear stagnant energy.
- Sit cross legged or on your heels, use a cushion or meditation stool to ensure your hips are above your knees.
- Make sure your back is straight and shoulders are back and relaxed. You are neither tense nor relaxed, put poised.
- Scan your posture and then put your awareness into your relaxed normal breath that is traveling in and out of the nostrils.

It is much better to meditate for ten minutes a day than for fifty minutes every few days, and also try to meditate around the same time every day, a time when you are not tired. Many people state that are too busy to free up time for meditation, these people are too obsessed with the illusion.

The hardest part people find is the ceasing of thoughts, emotions, memories, future projections and daydreams. There are three main ways to do this, the first is to deny them with your will, the more favorable second way is to just let them go, and the third way is to place your awareness just behind and above your throat (where the skull seems to join).

Meditation is the only way we can slow down the waterfall of thoughts to a slow trickle, and then to a stop completely, but it is not easy and will take practice to really notice a difference. Meditation could be seen as us climbing out of the rivers flow of thoughts and sitting on the riverbank to watch them go past without giving them attention.

One monk told me once that thoughts and activity in the mind is like being in a cinema with our mind playing the movie on a movie screen. He said to become the projector and not the screen, to notice the thoughts (the screen of images), even label them, but not to give them any energy. If not involved with the pictures or related feelings, they will soon float away. It could also be explained as the natural state of mind being a blue sky and the minds activity being the clouds. If we don't give the clouds any energy they will soon disperse.

At first we will have activity in our mind for sure, and it will be helpful to know that all mental activity and chatter can fit into this small grouping:

Feelings and sensations (pleasant, unpleasant, or neutral).

Mind states (happy, sad, angry, neutral).

Mental contact (thoughts, ideas, concepts).

We just need to let this activity arise and pass, to witness without commentary, to be the silent observer.

Soon in our practice we will find a small gap, a nothing, the true nature of mind, the blue sky, and if we put our relaxed attention into this gap, it will soon get bigger and bigger until most of our meditation is performed in this place. Don't ever get frustrated or annoyed when you have a few intruding thoughts as the mind's ocean is a big enough sea for a few fish to swim in without hurting. Just know that all fleeting appearances arise in the clear space of mind and observe them without impulse or grasping.

Just meditating twenty one minutes a day for twenty one days will guarantee results. With meditation it is quality and intensity and not quantity that we are seeking; ten minutes a day with full motivation and focus is better than three hours half heartedly. If one is finding meditating extremely hard, one could use some of the audio guided mediations that use technology to alter brain wave patterns.

We are aiming to enter the unknown, where there are no signposts, where the I is erased, where there is no comparing, no honor, no definitions, and no judgments.

For we are not the intellect and we are not the mind, but mind gets in the way and tells us we are the body. We need to go behind this, and the best way is through meditation. We can go with our consciousness to the energy field of potentiality, to the Infinite space of pre-thoughts where there is no form, to the field of consciousness which is the un-manifest from which manifest comes. We soon realise that all thoughts arise independently from nothingness.

When you do no-thing, other than be fully aware that the three dimensional experience is an illusory deception conjured up through the thought process that disconnects us from true reality, then you have reconnected to your original eternal wisdom state. There's nothing to do except just simply become aware of what is transpiring. Perfection and purity is what we are already, this is wisdom and this is liberty, and this is the freedom and the power and strength of what we always have been. The trick with meditation is not to learn anything, it is to remember.

When one can achieve this state for at least twenty one minutes then one can meditate upon decisions, people, events, or absolutely anything else with some super razor sharp insight, or even levels of clairvoyance.

It is the ability to induce an altered state that is the key we wish to claim from the treasure ridden cave of meditation. The emptying of one's mind is the doorway to all metaphysical activity.

> *"Meditative awareness is the seat of the warriors' world."*
> *Shambala, The Sacred Path of the Warrior*

Mantra

The use of chants and mantras raise vibration for sure. Using one of the ancient Sanskrit mantras has extra zest due to the many millions of people that have used these sacredly. A mantra is a phrase that is connected to a spiritual force, or a concept. By the repetition one becomes aligned to that energy.

A reservoir of associated energy has built up in the astral plane akin to a deity, and mantra is similar to a deity archetype but in resonant vibratory form. Our being is affected by vibration because we ourselves are vibration, it cannot be any other way, for instance, if someone says they hate you or love you, even in a language you don't understand, the resonance of the sound and the associated intention, will, and energy will attach to your aura. This is basically how mantras work.

Certain sounds can affect our circulation and nervous system, and whatever change such vibrations cause, extends to the mind of a person and also to the surrounding atmosphere, causing warmth or coolness. Just think of two thousand people chanting aggressively at a football match or one thousand Tibetan monks chanting a mantra that has been held sacred for millenia, or a rock or a classical music concert. It is all resonance and atmospheres are severely affected and manipulated by it.

Spiritual scientist, Dan Winter has shown that when Hebrew or Sanskrit are chanted they create a vibrational frequency that moves tiny elements of matter into geometrical patterns. Chanting the Sanskrit vowels ee-eh-oh-oo-ah from the pineal to throat to heart to solar plexus to abdomen, placing your being in the state of intent to wisdom to oneness to experience to presence will yield quick results.

Swami Murugesu has chanted Sanskrit whilst watching a flame and claimed that flames change. From my own experience of working with mantra, some amazing things can happen; Once with a shaman in Guatemala I performed the 'Aum Mani Padme Hum' (translating to "oh, jewel in the lotus" meaning "the spark of divine within me") mantra in an altered state and went to a very special place where I was shown compassion on some deep levels.

Sitting in a circle with just two others chanting 'aum' correctly for ten minutes with eyes closed and a straight back will open the door to mantras, and if one finds mantra a bit strange or weird then one must ask themselves why they live with self limiting barriers that are built only by the self. I have cold showers often to clean the aura and I use a self made mantra that enables me to switch off the part of me that does not desire the cold shower. With mantra, there are again no rules, and imagination, will and intent are all so important.

"Sound and resonance interacts with life and intent."

Pineal Gland or Third eye

The pineal gland has always been tied to the esoterica of the sixth chakra, the third eye, and the ancient Greek's Seat of the Soul. This gland has long been known to the ancients; with the Eye of Shiva, the Eye of Horus, the Hindu Tilak, the Cyclops, the Unicorn, the Vesica Piscis, and The Temple of Maat from early Egypt all dedicated to the process of opening the Third Eye.

Lesser known is that the pinecone (from the Latin 'Pineus') resembles the shape of the pineal gland, or that pinecone symbolism has been used throughout history to resemble the secrets of the pineal gland.

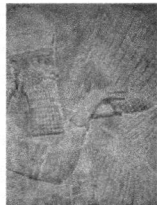  

Above we see the Assyrian winged God, a Mexican God, and a Hindu God each with the pinecone.

Dionysus (Bacchus in Rome were both were depicted with the pinecone on a staff.

In Catholicism, the pinecone is seen in statues, architecture, and even on the Popes staff. The oldest symbolism we find is the staff of Osiris from Ancient Egypt.

The Hebrew word for eyes is not plural but singular, so a correct translation of choice biblical scripture shows that it can only be talking about the eye of the soul.

> "For God doth know...then your eye shall be opened and ye shall be as Gods...knowing Good and Evil....And the eye of them both opened. "
> Genesis. 3:5-7

> "The light of the body is the eye: if therefore your eye be single, your whole body shall be full of God".
> Matthew 6:22

> And Jacob called the name of the place Peniel: for I have seen God face to face, and my life is preserved.

Matthew 6:22

Blavatsky wrote in her 'Secret Doctrine' that the Pineal gland was once an active organ before the fall of mans spirituality. This comment has added weight when we realise that the evolutionary older animals such as amphibians and birds have a pineal gland with a retina, cornea and lens.

While the physiological function of the pineal gland has been unknown until recent times, mystical traditions and esoteric schools have long known this area in the middle of the brain to be the connecting link between the physical plane and the higher spheres.

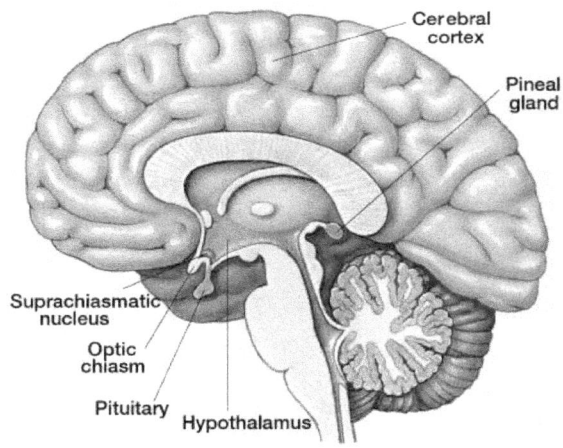

The pineal gland in the centre of the brain is about the size of a pea and lives in a tiny cave behind and above the pituitary gland weighing only 0.1 gram. Activated by light it controls various biorhythms of the body, and by working in harmony with the hypothalamus and pituitary glands, it directs the body's thirst, hunger, sexual desire and the biological clock that determines our aging process.

The pineal gland secretes melatonin during times of relaxation and visualisation, and as children have abundant melatonin levels before puberty, this is believed to be the inhibitor of children's sexual development. Furthermore, the pineal gland is large in children before puberty and then shrinks.

Further poignant study of the pineal gland has discovered it is the only part of the brain that isn't divided into two hemispheres and it's the first gland to be formed in the fetus, even distinguishable at only three weeks.

An active third eye acts as a sensitive receiver and transmitter, by which vibrations of many different types can be translated, interpreted and dispersed into our third dimensional brains to gain wisdom and illumination. Through this eye, inner planes, thought-forms, and higher archetypal entities can be perceived. Consciousness is raised from an emotional nature into an illuminated awareness, and when the pineal gland is lifted from dormancy this leads to astral vision, or vision of the higher spheres.

"Developing the third eye is a direct way of expanding your conscious universe and discovering your essential values, so that you may fathom your own mystery."
Samuel Sagan, 'The Awakening of the Third Eye.'

As human beings continue to evolve, further out of matter, on the journey from spirit to matter back up to spirit, the pineal gland will continue to rise from its state of age long dormancy, bringing back to humanity astral capacities and spiritual abilities.

In 2010, the fluoride in the tap water and the female contraceptive pill are both working toxically on the pineal gland, this is surely not a coincidence because if humanity had their third eyes open, then the levels of control in the world would disappear overnight.

Techniques

There are many techniques that are sure ways of opening and awakening the third eye, we will come to some more of these later on but for now, just using a selection of the following will give quick results. This can be used as a reference section for later.

To perform any of these techniques can be harmful if one is not meditating frequently, or has emotional problems, or is ingesting toxic stimulants.

The key words in all of these are visualisation, imagination, intent, and will, and hold in mind that esoteric master Paul Foster Case once stated that concentrated attention is really the packing together electromagnetic force.

- Simply mediate with fixed point awareness upon the area between your brows.
- Stare at a candle trying softly not to blink for eleven minutes, and then close your eyes and 'keep' the candle in your third eye until it disappears.
- Do the same as before but move the candle in your third eye to the centre of the brain, hold it there, and/or move it back and forth. Use your breath.
- Lie down and visualise each chakra starting at the root chakra. Imagine the correct number of lotus petals opening and feel the energy centre. Breathe the colour into the area.
- Create a resonant, deep, strong constant noise that vibrates into the root chakra. Work up the chakras raising the pitch of resonance each time. Calibrate the resonance to vibrate the internal area of the relevant chakra.
- Breath in through the nose fiercely to the centre of brain for five minutes, relaxing on out breaths, and then relax with attention placed on the third eye.

- Meditate with single pointed focus on the centre of a mandala (meaning sacred circle or container of essences) with relaxed focus within the third eye for twenty one minutes.

- Stare at your third eye area under soft light in a mirror for twenty one minutes. Try softly not to blink, and without moving your eyes, allow your attention to move away from your physical eyes toward your inner eye.
- Sit two meters away from a friend and do the same, this can induce face changes as well as other phenomena.
- At the end of the day visualise the whole day in your third eye in the correct order, who you met, where you went, and what you felt.
- Hold an object up in front of your eyes, stare at it for a few minutes, and then close your eyes and keep the image in your third eye for ten minutes. Then do the same without closing your eyes.
- After a few minutes meditation, imagine for ten minutes with all of your will and intent one of the following; noises, smells, warmth, coldness, hunger, thirst, tastes, gravity, lightness.

When the third eye is awakened one will feel sensation, awareness, and even a pressure between the brows, with these increasing while visualising or meditating. This pressure can grow up to the size of a ping pong ball and will feel like added insight, or literally, a third eye. Those who have this active will feel even more pressure around the times of full moon, equinox, solstice and eclipse.

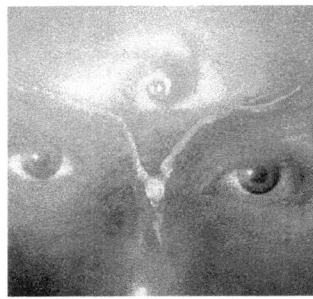

The best way to keep the third eye open is to make sure that you have enough energy flowing through it from the chakra directly beneath it. Actually, most of the energy which is moving through the third eye center has to come from your heart. This is where what is seen, heard, felt, and touched is absorbed by the inner self and given a final okay. It is there where we find the doorway to all other chakric doors, and if this chakra is not clear, the third eye cannot be clear and insightful.

To many the opening of the third eye is the ultimate goal, but for the great work of the adept, it is only the beginning, and the following alchemical art shows that it is only the start, at the roots of the tree.

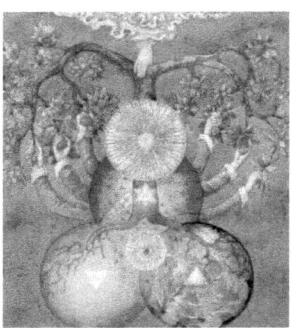

Sexual energy

Sexual desire is our most powerful and primal of urges, mainly because our DNA is programmed and hard wired to procreate. Due to the modern world using this primal urge to sell and shepherd people, many are left slaves to their sexual desires, hang-ups and frustrations.

Through the sexual act we seemingly transcend our isolation and physical boundaries and share in a greater reality, we discover, if only momentarily, that the other seems to become part of oneself.

For centuries Tantra has shown that a large amount of energy is created in sexual union, and that this energy can be directed instead of only being a stress relief born out of base chakra desires.

Tantric Vama Marga looks at sex as a fractal of the universal male and female principle, positive and negative, or we could use the Qabalistic terms, active and passive, or Chokmah and Binah. In sex we are drawing a fractal union of these polarities together at a centre, into a nucleus, into an explosion, into a singularity, and it is this singularity of love chaos that creates universes as well as baby humans.

We can move this powerful energy to higher centres using our will, focus, and concentration.

Instead of holding tension within the groin area, a man can breathe deeply and relaxed whilst sending the energy up the spine to the crown or around the whole body. A women can concentrate solely with fixed point focus upon her base chakra, at the cervix just behind the opening of the uterus. Both can also breathe in unison, and inwardly breathe energy up the spine, and breathe out energy into the heart or third eye.

At the time of orgasm, both can launch the energy up the spine and either a) to the heart chakra, and then blast out the energy to the whole body, or b) to the third eye. Either way will keep the vast amount of life force within the aura and not expel it. Eastern philosophy often states the following phrase that is worth some contemplation, "Orgasm is self destruction of the individual."

Tantra does not have to be about learning lots of techniques, having ten hour sex marathons, or having ritualistic orgasms visualising sigils. There are different levels. It is mainly just a change in mindset that sees sex as an intermingling and interplay of energies, not as a physical stress relief.

What is most important to know is that sex creates the sharing of karma and that you absorb their very essence mixing it with your own essence. You literally absorb their good stuff as well as their bad stuff. Scientifically, the two auras become entwined for days to come and a connection is maintained in the astral plane for much longer.

Synchronicities

"The way is patterned on nature."
Lau Tzu Tao Te Ching

If one has taken to any of the past texts regarding raising vibration, it is highly possible some synchronicities have entered ones experience or are just about to.

What is a synchronicity?

It is the *meaningful* coincidence of an unlikely conjunction of events. Who hasn't had it happen in their life? You think of someone for the first time in years, and run into them a few hours later. An unusual phrase linked to something you're thinking about, but you'd never heard before, jumps out at you three times in the same day. A book falls off the shelf at the bookstore and it's exactly what you need.

Many brush these events off as laws of probability, but the first person to study synchronicities was Carl Yung, and he believed it was a glimpse into the underlying order of the universe.

Jung believed the traditional notions of causality were incapable of explaining some of the more improbable forms of coincidence. Where it is plain that no causal connection can be demonstrated between two events but where a *meaningful* relationship nevertheless exists between them, a wholly different type of principle is likely to be operating. Jung called this principle "synchronicity."

He used the term synchronicity to describe what he called the "*acausal* connecting principle," meaning literally that the intrapsychic state and the objective event are not causally related to each other.

Such synchronicities occur, he theorized, when a strong need arises in the psyche of an individual. He described three types that he had observed: the coinciding of a thought or feeling with an outside event; a dream, vision or premonition of something that then happens in the future; and a dream or vision that coincides with an event occurring at a distance.

The most famous example was written by Jung in 'The Structure and Dynamic of the Psyche.'

"A young woman I was treating had, at a critical moment, a dream in which she was given a golden scarab. While she was telling me her dream, I sat with my back to the closed window. Suddenly I heard a noise behind me, like a gentle tapping. I turned round and saw a flying insect knocking against the windowpane from outside. I opened the window and caught the creature in the air as it flew in. It was the nearest analogy to the golden scarab that one finds in our latitudes, a scarab beetle, the common rose-chafer (*Cetoaia urata*) which contrary to its usual habits had evidently felt an urge to get into a dark room at this particular moment. I must admit that nothing like it ever happened to me before or since, and that the dream of the patient has remained unique in my experience."

The Scarab represents self-generation, resurrection and renewal, and caring not for those who won't believe me, minutes after reading this example for the first time when I was 35 days into a silent meditation I too found a golden scarab beetle, the only I have ever seen.

But this is all not to say normal but improbable events from the causal plane don't exist. The following is such an example to display the difference:

"A wife gives a man a new pipe for his birthday. He takes a walk and sits under a tree in a park. Sitting next to him is a man smoking the same kind of pipe. He tells the man his wife gave him his pipe for his birthday. The man says, "Mine did too." It turns out that they both have the same birthday. They introduce themselves. They have identical Christian names."

This is not a synchronistic event because there is no simultaneous, inner-meaningful, subjective event. This is something many new age fluffies may need to understand.

For Jung, a synchronistic event usually involves an archetype, with his explanation of archetypes being points or components of the collective unconscious that govern or influence our patterns of behavior. We will be venturing into sub-conscious archetypes within Qabalah and Tarot later on.

Synchronicities changed my own life, I had started meditating and studying progressive ancient history when for two weeks books about the Maya fell off shelves, or I would meet someone by chance outside a travel agent and there would be Maya temples in the window. This went on and on for days, resulting in me packing my belongings and flying to Mexico to study the Maya. When I landed, the flow of synchronicities really fired up, and from that time I have always lived in the cockpit of the synchronistic super jet. I know many others who live in similar super jets, and many have links to the numbers 11:11, as if this is the logo or uniform for the cosmic wink. It certainly seems that if we focus mentally on something that is on the path of our purpose and fullest potential, we draw synchronicities towards us.

The unwritten Qabalah can fire up synchronicities, but we cannot go there until more ground is covered. If you catch one synchronicity you need to chase it down, study it, draw it, meditate upon it, look at all the related factors, follow it, lead your life by it, and then the wink from the cosmos will gift you with more.

Via synchronistic experiences in life we begin to realise that we are all interconnected regardless of time and space. Following your intuition also often results in events coming together. Tasks and goals you want to accomplish in life somehow seem to happen without you consciously directing or controlling it. You can learn to become more in touch with this "flow" to the extent that you can live by it and be totally dependent upon it.

But to live life sailing in the ethereal world of natural signs and signposts from the edge of the fabric of our reality, a raised vibration is a must.

People who have been bound too long to the causal paradigm begin to wilt in this life, with the magical spark in all of us dimming each day. The Sufi mystics say these words of wisdom, "die before you die," by this they mean that in such people a new conscious orientation should take place which enables one to be more connected to the principle of synchronicity instead of causality. Such people begin a second life which falls under the principle of synchronicity, meaning they begin to let themselves be led by 'meaningful coincidence' and to take assistance from their dreams in order to understand wherein the way of life further leads. In greatly critical moments synchronicities come to pass which show the real goal of life, which cannot be found by will and critical thinking.

Jung said synchronicity is not sought or anticipated but it is discovered, and I agree, even though there are ways to initiate the first one. For instance, a five day silent fast in solitude is a pretty sure fire way to bring about synchronicities on the first day back into the 'real world.' It is this that is meant when the Sufi said 'death,' it is an inner death, to kill the self, and go within to the psychic archetypal world Jung wrote so much about.

It's really a way of tapping into a dimension that goes beyond time and space, allowing for temporal and spatially distant events somehow involving themselves in the here and now without the normal channel of cause n effect. This is suggestive of the theory that our life paths are woven into an order of meaning that even transcends our human perspective, and this links us back to the section on evolution.

Some fringe scientists now see a theoretical grounding for synchronicity in quantum physics, fractal geometry, and chaos theory. They are finding that the isolation and separation of objects from each other is more apparent than real; at deeper levels, everything, atoms, cells, molecules, plants, animals, and people all participate in a sensitive, flowing web of information. Physicists have found that if two photons or electrons are separated, no matter by how far, a change in one creates a simultaneous change in the other. But science will never be able to prove or measure synchronicities, and that means they sit firmly in the pot of mysticism and metaphysics, and for the wise, that is just fine.

Synchronicities are the ultimate glitch in the matrix, they are the easiest way for the fabric of reality, it's the supreme case of like to like; there is less energy expelled by the matrix and a simpler fractal is conjugated.

DMT & Shamanism

DMT, or Dimethyltryptamine is a relatively small molecule that exists in all of us and is produced naturally throughout the plant and animal kingdom. DMT is amazingly produced naturally by our pineal glands when we are born, when we dream, at death, when we induce mystical states, and during near death experiences. Strangely enough it is illegal.

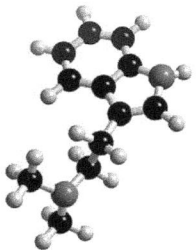

For thousands of years shaman in many parts of the world have used the ingestion of DMT and other psychotropic plants in ceremonies to create altered states of consciousness and journeying experiences. In the Maya, Peruvian and Egyptian cultural remains, there are statues and art all commemorating the use of shamanic medicine from long before 1000BC. There are hundreds of such plants, but the most well known are:

- Ayahuasca
- Peyote
- Wachuma "San Pedro"
- Mushrooms

Later we will look a little into the mushroom cults within religion, but for now we can just show one of the many mushroom statues found in Guatemala, plus the Old Temple at Chavín de Huantar in Perú depiction of a shaman holding the Wachuma cactus. Both are dated at beyond 1500BC.

Nearly all of the firsthand accounts of DMT are astonishing. In the altered states most people feel like they have been shot out of their bodies to another dimension where resides a place of animal spirits, amazing colour, fractals, wisdom, teachings, entities, past lives, love, truth, and deep insights into life, love, and direction. Deep teachings at the level of the soul can occur, as can major healings, major realisations, and the end of addictions. One usually feels totally refreshed and reborn after such experiences, with a new lease of creativity and a deeper connection to nature.

As stated earlier, it is only shock and experience that really change man and these shamanic journeys really tick both of these boxes with a big fat marker pen.

More and more people are heading to places like Peru, or even the underground circuit in Europe to participate in these ceremonies, usually people seeking truth, insight, and purification.

Once out of 'group think' it is easy to see that the ingesting of shamanic plants is of an anti-drug position because drug dependencies are the result of habitual, unexamined, and obsessive behavior; exactly the traits that the plants mitigate. Many people have such an amazingly deep profound experience that their core being is changed for the better.

I have had experiences along this path, and though this is to be shared in other writings but I will share some highlights:

- I was completely out of my body, in another place, and something told me to turn around, when I did I saw thousands of photos of my life, and I could play a movie clip of any of them.
- I felt like a naughty child in a giants house and then an organic machine of sorts plucked me out, threw me through
  some tunnels at amazing speed and I ended up at a table with some higher intelligences and an audience. They wanted to know what I was doing there. I laughed and asked them some questions about reality. They waved some keys and
- told me that wiser men than I are not allowed to play with these.
- A soft feminine energy gave me fluorescent teachings about patience, humility, and how love chaos creates.
- I was shown some synchronicities in my life and the geometry and fractals behind them.
- I started singing the words of the song the shaman was singing but I had never heard the song before and it was in a language I didn't know.
- Deep connection and merging with owl and panther animal spirits/energies.
- One time I was in a scary place and when I eventually let go of fear and surrendered a whole world of beauty opened up,

It became clear to me that one cannot discover the limits of the soul however far you go, and that our physical vessels store a lot of auric trash that needs clearing, and this goes for everyone, no exceptions.

I like this account from writer Mathew Delooze after one of his Ayahuasca journeys, "the face said all I am experiencing in my life is a dream and has nothing to do with the ayahuasca medicine. The face said the ayahausca side of things is simply on a par with a commercial break in a movie. I was told that the ayahuasca simply provides 'a commercial break dream in a bigger dream' and that the 'commercial breaks' provided by the ayahuasca can either provide the tools we need to break from the bigger dream or it can provide us with golden ticket dream tokens to keep the bigger dream going."

The shamanic medicine path is the back door in, the less graceful way of peeling back the veil of Isis. Using the Hermetic Great Work, we can be invited in through the front door and offered a chair in the living room with a cup of tea waiting.

The truest way is to get to this place naturally and that is what part III of this book is all about. The meditative way is slower, more systematic, but encompasses the same realms and spaces. As it is more gradual there is much more control. One can stop and look at the road signs instead of flying past them with galactic neon butterflies at the speed of light being chased by demonic entities. One can process the insights gleaned more slowly and therefore the full integration will never leave you. It is a purer trip, and the people I know who have trodden both paths have more awe for the natural fork in the road.

Life is a real mystery, and there are very few ways to actually crack through the surface. The shamanic medicinal route is one of these cracks in the matrix for sure, and more and more warriors are peeking through this crack in a serious way.

> "To go far away sit in one spot alone, fast for a day, then ingest some Wachuma. Man in his folly looks to cars and planes to alter the external reference frames in order to journey. A journey is always internal, until you realise this you are flapping in the wind."

The Journey is to the Self

> "The biggest conspiracy in this world is about you. Solve that and the rest will follow."
> Matthew Delooze

All orthodox religions have the journey to the self at the core, but it is often hidden. In the Gnostic gospel of Thomas that never made it into the Bible it states that if one does not know thyself then one will live in poverty. The entrance to the Delphic Oracle had the sign "Gnothi Seauton" (Know Thyself) and this comment was associated also to Socrates.

The only real freedom is authentic selfhood, and this is claimed once one has won the struggle against the false I, only when one has cleaned and re-orientated the furniture inside the inner shadow self.

As we will see, the sleeping of the body is the waking of the soul, and the waking of the body is of the sleeping of the soul. Man has two ways of life; one where the senses are awake and the soul sleeps or where the soul is awake and the senses sleep, we all have the choice.

> *"To live solely in the five senses keeps your soul asleep, we need to awaken the soul and realise the five senses are just inputs and ways of experiencing just some of this realm. The mind therefore can be the slayer of reality. We need to slay the slayer with the sword of our souls."*

> *"Your vision will become clear only when you look into your heart, who looks outside is dreaming, he who looks inside, awakens."*
> Carl Jung

Gurdjieff was once asked why truth was so carefully concealed and why mystics do not pass it on to the public to help the world. His answer was, "It is not concealed, by its very nature it cannot become common property. People do not want it, or more commonly, are unable to receive it. There is a definite amount of knowledge, lots of people get a little, or a few people get a lot. Large quantity of knowledge in a few people is strong therefore it is better not to be dispersed. If in the hands of a few, each will not only receive enough, but they will or can increase what they receive. Also to get at the real knowledge takes much time and labor, the crowd does have not time, and seek no labor save that which gives them money. But arts like music and painting take years of arduous labor to perfect, this art there is no difference. One can only obtain knowledge from those who posses it. To speak the truth, one must know the truth, but firstly, oneself, and this, nobody wants to know. People do not value a thing if they do not pay for it."

> *"People are always saying that they want truth, but they don't really want truth. They want something which is familiar. They want a guarantee that if they come into the next step to waking up they'd be guaranteed to be able to handle it and that isn't the case. Not everyone can truly wake up. Many people can wake up to the first step, which is simply understanding what's happening in the world around them and to them and where it's going and they can follow the speeches given by various people down through the last hundred years or so and it all begins to make sense to them, but that's only one level of this whole process."*
> Alan Watt

There is so much information out there now that we need to go within more than ever, there is so much mind control, disinformation, fanaticism, and false debunking. We are amidst an information and spiritual minefield, but we need to go within, and to use an ancient system that can help us; a system that has not been bent or tampered with.

***

There are so many systems that one can choose it can get very messy. Many of these require a guru, the remembering of lists, and the performing of strange dogmatic physical traditions that do nothing for vibration.

Nobody can be a part of a collective shift in consciousness by giving their own consciousness away. No one can shift their own awareness by leaving it to someone else to do it for them. You can't hire someone to do your shifting for you. We need experience, we need shock, self initiation, so we look to a system that can give us this independently. Alas, it seems in this day that people seek a father figure, an expert, a leader, a hero, a something to attach to so one doesn't have to look at the self, from the self.

One thing is for sure, we need to carry out a system in its entirety and not fleet from system to system, or one will just become a dabbler.

The main respectable routes or paths that can really help us achieve the aim of going deep to the authentic self are few. The paths worth their salt have to be ancient and use archetypal meditation to achieve altered states and altered physiology as this is the only real way to activate dormant cells and DNA.

The Sufi path is based upon the Enneagram nine pointed star. This path uses archetypal concepts to push mind and consciousness, but alas there is very little text on this subject. This is the path Gurdjieff took when spending years in a Sufi mystery school.

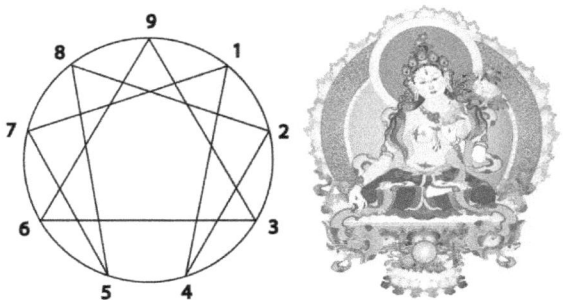

The Tantra path uses archetypes and energy based initiations, but one pretty much needs a guru, and for the westerner the language barrier may prove a problem. Unfortunately alongside Tantra, there are now many Buddhist schools where there are more rules than spark, more dull energy than life, and groups all huddled around one teacher. This really cannot be the way, and may start to cloud what is a beautiful core philosophy.

The highly acclaimed author, Dion Fortune, stated that Qabalah is the best system for the western mind. I agree, it is based on universal laws, uses your inner guru, has a language that is easy to understand for the westerner, and other theologies and theosophy fall into it.

Qabalah is not really a system, it is more a vehicle that is traveled upon in an individual way.

Most importantly, the Qabalah is about how *your* inner self interprets and grows, not from what anyone has told you. One learns about the archetypes and the meditative glyph, the tree of life, and goes from there in his or her own way. It is for those who are seeking a spiritual quest and adventure, not just more knowledge and theory.

This is the path we will study, and a path that has a lineage that traces back to the Egyptian mystery schools.

Each of these paths have a similar theme; they each peel the layers off of a human, akin to the peeling of an onion. They each go in reverse, they don't add, they actually take away and then enable one to travel to the core essence of our true selves. The Qabbalah I know for sure allows one to see the world without labels and concepts.

Before we enter the rich world of Hermetic Alchemical Qabalah, we need to cover some information that was left out of the science and history books within the child indoctrination centres (schools).

"Truth agrees with truth, and when you get to the summit of the truth mountain, it matters not which path you took to get there."

PART II – PROGRESSIVE KNOWLEDGE

New truth does not triumph by convincing its opponents and making them see the light, but rather because its opponents eventually die, and a new generation grows up that is familiar with it."
Max Planck

I did not wish to call part II science and history as these words conjure concepts in the mind I wish to steer clear from. With science and history humans always seem to leave it to the academics to tell us how things are, what has happened, and where we come from. This is surely not the way, especially when one finds out how any word against the official line is often aggressively quashed, or confused with disinformation. Even children are taught lies about ancient Egypt as young as seven years old, and the main history and documentary TV channels often air programs of disinformation via premeditated simplistic lies or confusion. I may sound like a conspiracy theorist but spend a few years independently researching these areas with people that do not rely on umbrella funding and you will soon get the full picture.

"Science is but a perversion of itself unless it has, as its ultimate goal the betterment of humanity."
Nikola Tesla

Science stands in the corner shouting that it is only them that understand life, and the philosophers and mystics are ridiculed. But the scientists are always looking at the how, and never the why, always looking at matter and never consciousness. The scientist is always shouting about what they do know, whereas the philosopher and mystic always concentrate upon what is not know.

Science looks external and the only way to further in the hunt for knowledge is to go internal. The deep rooted materialistic view in science can be summed up by trying to weigh and measure a myth, it cannot be done but this is not to say the myth does not exist upon real facts.

Have there been more mainstream scientists who became mystics, or more mystics who became mainstream scientists? I rest my case.

There are some facts about our reality and past that need to be shared, and this is what Part II is about.

> *"Life is a mystery, trying to solve it with the intellect is like trying to empty the ocean with a spoon."*

> *"The most dangerous and the saddest of sciences is Theology, for it constitutes itself wrongly a science of God. Rather is it a science of the foolishness of man when it seeks to explain the inscrutable mystery of man and when it seeks to explain the inscrutable mystery of the Divine."*
> Eliphas Levi

Glitches in the Matrix

Our reality has some clues about "our reality." There are some very big glitches in the matrix and most of these are brushed under the carpet. The immediate list presents some very real phenomena in our realm that society and science pushes into the baskets of weird, paranormal, and nonsense.

- Twins sharing telepathy.
- Blind people feeling colour.
- Deaf people feeling music.
- People being hypnotised.
- People being mind controlled.
- Amputees experiencing the phantom limb effect.
- Organ transplants experiencing personality traits of the donor.
- Crops circles.
- Residual energy from people long deceased.
- Leylines.
- Sungazing for energy.
- Placebo effect.
- Dowsing.
- Near death experiences.
- ESP and precognition.
- Hive mind animals.
- Disappearing bees.
- People awakening from comatose with new traits such as a new language.

- Animals with a sixth sense.
- The hundred monkey effect.
- Hot ash walks.
- We can't measure velocity and position at same time, it is one or other. A pendulum is never at rest, it is a violation of the particle uncertainty principle.
- Ripples in a lake, pendulum swings within clocks, and women's menstrual cycles all falling into in synch within a local environment.
- Ancient phenomena such as The Great Pyramid, The Sphinx, the Nazca Lines, Baalbek, Fatima, Easter Island, Teotiuhacan, Tiahunaco, Ollantaytambo, Sacsayhuaman, Kailasa Temple, The Red Pyramid, Machu Piccu, Chichen Itza, Tikal and Palenque.

Glitches are evident in the solar system and universe too.

- The moon is four hundred times smaller than the sun, and the sun is four hundred times the distance from us than the moon, giving us a perfect eclipse. Some call this a coincidence!
- The moon moves thirteen Degrees a day, and there are thirteen cycles in solar year.
- Venus orbits just over thirteen times for every eight orbits of the Earth, creating a pentagrammic pattern of inferior conjunctions.

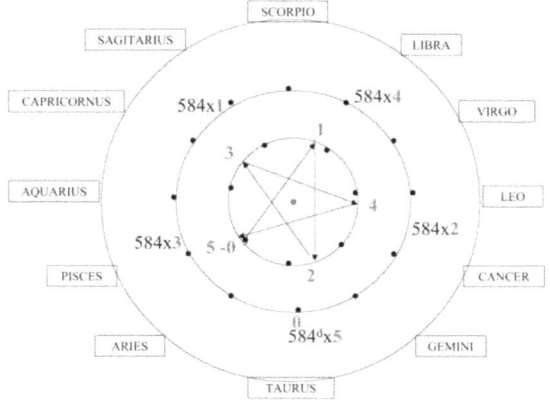

- Science states that atoms, planets, and galaxies are spinning due to the big bang and that this spin has been continuing ever since due to the frictionless environment. For this to be true all objects would have to be solid (try spinning an unboiled egg versus a hardboiled egg) which they are not. There is lava in the earth and plasma density changes in the galaxy, hence more like an unboiled eggs. Also atoms collide and interact with gravitational atoms, and this creates friction, as does the inside of the earth against the crust.
- The big bang was not a bang at all, but more of a singularity of condensed energy, a spark.
- The conditions of the universe and solar system are exactly just right to enable human life to live, these conditions are in their hundreds, but a few notable ones are; nuclear, gravitational, the suns distance, electromagnetic forces, ratio of electron to protein mass, entropy level of the universe, average distance between stars, universe and suns age, crust thickness, carbon dioxide levels, and soil mineralisation.
- The Sun, Venus, Jupiter, and the Earth have spots, volcanoes or major mountains at 19.5 degrees from their equators, the same as the vertexes on a star tetrahedron.

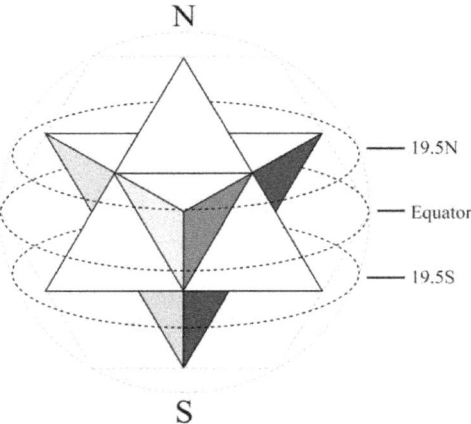

- Professor Paul Davis PHD estimates that if no intelligence is involved and our reality came about only by chance and mechanicals laws, then time requested to achieve this level of order and life we have now by random is 10(10)(80) years. Allot more than the sixteen billion years sited as the age of the universe.

"When it comes to the origin of life there are only two possibilities: creation or spontaneous generation. There is no third way."

Reality is an illusion?

Actually all of the leading theories in science actually seem to think so, which take us full circle back to the Vedic texts.

- Virtual reality theory.
  Given that any technological society would build many such artificial realities, in time, the number of those is expected to be higher than the number of real realities, making it more likely reality is a simulation. Think about that logic, it's actually hard to deny.
- Standard theory of Quantum Mechanics.
  In Quantum Mechanics, mass is actually caused by virtual particles that very briefly pop in and out of existence, quite probably by causing twists in time space. In addition, things only have a definite place in space and time when they interact.
- Bohms Theory/Holographic universe.
  In Bohms theory reality is in fact one thing, folded many times through another dimension, to look like many things e.g. reality. They discovered that under certain circumstances subatomic particles such as electrons are able to instantaneously communicate with each other regardless of the distance separating them by an unrecognized force. It doesn't matter whether they are ten feet or ten billion miles apart. In holographic universe, all information is in the whole and in the part.
- Torsion wave Physics. Reality is constantly being created by spinning vortex waves coming out of the ether.

According to Nassim Haramein, a deeper fractal reality is occurring in which atoms are like little black holes. The universe is learning about itself, "the information that it gathers, coalesces and synergizes to produce the next set of questions," in a kind of "self organising feedback structure," he recently explained.

Matter is just energy translated by the brain as reality, energy fields are decoded by our brains into a 3D picture, to give the illusion of a physical world. How often do you dream and in your dream you don't even realise you are dreaming?

Our existence is not what is being questioned, we all undoubtedly exist as consciousness but the question is does the universe exist? Is it really there or is it (just like our dreams) an illusion *created* from apparent nothingness.

Most people, even if they begin to understand that we live in an illusion will stop at the five sense level of it.

> *"If it changes it wasn't true in the first place, and scientific results are always changing."*

Consciousness

We can place our consciousness into an atom, into space, and into a connection with other people by thinking about them. We can lucid dream, astral travel, and remote view, and such techniques have been used by the military for decades. We can replay songs, films, experiences, feelings, and stories in our mind, and we can comprehend the size of the universe and visualise future scenarios. Wow!

Consciousness has no mass or volume, therefore it cannot be sampled, or measured. It is a field with no charge, polarity, density or effect. It is a state that cannot be observed, created or destroyed.

Many scientists have said that without a consciousness there to observe the big bang, the big bang exists only as a probability state, and the late physicist John Wheeler advanced this notion by stating that light from distant quasars only existed when it was observed.

Every physical manifestation is light energy. $E=mc2$ states this fact. Multiply mass by the speed of light times the speed of light and the mass becomes light energy once again. Slow it down and it becomes mass and visible. Speed it up again and it disappears to the naked eye. The only thing capable of manipulating energy in this way is a thought. A thought is the concept of living outside the moment that appears to create light energy. This thought, when combined with sound, slows and drags the energy down to make everything physical appear. This is the fundamental theory to all occult practice.

The manipulation of a light beam produces symbols, shapes, colours and sounds. Dogma directly and deceitfully throws a veil over our ability to connect to wisdom. This occurs because we have been tricked to believe we are physically created and that life is breathed into us. In reality we have always been present, but through hypnotic suggestion we believe our physical and mental being is reality. Life wasn't breathed into us, quite the opposite!

We don't see objects but we see reflected light, and we don't hear sound but interact with a wave. It is a trick to create our reality.

The body computer is like a space suit that allows our consciousness to experience this reality. If I didn't have an outer shell that vibrates within the frequency field of this 'reality' then I wouldn't be able to type these words. I would have no fingers and, even if I did, they would pass through the keys just as radio waves pass through the walls.

The brain is really just the electrical transmitter *for* consciousness, and the paradigm of consciousness being non local is one that can be looked at in a similar way to Dr Darfatti, "imagine your brain is a computer, now imagine the whole universe as a mega-computer. Then imagine the sub-quantum realm being made up of mini-computers. The hardware of all of these computers is localised somewhere is space-time, but the software, the information, is non-local. It is here, there, and everywhere; now, then, and everywhen."

Akin to Russian dolls there exits the local "I" consciousness, then the family consciousness, the tribal (local environment) consciousness, the global collective consciousness, the galactic consciousness, and then the universal consciousness. It is the only way it can be.

To science, consciousness is the ghost in the machine, but to the mystic it is the centre of all investigation.

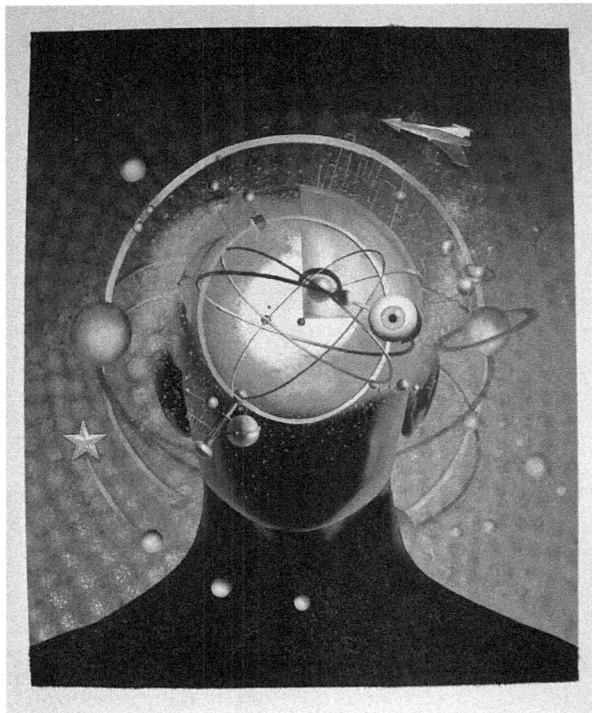

Sacred Geometry

Vibratory infrastructure of energy pathways are formed by geometric patterns, therefore at all times when we think or feel, we are sending out geometric patterns into the field, and likewise we are constantly receiving geometrical patterns.

Without going into the flower or life, the platonic solids, metatrons cube, and all the other wonderful complex shapes that are inherent within creation, we can just simply say that sacred geometry is a prime conduit to source. This is because it bypasses dogma, philosophy, intellect, belief and disbelief. It simply charts the unfolding of number in space, from point to line to shape to 3D, and then charting back. We could look at geometry as number in space and music as number in time.

When we interact with sacred geometry we interact with its energetic radiance and so enter into commune with the base blueprint of creation.

Cymatics has recently shown that sound vibrations can be translated into geometry too. This is usually done by vibrating a fine powder or a liquid on a plate connected to a speaker (sine wave vibration). The images that can be produced with different frequencies are complex and beautiful and can often look like mandalas, and one can immediately comprehend the link to science of mantra too.

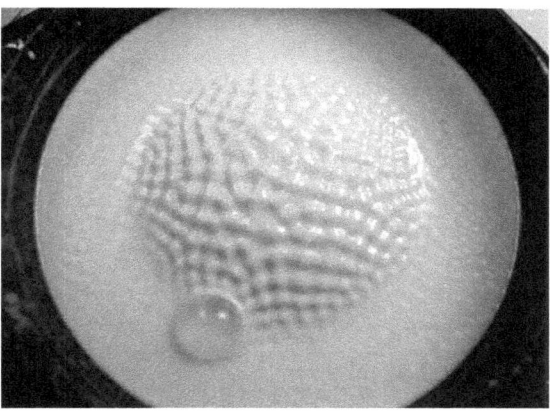

There is no need for expensive new age courses, it is simple; be close to the geometry in the natural world and feel it. There is no better way to do this than to align with Golden Phi.

Phi, which is a ratio of 1.6180339887...(into infinity) was described by Johannes Kepler as one of the "two great treasures of geometry," with the other being the Theorem of Pythagoras.

Phi is a ratio seen everywhere in nature, so one could say it is an infinite number showing infinity. A coincidence to scientists who really keep well away from thought constructs like infinity.

The simplest way to first comprehend Phi is to look at line. The ratio of the whole line (A) to the large segment (B) is the same as the ratio of the large segment (B) to the small segment (C).

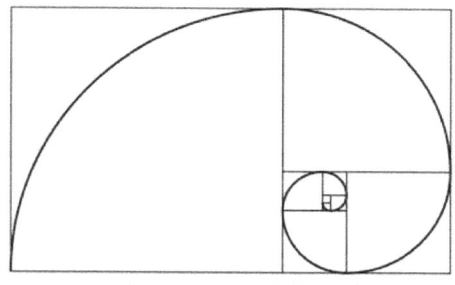

The ratio the rectangles grow in size by a ratio of 1.618...... and if a curve is drawn through them we achieve what is known as the Golden Section.

This is seen throughout nature as a fractal within shells, flowers, clouds, galaxies and much more.

Golden phi is also found in water, butterflies, music, arches, sunflowers, pinecones, leaf arrangements, music, and even the family trees of cows, bees, and rabbits.

There other places of interest where can we find this amazing natural number that's never mentioned in modern day "schools."

In the human body; teeth, bones, feet, ears, face, self organising DNA nucleotides, and more.

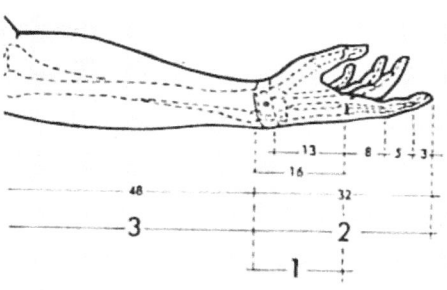 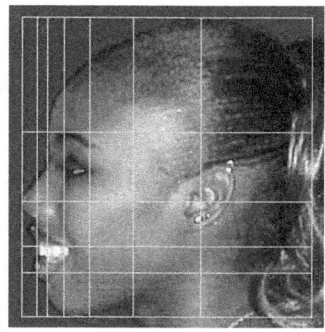

It is found in paintings, mainly those from the renaissance period where Hermetic alchemy was rife, such as work from Boticelli and Leonardo Da Vinci.

It is found in Cathedrals, the Great Pyramid, the Parthenon, the Taj Mahal, the United Nations building, and even the ancient Egyptians built these irrational numbers into temple doors so that the human spirit would feel good upon entrance.

Phi is found in the ratios of planets distances from the sun, and also in orbits relative to earth. It is even used in modern day logos, product and package design.

**

Why have we looked at phi so much? How is it relevant to this book?

It is a pure fractal, infinity shown in number, above and below using the same laws, and this makes it a doorway into Hermetics and backdrop to Qabalah.

With golden phi we really can call upon Plato's quote of "learning is remembrance," because in Phi we can find unity and cease the illusion of ego. It is hard wired into our reality and this is an ultimate glitch in the matrix.

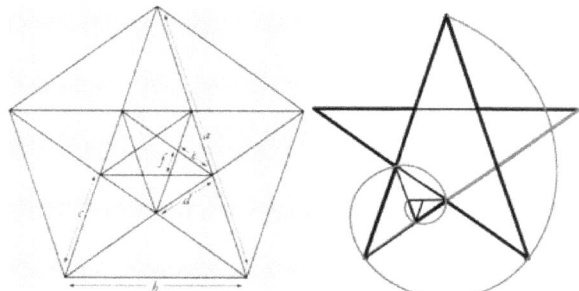

Times Past

Much could be, and has been written about the history of hidden knowledge and its flow through humanities evolution. This chapter will divulge a slither of some of the knowledge within the mystery schools that are around today. In the following sections I wish to lie down a few seeds of information that can open up new avenues of investigation and thought.

"To know where you are going, you need to know where you have come from."

Ancient Egypt Snippets

There is increasing evidence for advanced civilizations before Egypt in Atlantis, Lumeria, and beyond.

We can notably pick up the trail of the mysteries in Egypt where hundreds of Gods personified nature and human traits, thus being inner and outer archetypes of the reality lived within.

In the Egyptian initiatic mystery religions a human death did not destroy an individual but only gave the person a different form and closer association with one of their many polytheistic Gods. The Pharaohs who were often looked upon as Gods viewed life as a passage to the celestial worlds, and the concept of a soul was highly developed in the Egyptian mystery religions.

The Osiris, Isis, Horus trinity and the *Egyptian Book of the Dead* is a certainly one source of Christianity, and the two pillars of Osiris and Isis at Nysa in Arabia are the source of all modern day paired pillars found in theology and the mystery traditions.

The God of the dead Osiris was resurrected by Isis from the underworld, and the cult of Osiris exited for centuries throughout Egypt, if not millennia.

The Bible talks of a mass exodus from Egypt across the Sinai Desert but there is no record of this in Egypt. Many progressive historians are linking this event to Akhenaten (previously named Amenhotep IV), and some even state he was the real Abraham or even Moses (though both of these characters are allegorical). What can we look at to add weight to this link?

- Egypt was polytheistic with its capital in Thebes with the highest God being Amun.
- A few years after Akhenaten came to power around 1350BC he declared Aten (the Sun God, the solar disk) as the only deity. He outlawed all worship to any other deities and the polytheistic priesthoods and clergy were dismantled. Monotheism was born.

- He moved the capital over 150 miles away to middle Egypt and named the city Akhetaten, meaning 'horizon of the sun-disc' (now known el-Amarna). The city was full of gold, artists, and princesses, and was the centre of the monotheistic cult.
- A few years after Akhenaten died aged 25 in 1332BC, his son Tutankhamun took the throne as a child with the hidden hand of Smenkhkare behind the scenes.
- Around 1330BC the deities of Polytheism with Amun as the chief God was restored and the capital moved back to Thebes. As time went on all remaining links to Aten were destroyed, as was the city Akhetaten.
- It is during this time that the residents of Akhetaten were forced to flee due to reprisals. This is the only possible exodus in the whole of ancient Egypt, and has to be the one within the Bible (Exodus was written 700 years later). It is these people that were probably the originals Jews (the word Jew and its meaning has been changed over time by Judaism, which is really more of a political and social movement).
- In the Exodus 1:22 it states the Pharaoh orders the death of all first born Hebrew sons, this does not fit with any other time in Egyptian history, and there is much evidence of many delivery rooms in Akhetaten as breeding was promoted. Exodus also tells of how the one God was revealed to the patriarchs.
- Abraham fits no one else in ancient times nowhere near as well as Akhenaten. Abraham broke the idols of his fathers, and the Bible states YHVH said to Abraham, "leave for your own sake, out of your country, away from your native land, and from paternal home, go to the land I will show you. I will make you a great nation."

There is also much recent evidence to suggest that the Biblical Moses was based upon the Pharaoh Ramesses I but the seed I am trying to plant is that the Bible is plagiarised and it meshes stories and myth across centuries and is riddled with allegory. For instance, when Moses saw the bush consumed by fire in the desert it is probably stating that the self never dies within retreat. The secret societies of the past few centuries make it their first task to deprogram new members from Christian thought, this has been told to me from high members of the O.T.O (Ordo Templi Orientis) whose invitation I declined.

In Egypt Melchizedek was probably a very high order of priesthood, and the Eye of Horus mystery schools are one of the main roots of modern day secret teachings.

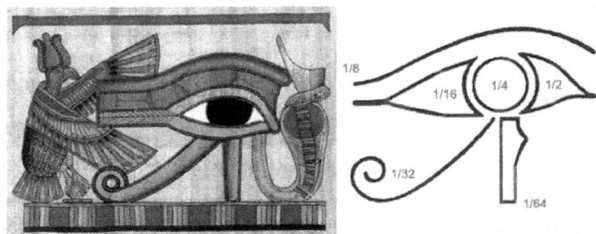

The eye is made up of parts which are associated with fraction values, these relate to Touch, Taste, Hearing, Thought, Sight, and Smell. Added together they equate to 63/64 which leaves a hidden part, such as the myth of Osiris (were Isis put him back together save his penis), such as YHVH having a missing letter, and such as the Tree of Life having a missing Sephirah.

> "Come, the Eye of Horus hath delivered for me my soul, my ornaments are established on the brow of Ra. Light is on the faces of those who are in the members of Osiris."
>
> The Pyramid Texts

Egypt was never to be the same again after Greek King Alexander the Great invaded Egypt in 331BC, and the later Roman invasion and rule of Egypt in 31BC. Between these times Rome had also invaded and controlled Greece after the battle of Corinth in 149BC.

At the beginning of the 3rd century BC, during the reign of Ptolemy II of Egypt, the great library in Alexandria was built. At its peak it held between 400,000 to 700,000 parchment scrolls containing knowledge of mystery traditions, of maps, and of ancient civilizations. In 46AD a battle between forces of Caesar and his ally Cleopatra VII of Egypt and those of rival King Ptolemy XIII of Egypt saw the library burned down. It is here that we find many mysteries and stories relating to many parchments being taken back to Rome before the planned fire. Any remnants of the library were crushed by Muslims in the 17th century.

Knowledge from ancient Egypt spread to Greece, Arabia, and Rome where many initiatic, mystery, and alchemical schools and cults were formed.

Religious Cult Snippets

The Cult of Pythagoras

Pythagoras was born in 560BC and spent much of his youth travelling and learning. He was initiated into the mysteries of Tyre and Byblos and had to perform a forty day fast using strict pranayama before being allowed admittance into the mystery school at Diospolis. He spent the next twenty two years in Egypt being initiated into the Egyptian mysteries before an invasion by the king of Persia placed Pythagoras in Babylon. There he spent twelve years with Chaldean Magi before going to learn even more in India with Rishi descendants.

He was fifty six years old when he returned to his homeland in Greece where he opened a mystery school. A statue of Hermes Trismegistus was placed at the door of the inner school with the words on the pedestal "let no profane enter here."

The school had a very strict discipline of silence and cleanliness, and most teachings were based upon numbers, geometry, astronomy, spirit, and sound. The core beliefs in the schools of Pythagoras were:

- That all form is a thought expressed through sound.
- That at its deepest level, reality is mathematical in nature.
- That philosophy can be used for spiritual purification.
- That the soul can rise to union with the divine.
- That certain symbols have a mystical significance.
- That all brothers of the order should observe strict loyalty and secrecy.

Plato had most of his thoughts and beliefs firmly rooted in Pythagorean thought, and Plato taught Aristotle, who in turn taught Alexander the Great.

Pythagoras was much more a magus than a modern day professor but in 2010 schools stay clear of such truths and simply focus on some of the basic geometry.

The Cult of Dionysus

Dionysus (the bastard son of Zeus from around 1440BC in myth) was also commonly known by his Roman name Bacchus and was seen as the Greek God of mystic illumination.

On the one hand, Dionysus was the God of wine, agriculture, and fertility of nature, who is also the patron God of the Greek stage. On the other hand, Dionysus also represents features of mystery religions such as those practiced at Eleusis; ecstasy, personal delivery from the daily world through physical or spiritual intoxication, and initiation into secret rites. Scholars have long suspected that the God known as Dionysus is in fact a fusion of a local Greek nature God and another more potent God imported rather late in Greek prehistory from Phrygia (the central area of modern day Turkey) or Thrace.

The cults throughout Europe and Asia used wine fuelled orgies, dance, mushrooms, and music to create trance induced states to remove inhibitions and material constraints. During the Dionysia festivals the maenads would enter a trance dancing to the beat of drums and waving thyrsi. Sometimes they would go into a frenzy during which they gained supernatural powers it was claimed. It was said that the maenads could tear apart animals and even humans with their bare hands.

The cult was initiatic and performed closed masked rituals as well as public plays and theatre sacred to Dionysus,

Large scale worship of Dionysus was evident in Thebes in Greece in 1500BC and only later was the cult introduced into Rome around 200BC.

This cult is very much alive today in 2010 within various secret societies and power groups. The movie "Eyes Wide Shut" gives a very accurate detail of what goes on, and strangely enough the director Stanley Kubrick died just after the film was completed.

The Cult of Mithras

The roots of Mithraism go back to ancient Zoroastrianism, a Persian religion of Magi that became popular in Greece around 400BC. Many scholars also outline Vedic roots in Mithraism too.

Mithra was a pagan sun God, the lord of light, and was usually depicted killing the bull which shows his links to the end of the age of Taurus around 2150BC. The astrotheology linked to Mithraism is vast and the lions head in one of Mithras' depictions is obviously the sun, and in other remnants of the cult the twelve animals of the zodiac are seen.

During the 1st century BC the cult of Mithra made much progress in Rome and soon most Roman soldiers became members, and then Emperors.

Mithraism maintained strict secrecy about its teachings and practices revealing them only to initiates. Small Mithraic congregations were like Masonic lodges and allowed only men. In underground caverns (later found scattered all across Europe) they shared ritualistic meals with bread and wine, and performed initiations using blindfolds and shock-based rebirth rituals.

Mithraism had a complex system of seven grades of initiation:

CORAX (Raven) – Mercury
NYMPHUS (Male-bride) - Venus
MILES (Soldier) - Mars
LEO (Lion) - Jupiter
PERSES (Persian) - Luna (moon)
HELIODROMUS (Courier of the Sun) - Sol (sun)
PATER (Father) - Saturn

Born on the 25th December, Mithra later had a final meal before being called to heaven only to be later resurrected as the sun of God, and by 200AD worship of Mithras outnumbered those of Jesus massively.

In 274AD Emperor Aurelian had declared Mithraism to be the official religion of the Roman Empire, and the same man officially named 25th December (the after the previous seven days known as Saturnalia) as the "Birth of the Unconquered Sun celebration."

Well into the 4th century, the 25th December had nothing to do with Jesus anywhere on the planet. It was celebrated in link with the solstice, the death of the sun (winter solstice), Saturnalia, and Mithra.

To diverse for a moment, all of today's Christmas symbolism from trees, to ivy, to mistletoe, to Santa Claus, to stockings, to gifts, either come from this period in Rome or a splattering of other European paganism. It was Charles Dickens' book *A Christmas Carol* that sold the idea of what we now know as Christmas to the masses in the mid 19th century.

***

In 307AD, Mithra worshipper Emperor Diocletian burned much of the Christian scriptures, but Christianity was still on the rise mainly due to women not being allowed into the core traditions of Mithraism.

Emperor Constantine merged the cult of Mithra with the Christianity that was developing. He declared himself a Christian but at the same time maintained his ties to the Mithra cult. He retained the title "Pontifus Maximus," the high priest, and on his coins were inscribed "Sol Invicto comiti" which meant "committed to the invincible sun."

This new blend of the two faiths he officially proclaimed as Christianity in the Council of Nicea in 325AD.

Once the Nicea Council meeting was underway Constantine demanded that the three hundred bishops make a decision by majority vote defining who Jesus Christ was. Constantine commanded them to create a "creed" doctrine that all of Christianity would follow and obey, a doctrine that would be called the "Nicene Creed" and upheld by the Church and enforced by the Emperor.

Jesus became the "Son of God" from the "Sun of God" and the official definition of the Trinity was also born; the deity of The Father, Son, and Holy Spirit under one Godhead.

The early Christian fathers were worried about the pagan roots and soon outlawed Paganism, Gnosticism (explained soon), and Mithraism.

Temples were destroyed for churches to be built on top of the remains (to harvest the energy). Many people were burned alive.

The Church began to suppress initiatic teachings and reduced its own teachings to dogma. Mithraism soon died and the church went onto rise in power, and from this time the occult knowledge went underground only to resurface in sporadic fits and spurts as we shall soon see.

"Spirit of Spirit, if it be your will, give me over to immortal birth so that I may be born again - and the sacred spirit may breathe in me."
Prayer to Mithras

The Essenes

Around 150BC a group called the Essenes was prevalent. Some say they came from Egyptian or Hindu origin, and others state all had Jewish births, whatever the origin they all denounced the Jewish majority as apostate, and temple worship in Jerusalem as polluted.

Around four thousand strong went to live in pious isolation mainly on the western shore of the Dead Sea in what was probably one of the first existences of organised monasticism.

It is not clear whether the Essenes proceeded from some sect of Judaism or whether elements of Greek and other foreign philosophies had an influence in their origin. It does appear that even though the Essene theology was basically Jewish (an absolute belief in God and angels), Buddhism, Parseeism, Syrian heathenism, and Pythagoreanism were at all play.

Admission required two to three years of preparation and new candidates took an oath of piety, justice, and truthfulness. Each member had little or no private property, each wore white linen, and each honored virtue by foregoing all riches and pleasures. Purification, silence, cleanliness, meditation, and farming were the firm bases for the Essene communities. Many scholars state they lived with women and made love under strict rules, but more reliable sources such as Pliny the Elder state that they lived without women.

The Essenes are not mentioned directly in the Bible even though scores of scholars state Jesus spent time with them. However, it is thought that Matthew 19:11-12 includes indirect references to the Essenes. In any case, the Essenes disappeared from history after the destruction of Jerusalem in 70AD and an earlier Earthquake in the Qumran region.

The importance of the Essenes is that they had in their possession a great number of very ancient manuscripts. A portion of the members spent their time decoding them, translating them into several languages, and reproducing them in order to perpetuate and preserve this advanced knowledge.

These are what became famously known as "The Dead Sea Scrolls."

The Dead Sea Scrolls were the find of just under nine hundred documents discovered between 1947 and 1956. All were located in clay jars in eleven caves in and around the ruins of the ancient settlement of Qumran, on the northwest shore of the Dead Sea. Written on parchment and papyrus in Hebrew, Aramaic and Greek, these manuscripts were carbon dating to between 150BC and 70AD and included many texts that ended up within the Bible.

Over the few years following the original find, cave hunting, scroll smuggling, and international selling became rife. By 1951 the area had became a military zone.

The next few decades saw the Vatican, the newly formed state of Israel, and the Rockefeller museum (see my last book for corruption linked to the Rockefellers) gain control of the scrolls. The official line released to the public over the decades was that the scrolls are just some Biblical and historical fragments.

A Catholic conclave came to dominate the Qumran scholarship over the years, and only one of the seven members deciphering the scrolls spoke out, "there is no doubt that the evidence from the scrolls undermines the uniqueness of the Christians as a sect. In fact we know damn all about the origins of Christianity, however these documents lift the curtain" said John Allegro who was crucified by the Vatican and the press. Allegro was of Gnostic thought and was the only non Christian on the scrolls team.

Many scrolls to this day have never even been released to public eyes, and even nowadays independent scholars with the correct academic credentials in relations to Christian theology are refused a look at the scrolls by the Vatican. The scrolls and the truths they reveal obviously are a slap in the face of Catholic dogma, and they currently gain dust along with the ancient Maya doctrines and more from the Library of Alexander.

***

Just what did these scrolls contain? We know that the Gospels within the Bible cover nothing of the climate of the supposed time of Jesus; there is no reference to Nero, the burning of Rome, or the 39AD exile of Herod Antipas.

The story of Jesus does not have a backdrop of what was happening in that area at that time. The historians of the time don't mention Jesus either.

In 74AD the fortress of Masada was under Roman siege and the defenders voted to commit mass suicide rather than be captured. It is obvious they wanted to keep certain knowledge safe rather than have it tortured out of them. It is said by many scholars this knowledge was the doctrine of the Essenes.

Josephus recounted a testimony of a women on her interrogation by roman officers:

"Ever since primitive man began to think, the words of our ancestors and of the Gods, supported by the actions and spirits of our forefathers, have constantly impressed on us that life is the calamity for man, not death.

Death gives freedom to our souls and lets them depart to their own pure home where they will know nothing of any calamity; but while they are confined within a mortal body and share its miseries; in strict truth they are dead.

For accusation of the divine with the mortal is most improper. Certainly the soul can do a great deal when imprisoned in the body; it makes the body its own organ of sense, moving it invisibly and impelling it in its actions further than mortal nature can reach. But when, freed from the weight that drags it down to earth and is hung about it, the soul returns to its own place, then in truth it partakes of a blessed power and an utterly unfettered strength, remaining as invisible to human eyes as God himself. Not even while it is in the body can it be viewed; it enters undetected and departs unseen, having itself one imperishable nature, but causing a change in the body; for whatever the soul touches lives and blossoms, whatever it deserts withers and dies: such is the superabundance it has of immortality."

> *"Catholicism is the enemy of history and science."*
> Edmund Wilson

The Gnostics

Gnosticism is the teaching based on Gnosis, meaning knowledge. It is a philosophical and religious movement which started in pre-Christian times consisting of many syncretistic belief systems which combined elements taken from Asian, Babylonian, Egyptian, Greek and Syrian pagan religion. Many state Gnosticism came from the Essenes and others state it predates Jesus but there is lack of evidence to fully commit to either notion.

Gnostics disagreed with the theory that man was sinful by nature, but believed man erred through ignorance; by knowledge man could correct his ways and gain salvation.

They had no deity save the wisdom of God, or Sophia who is a feminine creative force that creates through emanation. They looked at Jesus not as a divine person with a human form, but as a spiritual Christ (meaning anointed) that dwelt in Jesus. The term "only begotten son" was a Gnostic term meaning "cosmic principle in creation" or " Divine Nous" (Greek for mind).

Gnosticism was really a spiritual path of experiencing God force within oneself.

Gnosticism has many links and parallels to Platonic, Pythagorean, mystic, and Hermetic thought, and many Gnostics blended with Christianity or Hermetics which ensured the edges of Gnosticism became very grey. This led to many Gnostics being seen as heretics by the Church in different periods in history.

The Gospels of Thomas, Mary, Truth, Philip and Judas are all Gnostic and were all excluded from the Bible.

The Cathars

Known as the "pure ones," the Cathars were a religious sect that flourished in the Languedoc region of France between the 11th and 13th centuries. Their beliefs were a mix of Gnostic and those thought to have come originally from Eastern Europe and the Byzantine Empire by way of trade routes.

They meditated and believed in reincarnation and transcending matter. They renouncing anything connected with the principle of power and thereby attained union with the principle of love. They pushed that everyone should be able to read the Bible via translations into local languages.

The Cathar religion was presumed to hold enough information of substance as to expose fundamental concepts of the Catholic church. There was only one solution for the desperate and fanatical church, to kill them all. From 1208-1244, 30,000 knights from northern France and Germany made up the Albigensian Crusade and savagely attacked the Cathars. During this period an estimated 500,000 Languedoc men women and children were massacred in Genocide.

During this time the Synod of Toulouse in 1229 forbade laymen to own a Bible.

Christian Snippets

Jesus

We will look at the roots of the word "Jesus" later within Qabalah, but now we should look at some facts regarding the possible existence of this figure a little more.

The official stories of the Christian "deity" Jesus share many similar traits to other deities that preceded him; Mithra, Krishna, and Attis to name a few, but there are striking similarities to Horus, Dionysus, and Osiris. Even the "deity" Mary has far too many similar traits to Isis, Ishtar, Inaana, Semiramis, and Hecate. But this is not to say Jesus did not actually exist. The main question that needs raising is where was Jesus from the age of 12 to 30? The Bible has no mention of these 18 years.

The Lost Years of Jesus by Elizabeth Clare Prophet, *Nine Faces of Christ: Quest of the True Initiate* by Eugene E. Whitworth, and *The Yoga of Jesus* by Paramahansa Yogananda are arguably the best sources of investigation into these years. Each state that Jesus wasn't a man born a "divine perfected being" but had to earn his "Christ consciousness" through training and challenges. Within these are the statements that Jesus became a master initiate in many of the mystical teachings, from the Zoroastrians, the Jains, the Vedas, the Hermetists, and probably even Buddhists, travelling through India, Tibet, and Persia.

Even Madam Blavatsky wrote that Jesus was an adept and a magus steeped in Essene and Gnostic tradition.

When reading the Gospels with the thought construct that Jesus was a master adept of the mystery traditions, a Magi, the book takes on more of an esoteric allegorical feel. The Bible states that Jesus once said "the secret of the kingdom of God is given to you, but to those who are outside everything comes in parables."

If such a man named Jesus did exist, it appears that he had nothing to do with the crucified Christos from Paul's theology.

I do not wish to get too deep into Jesus (the man or the deity), nor the corruptions surrounding the creation of the Bible. I will however ask you to remember just one quote related to Jesus that will take on new meaning later on.

> "The kingdom of God does not come with observation; nor will they say, 'See here!' or 'See there!' For indeed, the kingdom of God is within you."
> Luke17:20-21

Murderous Events In Catholicism

After the council of Nicaea in 325AD the Catholic Church grew in power and believers (most who could not even read) by preaching Christianity far and wide. Growing in tyranny the Catholic Church after many small inquisitions launched the Spanish Inquisition in 1478, an inquisition that would last well into the 1800s. This allowed the Church to use cruelty, oppression, torture, and execution to what is said to be up to five million people that were seen as heretics to the word of Christianity.

The inquisition included the murder of witches, shaman, Hermetists, alchemists, Muslims, Jews, Incas, Maya and Aztecs. It also included many of the Protestants who formed after Martin Luther in 1517 famously nailed his 95 Theses of Contention (a list of heretical theology and crimes of the Roman Catholic Church) onto the church door at Wittenberg. The Catholic versus Protestant troubles on one level were a struggle between the Vatican and Hermetic Alchemical thought, the exoteric versus the esoteric.

In this time the Vatican order of the Jesuits was born.

The Jesuits

Founded in 1540 the Jesuits (also known as the Society of Jesus) were religious soldiers of the Vatican created to stamp out heresy. They were the chief assassins for the Vatican. One of the founding members, St Ignatius of Loyola, wrote *Spiritual Exercises of St. Ignatius of Loyola* in which he shared esoteric techniques of meditation, pranayama, active imagination, and lucid dreaming all the way to "Christ consciousness." Therefore the Church was killing witches, pagans, and heretics but they themselves at a high level were creating and following esoteric teachings.

At the time of Ignatius's death in 1556, there were about a thousand Jesuits. One century later, there were over fifteen thousand, and near the end of the following century, almost twenty-three thousand.

Jesuits had involvement in hampering the activities of Protestant trade and controlling education systems. Even some Catholic nations became upset as every time a new King or Queen died under the Jesuits watch, the noble families of Europe became more agitated. In 1572 the Jesuits engineered the infamous St. Bartholomew's Day massacre as well as other wars such as the seven year war between England and France in 1756.

The Jesuits had places of power in governments and also within the new world by the 18th century, but as protestant countries leapt ahead in commerce, industry, and wealth, many Catholic states started to expel the Jesuits. In 1754 from Brazil, 1758 from Portugal, 1764 from France, 1768 Parma, and in 1773 Pope Clement XIV (trained as a Jesuit himself) disbanded the Jesuits after increasing pressure from the Monarchs of Europe.

Pope Clement XIV died a year later from being poisoned, and on his deathbed he declared, "alas I knew they would poison me; but I did not expect to die in so slow and cruel manner."

From this moment the Jesuits went more underground and in 1776 Jesuit trained Bavarian law professor Adam Weishaupt created and established the Illuminati (secret order) specifically to be a front organisation behind which the Jesuits could hide.

Other secret societies had oaths based upon the oath of the Jesuits; Knights of Columbus, Knights of Malta and Rhodes Scholars to name a few among many.

From 1776 the French and US revolutions, the two World Wars, economy crashes, globalisation, the EU government, and many other global policies and events have all had a part of the hidden Jesuit hand behind them. According to the late Jesuit priest, Fr. Alberto Rivera, it was actually a fellow Jesuit named Fr. Staempfle who wrote Hitler's book *Mein Kampf*. I could write another five books on Jesuit truths but all I will do is ask you to research this for yourself and take into account the following quotes:

> "My history of the Jesuits is not eloquently written, but it is supported by unquestionable authorities, [and] is very particular and very horrible. Their [the Jesuit Order's] restoration [in 1814 by Pope Pius VII] is indeed a step toward darkness, cruelty, despotism, [and] death. ... I do not like the appearance of the Jesuits. If ever there was a body of men who merited eternal damnation on earth and in hell, it is this Society of [Ignatius de] Loyola."
> John Adams (1735-1826; 2nd President of the United States)

> "The Jesuits are a MILITARY organisation, not a religious order. Their chief is a general of an army, not the mere father abbot of a monastery. And the aim of this organisation is power – power in its most despotic exercise – absolute power, universal power, power to control the world by the volition of a single man [i.e. the Black Pope, the Superior General of the Jesuits]. Jesuitism is the most absolute of despotisms [sic] – and at the same time the greatest and most enormous of abuses."
> Napoleon I

> "The war [the American Civil War of 1861-1865] would never have been possible without the sinister influence of the Jesuits."
> Abraham Lincoln (Eric Jon Phelps, 'Vatican Assassins')

> "The public is practically unaware of the overwhelming responsibility carried by the Vatican and its Jesuits in the start of the two world wars - a situation which may be explained in part by the gigantic finances at the disposition of the Vatican and its Jesuits, giving them power in so many spheres, especially since the last conflict."
> Edmond Paris, 'Secret History of the Jesuits'

"The purpose of the Jesuit Order is, and has always been, to covertly or overtly force the 'new' variant of Sun Religion from old Babylon, Christianity, upon the world, while other branches, in conjunction with the Jesuits, are working on destroying Christianity. This is how the Illuminati works; the right hand is doing one thing and the left hand the opposite, but it all fits with the Great Plan and they achieve what they want by deception and to divide and conquer."
Wes Penre, Author

"If you trace up Masonry, through all its Orders, till you come to the grand tip-top head Mason of the World, you will discover that the dread individual and the Chief of the Society of Jesus [the Superior General of the Jesuit Order] are one and the same person."
James Parton (American historian)

"[Courageous Mexican President Benito Pablo Juarez] was the most dreaded enemy of the Society of Jesus while hating the Temporal Power of the Papal Caesar in Rome. He expelled 200 JESUIT priests…In 1872 he died at his desk, a victim of 'the poison cup."
Eric Jon Phelps, 'Vatican Assassins'

"All these things cause the Father-General [of the Jesuits] to be feared by the Pope and sovereigns… A sovereign who is not their friend will sooner or later experience their vengeance."
Luigi Desanctis (Official Censor of the Inquisition; 1852

Symbolism in Catholicism

The Vatican has symbolism around us today clearly showing its true roots, and even though I don't wish to fall too far into this pit I will share some of the symbolism.

The Black Virgins, or Black Maddonas are seen as an icon to Mary, but really they represent Isis; the divine feminine, mother earth. Historically the black virgin has ties to the Crusades and the Moorish occupation of Spain, roots with the Conquistadors who brought her to the New World and to the Merovingians and Knight Templars.

In the Afro-Brazilian tradition, the Black Madonna is the Orixá Oxum, Great Mother, patroness of pregnancy and of babies, of the rivers and of the seas, of gold, of honey, of laughter, of beauty, of seduction, of shrewdness and wisdom, the supreme ancestral mother: Iyami-Akko.

Many European churches contain the Illuminati symbol of the pyramid with the all-seeing eye and there exists scores of different imagery pertaining to Sun Gods.

"The Christian church is an encyclopaedia of prehistoric cults"
Nietzsche

John Allegro (who we mentioned earlier) wrote two books regarding the idea that all religions come from altered states. We know that mushroom cults existed in the Middle East, India, the Americas, Mesopotamia, and Europe, and that the mushroom experience gives one a rebirth experience of visions and heightened consciousness.

Shared below is mushroom symbolism shown in famous Catholic churches and paintings. Make of it what you will.

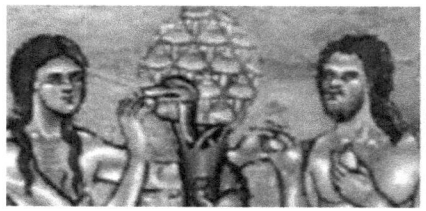

***

Christianity in 2010 is about money, fear, and control. It is founded upon dishonesty, has killed millions, looks at women and sex poorly, and encourages guilt. It takes self power away by ensuring believers feel power is within an external God.

Christians don't meditate or attempt to connect with omnipresence or "Christ consciousness," and as most are materialists surely they can be named heathens?

The Christian doctrine is a false doctrine based upon the plagiarisation of personified astrotheological, pagan, and sun God archetypes beforehand. Mythology never ended, and the deity of Jesus is just another myth. All religions were made to create barriers so that we did not understand our true nature. most people pray out of fear.

Their refusal to face facts comes from the subconscious and is part of the matrix programming.

However, within the Bible there lies a hidden essence and flow of truth that can only be found with Qabalistic eyes as we shall soon see.

In 2010 there are many more than one billion Christians on the earth.

The occult and hidden spiritual sciences first deprogram this most floored theology before any serious undertaking can commence. This is not to say a Christian cannot be a good loving person with faith, it is just to say that the dogmatic exotericism of Christianity is just not based upon truth.

> "Religion says believe, science says understand, but the adept seeks to understand the science of belief."

The personal realisation of truth is the science behind all sciences. The science of religion is about universal laws and truth which transcends dogma and beliefs. Truth is the ultimate religion.

Throughout the history of the Christian theology the flow of truth has been kept alive within the mystery traditions, no more than Hermetics and Qabalah.

Hermetic Snippets

The roots of the Hermetic traditions and its mix with Qabalah later on are hard to get a grasp on because the traditions were mainly passed orally from mouth to ear. However there are some notable dates and times in our past we can look upon to gain a picture into the flow of these traditions.

Hermetics is associated to Thoth and Hermes Trismegistus, two archetypal mythical deities that merged into one over time.

One could read a hundred books on this and read many different versions of the history but the truth is much is lost to antiquity. My teachings are that the roots are with the Atlantean priests, and that the Tree of Life itself was given to

Abraham (Akhenatun), but there are some common historical events that are undisputable.

10,000BC? - Thoth (known to many as the Atlantean) presided over the Temple cults and sacred ritual in ancient Egypt as the High Priest. He invented writing and was the Lord of wisdom. He was also the deity of all science and communication.

10,000BC? Zarathushtra founded the esoteric Zoroastrianism.

8,000BC? Osiris, Isis, and Horus myth.

2,200BC? The archetypal and mythical Abraham is stated by many to have been passed the Qabalah, and also the Sepher Yetzirah (Book of Formation).

2000BC to 1600BC: The Chaldeans of Babylon use astrology and alchemy. Their knowledge spreads to Egypt, India, and Greece.

1800BC to 500AD: The Eleusinian Initiatic Mysteries (12 miles from Athens) spread to much of Greece.

1700BC to 391AD: The Delphic Mysteries at Delphi exerted a tremendous influence in antiquity not only because of the oracles, but also because it housed a prestigious mystery school.

1130BC: The only exodus with any evidence from Egypt. Moses (highly likely an archetype) left Egypt and went to Israel after being "learned in all the wisdom of Egypt," he took the Qabalah with him.

570BC to 526BC: Greeks started to settle in Egypt under Pharaoh Amasis and associated Thoth with Hermes Trismegistus. They worshipped the dual deity as the messenger of the Gods. Hence, in the Hellenistic period, Thoth became the "word" or "logos," interpreting the divine will to humanity. Later the Romans would merge their messenger God Mercury into the same deity.

450BC: Orphic Mystery schools set up in Greece based upon mystical texts about an initiate named Orpheus.

400BC: The Hellenized Egyptian mysteries of Isis spread throughout the Mediterranean world.

46AD: The legendary foundation of the Rosicrucian Order, fusing early Christianity with Egyptian mysteries.

70AD: Rabbi Shimon bar Yokhai creates the Qabalistic *Zohar* (Book of Splendour) when hiding from the Romans. The manuscript was considered a work of mysticism and magic by the people of the generation. It was hidden for centuries from this moment.

204AD: Plotinus, a Neo-Platonism philosopher and mystic is born in Egypt. Plotinus was a major philosopher in the ancient world and is widely considered the father of Neo-Platonism.

250AD: The composition of *Corpus Hermeticum*, a core doctrine of Hermetics to this day that came out of the turbulent religious seas of Hellenic Egypt. From this moment the Hermetic tradition was honored by practitioners of Egyptian, Greco-Roman, Jewish, Christian, and the later Islamic religion. Many believe it represents continuity with the teachings in the Egyptian temples and Mystery schools. The seventeen short sections explain a dialog of Hermes who has visions and an audience with the divine mind. A world view, a philosophy, and a platform for how to be aligned to nature are all presented.

296AD: Roman Emperor Diocletian demanded all books in Egypt on alchemy be burned.

400AD: Church Father Augustine of Hippo thought Hermes was a contemporary of Moses.

529AD: As Christianity gained in strength, the Platonic academies were closed down because they were not conducive to the unity of the Roman Empire. This time was seen as "the end of antiquity."

550AD: The Sepher Yetzirah has its tangible traces in this time and had a large effect on the Jewish mind.

600AD: The rise in Qabalah within Jewish Mystics. Due to the strong connections to Neo-Platonism and the Sophia tradition in Gnosticism, Qabalistic magic became an important element in Hermetic and Rosicrucian theurgy.

776AD: *Sum of Perfection* and *Investigation into the Perfection of Metals* are written by Arabic alchemist Dschabir Ben Hayyan.

1118AD: The newly formed Knights Templar find something at Herod's temple. A religious military Order with a secret initiation ritual soon acquire a vast network of property and wealth from the European nobility.

1150AD: Alchemy is rife in Spain with Artephius writing *The Art of Prolonging Human Life*.

1200AD: The Picatrix is written offering talismanic and astrological guidance.

1206AD: Albertus Magnus, alchemist, scholar, philosopher, and scientist is born. He writes over twenty alchemical formulas.

1232AD: Raymond Lull, a Catalan Qabalist, alchemist, and philosopher is born. He went on to say about The Tree of Life that "its universal fruit is a language that serves to everybody. This book teaches that God created a universal language to talk in many languages." He was seen after his death as a great alchemist and the discoverer of ether in 1270. His monasteries and tomb are riddled with symbolism in Mallorca to this day.

For the rest of this century many alchemists were evident, and the search of the Philosophers Stone was at the front of many minds. Many monks and clerics were caught practicing alchemy and punished. The reason for the growth in Hermetic Alchemy is that people demanded wonders and the churches could not deliver spiritual experiences.

1270: Spanish Qabalist Moses Deleon uncovers *the Zohar* manuscripts in a cave in Israel. 1200 years had elapsed before *the Zohar* finally saw the light of day, just as Rabbi Shimon anticipated.

1312: The Knights Templar become extinct and they fled to Scotland only to resurface later as the Freemasons.

1345: The completion of the Cathedral at Notre Dame, just one of many Cathedrals that hid esoteric knowledge, gematria, and alchemy into its granite and marble.

Above are the alchemical steps at Notre Dame.

1378: According to the Confessio Fraternitatis, the founder of the Rosicrucian tradition is born, known as known as Frater C.R.C. and Christian Rosenkreutz.

1380: King Charles V the Wise issues a decree forbidding alchemical experiments.

1394: Christian Rosenkreutz, the legendary (perhaps allegorical) founder of the Rosicrucian Order (Order of the Rose Cross) visits Arabia, Egypt, and Morroco where he into contact with sages of the East who reveal to him the "universal harmonic science."

1403: King Henry IV of England issues a prohibition of alchemy.

1433: Marsilio Ficino, the Italian philosopher was born. Under the patronage of the wealthy de'Medicis, Ficino translates many Greek classics including *Corpus Hermeticum*. This went onto influence many of the Renaissance thinkers

1450: Printing technology is developed and Europe becomes awash with Hermetic and Alchemical texts and art. Cosimo de Medici asks Marsilio Ficino to set up the Platonic Academy in Florence.

1453: The fall of Constantinople to the Turks caused the dispersal and spread of Greek manuscripts and scholarship to Italy, increasing the changes within what became known as The Renaissance that would continue into the 17th century. A new vigor for philosophy, classical literature, learning and art ensued and flourished. It is the Renaissance mind that blended Qabalah and Hermetics into what became known as Hermetic Qabalah. Hermetic Qabalah was later viewed by scholars as Egyptian and Hebrew flavoured Neoplatonism.

Many religious paintings in this time included hidden alchemical symbolism.

1471: Sir George Ripley writes *the Twelve Gates leading to the Discovery of the Philosopher's Stone,* dedicated to Edward IV.

1488: The figure of Hermes Trismegistus was placed into the mosaic pavement in Sienna Cathedral near Florence.

1492: Ferdinand and Isabella expel the Jews from Spain, causing more dispersal and spread of Jewish and Qabalistic manuscripts and scholarship.

1493AD: Paracelsus, alchemist, physician, astrologer, and general occultist is born was born. His work and that of other alchemists deeply influenced many of the scientists of the 17th century, notably Isaac Newton. His terminology came to be adopted by mystics and theosophists too, including Heinrich Khunrath (1560-1605) and Jacob Boehme (1575-1624).

1527: John Dee, mathematician, astronomer, astrologer, geographer, occultist, and consultant to Queen Elizabeth I is born in London. After devoting years to alchemy and Hermetics he creates Enochian Magic.

1531: *Three Books about Occult Philosophy* is authored by Heinrich Cornelius Agrippa.

1540: Julius Sperber, alchemist, Qabalist, and mystical writer, is born. Sperber becomes one of the co-founders of the Rosicrucian Order. He states that the order is not new as it inherits the knowledge of the Chaldeans and Egyptians.

1550: *Rosarium Philosophorum* is published showing twenty illustrations of the themes of alchemy.

1552: Latin version of *The Sepher Yetzirah* is published by Guillaume Postel.

1558: *The Zohar* is printed.

1561: Francis Bacon, statesman, scientist, author, lawyer, and alchemist was born. It is highly likely Bacon was the real author of all Shakespearean work, and modern Rosicrucian groups claim that Christian Rosenkreuz is a pseudonym for Francis Bacon. Both subjects are too deep to go into within this book but one comment from Manly P Hall can divulge much, "Sir Francis Bacon knew the true secret of Masonic origin and there is reason to suspect that he concealed this knowledge in cipher and cryptogram. Bacon is not to be regarded solely as a man but rather as the focal point between an invisible institution and a world which was never able to distinguish between the messenger and the message which he promulgated. This secret society, having rediscovered the lost wisdom of the ages and fearing that the knowledge might be lost again, perpetuated it in two ways: (1) by an organisation (Freemasonry) to the initiates of which it revealed its wisdom in the form of symbols; (2) by embodying its arcana in the literature of the day by means of cunningly contrived ciphers and enigmas."

Bacon went on to write "New Atlantis" under his own name where he depicted the creation of a utopian land where generosity and enlightenment, dignity and splendor, piety and public spirit reigned.

***

The 16th century was seen as the Golden Age of Hermetism and for the next two hundred years scores of alchemical doctrines were published, most notable being Basil Valentines work, Christian Rosenkreutz *Chemical Wedding* and *the Golden Chain of Homer* by Kirchweger.

Kepler, Newton, Boyle and others used the alchemical process to push the fields of chemistry, astronomy, thermodynamics, and physics, and hence science was born. The scientific revolution ensured Hermetism declined, and from the late 17th century magus and mystics were ridiculed by science and condemned by the church…but both science and the church come from the very things they vilified.

1717: The United Grand Lodge of England of Freemasonry is formed, and keeps underground within its high ranks the secrets of the ancients.

1719: Georg von Welling's *Opus Mago-Cabalisticum et Theosophicum* is published. This esoteric work influences numerous subsequent authors, including Goethe, who perused it during his alchemical studies.

1766: The Golden and Rosy Cross order only admits Master Masons.

1776: Adam Weishaupt forms the Order of Illuminati of Bavaria. Many alchemical doctrines decline in circulation and become rare and expensive. Whether these events are linked I do not know.

1791: Washington City is designed by Freemasons with many esoteric teachings imbedded into the street map and overall layout.

1810: Eliphas Levi is born, and rejuvenates the interest in occult matters.

1831: Helena Petrovna Blavatski, adventuress, author, mystic, guru, and occultist is born. She goes on to write the epics *The Secret Doctrine* and *Isis Unveiled*, and was a cofounder of the Theosophical Society.

1856: Sigmund Freud, the Austrian neurologist and psychiatrist was born. His psychoanalysis method had many parallels to Qabalah, and David Bakan later wrote in *Sigmund Freud and the Jewish Mystical Tradition* that Freud had either consciously or unconsciously made use of Jewish mystical ideas in formulating psychoanalysis.

1861: Rudolph Steiner, philosopher, social thinker, architect and esotericist was born. Valentine Tomberg was for many years an enthusiastic student of Anthroposophy, the science of the spirit founded by Steiner. Valentine went on to author *Meditations on the Tarot*. Steiner went on to create his own idea of education based more on creativity, nature, and the inner worlds. The schools continue to this day with amazing results within the individuals.

1875: Carl Jung is born and goes on to shape the modern view of the subconscious. Jung studied alchemy and Qabalah, and during and after his 1944 heart attack he experienced Qabalistic visions which he described as "the most tremendous things I have ever experienced."

1888: The Hermetic order of the Golden Dawn is founded based upon Hermetic Qabalah and initiate grading. Early founders and members include Wynn Westcott, Kenneth Mackenzie, and MacGregor Mathers.

By 1900 Aleistair Crowley had already joined and infighting and politics had ensued. After many splits and infighting the Golden Dawn continues today with tens of thousands of members. It was the largest single influence on 20th century Western occultism.

The order maintained the tightest of secrecy by severe penalties for loose lips. Overall, the general public was left oblivious to the actions and even existence of the Golden Dawn, making the policies a success. This secrecy was broken first by Aleister Crowley in 1905, and later by Israel Regardie in 1940, each giving a detailed account of the order's teachings to the general public.

1890: Dion Fortune was born. She went on to write *The Mystical Qabalah* and was a member of the Golden Dawn before founding The Fraternity of the Inner Light.

1922: The mystic Rav Yehuda Ashlag established the very first Kabbalah Centre in the city of Jerusalem. Learning was made available to those who were steeped in religious studies, were Orthodox, and were over the age of forty.

In the late 19th century many films from Hollywood contained much esoteric, alchemical, and Hermetic symbolism. These include The

Wizard of Oz, Mary Poppins, Pinocchio, Sleeping Beauty, Alice in wonderland, The Matrix Trilogy, Snow White, Dark City, The Truman Show and many more.

Each could be elaborated upon but we will just share here that PL Travers was a 20th century disciple of Gurdjieff and his film Mary Poppins tells the tale of an adept who can turn world upside down inside out and bend laws of nature.

***

The history of true knowledge has its own flow though the ages and in 2010 some people look to Hermetic Qabalah amidst the swamp of new-age fads and money making nonsense. This will only continue as with the changes coming soon to the species the ancient knowledge will be more useful than ever.

PART III – HERMETIC ALCHEMICAL QABALAH

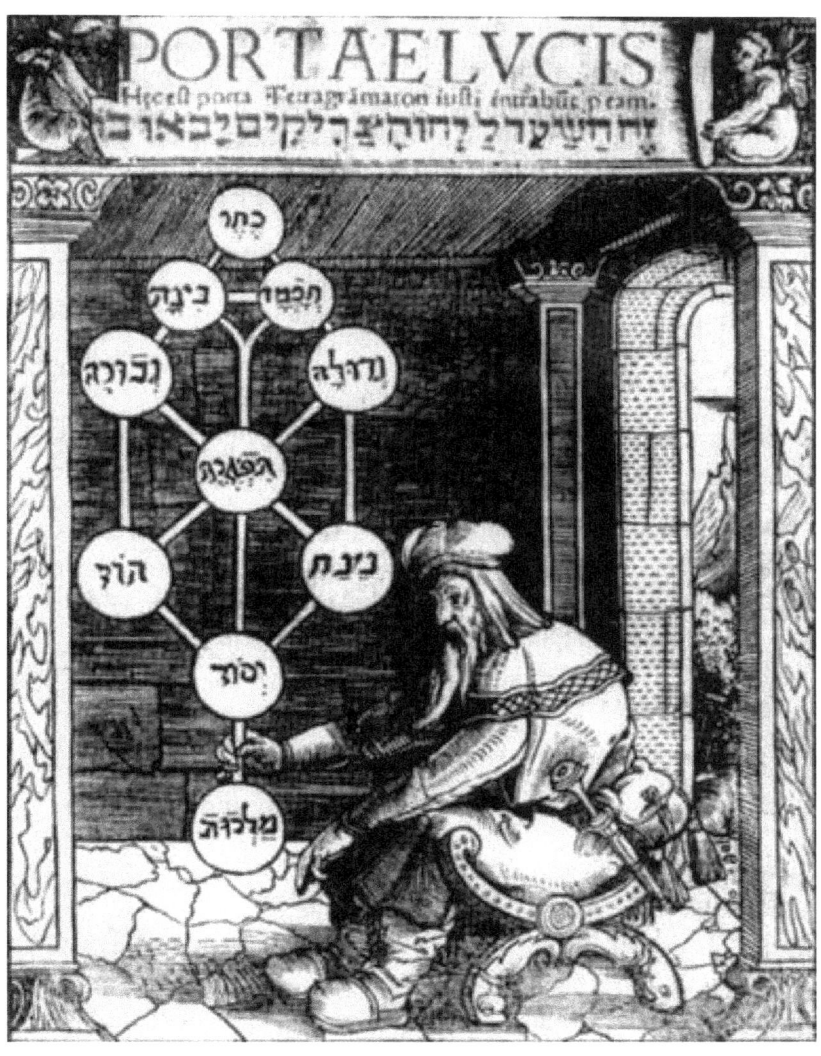

"I want to know Gods thoughts, the rest are details."
Albert Einstein

I congratulate those present, those who have stepped forth from the mass of unthinking beings. You are in for a treat. Much of part one was fierce to scare off those who did not seriously seek truth and wisdom, and Part II was to lay a backdrop, but now we are really ready to start the core of these writings. Content of Part III will be written in allegory, in a certain order, and in different ways with varied diagrams. There may also appear to be some awkward overlaps, but each comment is carefully presented and placed for a reason. The design is to open up one's *own* thought constructs and concepts from contemplating the material. I wish to stay clear of dogmatic Qabalah, but will be forced to dip in only when there are results to be gleaned.

Hermetic Laws
Before entering the world of Qabalah, we need some background into the long heralded Hermetic Laws. These laws are a fundamental backdrop for a richer path to the authentic self and many alchemists have stated that only one with an understanding of Hermetic doctrine can fully comprehend the Bible or the Vedas.

There are laws in our universe, some are conscious of them, some are not, but we all abide by them. With knowledge of these laws gained from contemplation we can begin to see and use these in the world around us.

> *"The lips of wisdom are closed, except to the ears of understanding"*
> The Kybalion

The Law of Mentalism

All is mind, the universe is mental held in the mind of THE ALL. THE ALL is the reality underlying all outward manifestations and appearances. Matter and energy are in fact spirit, and all is to be considered as a mental thought from the universal mind, THE ALL.

Only THE ALL is exempt from the laws of the universe. Within the infinite mind of THE ALL we live our human lives, for there is no power outside THE ALL. All that is, is within THE ALL, and THE ALL is within all that is; every particle, unit, and combination in the universe.

THE ALL possesses full unity, full will, full consciousness, and holds all the spheres and worlds and life within it.

We are all on the long journey back to THE ALL.

Plato gave teachings stating that everything visible was created or evolved out of the Invisible through Eternal Will.

The lips are sealed as to Why THE ALL stretched out with mental energy and created the universe.

(Is it because the mental divine-will fell in love with its thoughts? Was this the catalyst for archetypal man to fall downward from the stars?)

The Law of Correspondence

All that is above is as that which is below, and all that is below is as which is above. Man is a microcosm of the macrocosm.

All that which exists upon the earth has its spiritual counterpart on high, and there exists nothing in this world which is not attached to something above, and is not found in dependence upon it.

The arbitrary planes from below to above are the material, mental and spiritual, with no real edge or border to each. Gas, the electron, the worm, man, light, and the astral entities all live on a level of one of the planes due to the speed of their vibration.

The very planes themselves arise from vibration, and the laws of polarity, rhythm, cause and effect, and gender manifest on each plane. By studying the rock, he understands the archangel, everything is separated on the planes only by degrees of manifestation.

The Law of Vibration

Everything vibrates, nothing is at rest, everything moves. The musical scale is separated by vibration, as are the colours of the spectrum, as are different emotions and feelings within mind.

Matter, energy, mind, and spirit all vibrate, as does force and will. From the slow vibration of a rock to the infinite rate of vibrating spirit, the range of millions of degrees of vibration is prevalent within our realm. Low vibration equates to low consciousness but nothing is dead.

The Law of Polarity

Everything has poles, a pair of opposites. Opposites are the same, and are only different in degree of vibration.

Love	<>	Neutral	<>	Hate
Brave	<>	Neutral	<>	Fear
Hot	<>	Neutral	<>	Cold
Active	<>	Neutral	<>	Lazy
Light	<>	Neutral	<>	Dark

The range of vibration along polarity is a long one, where does cold start? Where does dislike start? When does like become love? Polar opposites are two degrees of the same thing.

We cannot change bravery to hot, but we can polarize on each with our will. It is possible to change the vibrations of hate to the vibrations of love, in our own minds and in the minds of others. We can choose our mental state within the law of polarity.

The Law of Rhythm

Everything flows in and out, everything has its tides, balance, and counter balance. The pendulum swing manifests in everything,

including the poles of polarity. This rhythm is found within the creation and destruction of galaxies, in the oceans tides, the seasons, empires, and the pendulum of a clock.

The swing to the right is the measure of the swing to the left, and by no means always to the extreme opposites of the relevant polarity.

Mental states are subject to the same law, some people are extremely sad and extremely happy, others a little happy and a little sad. Some experience extreme pleasure and extreme pain, and some little pleasure and little pain. The pendulum is always swinging.

However, the adept can overcome a negative flow of a pendulum by mentally neutralising at the point he desires to rest at via will, and then rise to a higher plane. The adept cannot cease the pendulum swing, but can escape its effects.

The Law of Cause and Effect

Every cause has its effect, every effect has its cause. Chance is a bad name for the law not recognised. Chance has an obscure cause we cannot see.

There are many planes of causation, with the higher planes of causation dominating the lower. Nothing merely happens.

Cause and effect deals only with events, no event "creates" another event, but is merely a preceding link in the chain of events flowing from the collective energy of THE ALL.

We have free will, but are determined by the plane of causality, they are each half truths. "I can do as I please" is a thought form that is an effect from a cause.

The adept mentally rises to the higher plane and becomes the causer instead of being carried along by effects. The adept rises above other's moods and characters, and above the local environment to become a mover instead of a pawn. If many causers are prevalent, the cause with the strongest will prevails.

Spontaneous right action means right choices at right moments. What are the consequences of a choice?

The Law of Gender

Gender is manifest in everything, the masculine and feminine principles are forever at work in the physical, mental, and spiritual planes.

Everything gives and receives, attracts and repels. The female aspect is negative, passive. The masculine vice versa. In the physical realm this principle can be seen in gases, chemicals, atoms, plants, people, and gravity.

Masculine also contains within it the female principle, and vice versa.

Gender is also in the mind. The I, the male, can will the me, the female.

Male	Female
Objective	Subjective
Conscious	Subconscious
Active	Passive
The I	Me
Just am	Likes
Thoughts	
Points of view	

"Obey above laws, rule those below."

"The practicing Qabalist is a theurgist, a God in incarnate, being able to apply the universal laws in the same way as the macrocosmic Gods."
Franz Bardon, The Key to the True Qabalah

Adepts of Hermetic Philosophy generally hold the following true:
- The physical universe is not the whole part of reality.
- Human willpower is a real force, capable of being trained to alter the local environment with physical effects.
- Willpower must be directed by the imagination.
- The universe is an ordered system of correspondences that can be understood.

Hermetic Qabalah Introduction

The word Qabalah is commonly written in different ways. Cabala came from the Latin based renaissance adepts and Christian mystics, whereas Kabbalah refers more to the Jewish tradition. Qabalah is the spelling used in most Hermetic western traditions, deriving from the root Hebrew word QBLH. QBLH literally means "an unwritten or oral tradition," coming from the Hebrew verb QBL, "to receive". The added 'H' (Heh) means window, and all windows let in light.

This meaning of "to receive" is extremely apt as the secret doctrine of Qabalah has always been passed orally, and initiations, realisations and core knowledge within the self can only be received by the adept and never given. Metaphorically speaking, if you would wish to speak with the Gods, you must first learn the language of the Gods and this does not decompose into text.

> "Ask and it shall be given you; seek and ye shall find; knock, and it shall be opened unto you."
> Matthew 7.7-8

So what is the difference between Judaistic Kabbalah and Hermetic Qabalah? The borders between the two are hazy but there are some core differences. The Judaistic Kabbalah is based more on the Jewish mystics penetrating the core meanings hidden in the first five books of the old testament (The Torah) by using Gematria, Notarikon, and Temurah (numerology systems). They perform a deep study of the The Zohar and the Sepher Yetzrah (which is a Book of Formation, as is the Eastern Baghavad Gita). Hermetic Qabalah does not look at these documents with as much vigor, and instead makes more use of Tarot, Astrology, and Hermetic laws and doctrines, and their collective relationship with the Tree of life.

But what actually is Qabalah?

The theosophy, mysticism, and science of Qabalah is not an easy one to explain, but the coming chapters will piece together the various jewels that fill up the treasure chest. In essence it is an unwritten doctrine that has a deep knowledge of man and creation. It presents insight into evolution, creation, force, form and consciousness, and also into poise, balance, and equilibrium. It is a domain of exploration into the human condition, touching the soul in a way little else can. It is a climbing frame for consciousness, and it gives archetypes and signs for where one is on the climbing frame. There are routes and archetypal guardians to all parts of the climbing frame as and when consciousness and core being is changing.

So what can this Qabalah "climbing frame" be used for?

- To know man
- To cleanse, heal and balance
- To expand our universe, thus expand ourselves
- To purify the soul
- To align with the energies of creation
- To align with the energies of nature
- To align with the energies of spirit
- To ascend

With humans being out of control machines, faulty and broken, this sounds like just what our species needs. With Qabalah's symbols, ideas, archetypes, and theosophy, it can also construct a customised and personalised high philosophy that can take one through life. Therefore, it is more of a guide and a vehicle than a system.

We will be using archetypes within the Qabalah so we need to explain how this all works. Every aspect of our consciousness has a counterpart in the greater archetypes of the universe, and If we focus on being receptive to an archetypal energy (e.g. Mars, Gabriel, Tipareth, White Tara), when we focus on the archetype it exists on the astral plane. Between the astral plane and the plane of physical manifestation is our consciousness, along with our imagination and mind. When we invoke an archetype we set up a resonance in our own consciousness through images. This builds a symbolic bridge using symbols, thus creating a circuit that the archetype's energy steps down to and activates its equivalent within us. It is now called into action, and in an organised and controlled manner we can direct and use archetypal energy upon the material plane.

To have any real results with archetypal energy, one must align will with divine will, the same as becoming a centre for divine macrocosmic consciousness.

"If a picture is worth a thousand words, then a symbol is worth a thousand pictures."

Parts of the Qabalistic creation story are fragmented, but a common theme among many is that the androgynous Adam Kadmon rests as the archetypal heavenly man, with all souls of all humanity in one being - the archetypal man. We here on earth being akin to tiny cells of this cosmic body or celestial man, all with a separate function to perform in the welfare of the universal soul. The archetypal Adam resided in unity (paradise, Eden) but was shunned out into material flesh during the fall. This coincides with the Elohim in the opening passages of Genesis, with the word Elohim from Hebrew meaning the male and female principle (in plural form), or even polarities.

The core Qabalistic system is unwritten, just as the core experience with a Shaman and ayahuasca cannot be written, but the vehicle of Qabalah can bring about a new vibration and creates mystical clicks about life and creation. It is initiatic but the master is yourself. The clicks and initiations are the fruits and can be different for everyone depending on how one has piloted the jet. It is a system that presents many doors that are usually locked, and we can only open these doors with intuition and inner feeling, and not with intellect. Paracelsus once said about the Qabalah that it opens us up to the hidden reaches of the mind, beyond the frontiers of reason, and that it enables us to read 'sealed epistles and books.'

From my experiences one can align consciousness and core essence with the forces that are abundant in creation; creation of a universe, a world, a man, an insect, a blade of grass, it is all the same force. From here we can ask questions, gain insights, and feel and unify with all that is.

It is impossible to write about Qabalah and to not include a few words about Magik which has been confused with witchcraft and demonolatry. We are all magus really, we are all creating our realities and placing energy via our will into thought forms that become manifest. Esoteric teachings are about giving love in the right way, and when you cooperate with the gracious forces that form the cosmos, the force flows through you in such a way you become conscious of it. This is called thaumaturgy or divine magic. Magik is essentially the method of mind to manipulate matter, and once the knowledge of universal laws and the secrets of nature are claimed, one's ability to manipulate forces increases. Using the allies of will, intent, and imagination, one can perform Qabalistic aligned rituals with sigils, metals, scents, herbs, talismans, colours, shapes and symbols to invoke higher forces for purpose. Magik can be deemed then as the spiritual reconstruction of one's whole universe. The Qabalistic Tree of Life allows one to map out their spiritual universe, thus, magus' use it as a filing cabinet to choose what energies to invoke for specific purpose. There are many publications on Qabalistic ritualistic magik which is not in the scope of this book, but one needs to be very careful because karma is multiplied and amplified when using magik. One really needs to know what they are doing and use the correct protection and caveats. We will leave ritualistic Magik alone as this book is fundamentally presenting the science that creates the alchemical wedding, but we need to keep in our minds at all times that the Qabalah *is* a magik formula.

> *"Magic has the power to experience and fathom things which are inaccessible to human reason. For magic is a great secret wisdom, just as reason is a great public folly."*
> *Paracelsus*

Many look at any sort of magik as evil, but evil does not exist. Cold doesn't even exist, it's just the absence of heat, darkness doesn't exist, it's just the absence of light particles, and imbalanced energy (what many refer to as evil) only exists where there is no balanced energy. Every single act of intention *is* a form of magik.

We must also state in this introduction the Qabalistic theosophy regarding God. Qabalah is not without archetypal or astral deity, it is swarming with them, but the supreme God is infinite existence, THE ALL, infinite consciousness, supreme consciousness, the source and force of all creation. The infinite existence from where the emanations of the Tree of Life perpetually pulse from. It lives within all things as the core essence, and gains a feedback loop of experience and understanding from all of the diverse lives and souls.

Ask a scientist what is energy, or ask a theologian what is God, they will both reply, "always was, always is, and contained in everything."

The adept holds this God in awe, and knows he himself has been created in God's image, and that he is actually a part of God. The master adept rises up and allows more of God to dwell in the vessel, aiming at union.

The following sections will delve into the core elements of Hermetic Qabalah, only then can we take the required gems towards the palace of the unwritten Qabalah. After which, we can venture even further upward within a Merkaba that can journey us all the way to the throne room.

El Arbol De La Vida

Core to Qabalah, The Tree of Life is a meditative glyph that is a blueprint of both creation and the soul of man. It is an attempt to show every force and factor in the manifested universe and within the psyche of man.

At first glance the glyph of 10 Sephiroth (Spheres) and 22 paths looks a simple and rigid structure, but as study and experience increase, the rigidity of the diagram begins to dissolve as the subtleties of its dynamics start to emerge. Its layers are so deep that a lifelong study could not collect all the fruits it yields.

The tree is so versatile it encompasses all things for all people, and herein lies its value. It is a method of elaborated learning that which, through observation, all mysteries can be understood and explained. It will open new angles of perception that help us to know where we come from, what we believe in, and the reasons why we do so. Those who roam the Tree of Life's paths and Sephiroth find themselves in a never ending field of self discovery.

Mind doesn't usually differentiate between the way it sees the world and the way the world really is, but the Tree enables the querent to see the world how it really is and not how one has learned it to be.

How does it do this? The Tree goes further than text, science and religion, yet different texts, sciences and religions all find their places upon the Tree. The Tree takes one further because it allows symbols, archetypes, and abstract ideas to ferment in the subconscious, and this activates dormant cells within the brain. What is within the Tree is purely gasoline to start the motors lying dormant deep in the self.

Man was created with the same laws as the universe, so a study of a law governing the universe tells us about man, and vice versa. God made man in his own image, so if we know man, we know God. Microcosmic man is an atom of the macrocosmic universe, it is the same laws above and below. The Tree will ignite its motors once meditated upon and contemplated, and it is these motors placing archetypes and abstract concepts into subjectively received subconscious minds that changes ones physiology.

The Bible states that eating the fruits from the Tree of Life will give everlasting life, this will make more sense later on, but for now just know that the Tree is a sure yogic method of peeling away the veil of Isis. One only needs a peek, and ones destiny can be seen.

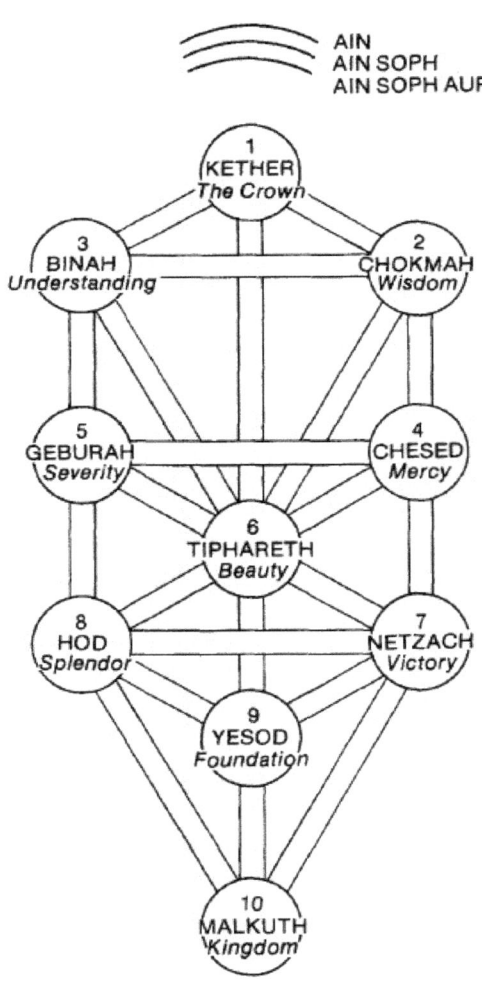

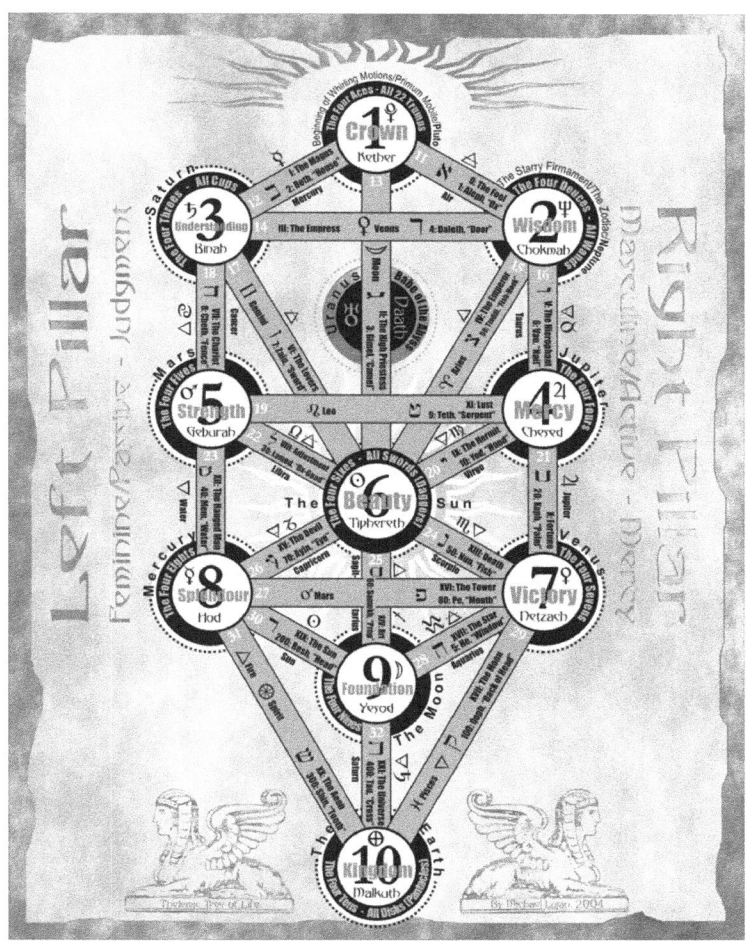

"The essence of the Unwritten Qabalah lies in the knowledge of the order in which certain sets of symbols are arranged upon the Tree of Life."
Dion Fortune, The Mystical Qabalah

We will now dissect the Tree to get to know it more intimately, only then can we look at it as a whole. We need to build the climbing frame before we climb. As we dissect don't worry when parts are not understood by the intellect, each is an important part of the jigsaw, and it will make more sense when the jigsaw is complete. Your subconscious will file away the information in the correct compartments.

The Lightning Strike, Pillars, & Triads

The ten Sephiroth are stages of emanations as spirit flows through to physical manifestation within the tenth Sephiroth, Malkuth.

Each Sephiroth is a stage along the way, remaining an energy centre of force once established, and then overflowing into the next Sephiroth. Each Sephirah (singular) emanates its successor without losing anything of itself, therefore, the first Sephirah is said to contain all those below it in order of creation.

The perfect and infinite Sephiroth represent different aspects of one thing, just as different rays proceed from light and appear different to the eye.

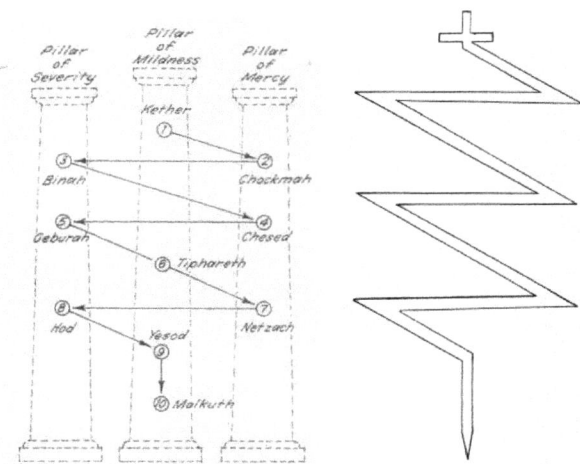

The lightning flash zig zags through the three pillars that represent the duality and polarity within the Tree and our reality. The pillars are present in all mystery lodges and stood tall at the entrance to Solomons Temple.

The pillar of mercy represents male, positive, active, fast, force, subconscious, light, and Joachin.

The pillar of severity represents female, negative, passive, slow, form, super consciousness, dark, and Boaz.

The pillar of mildness represents balance and equilibrium, the perfect pillar.

The lightning strike is an archetype for how all physical phenomena comes into manifestation from pure spirit. But the tree allows one to climb back up the same way whilst still in the vessel by balancing the internal pillars, thus restoring inner harmony and equilibrium of the soul. Only re-established unity can one go back up for a glimpse, and to regain ones primal spiritual state. The journey back up is one through the spirit worlds, the experiencing of the after death journey while still alive.

The climbing of the tree is represented by the serpent (Kundalini) that touches all 22 paths in reverse order on its climb to the crown. The serpent within the book of Exodus has too many allegorical links to this climb to be coincidental.

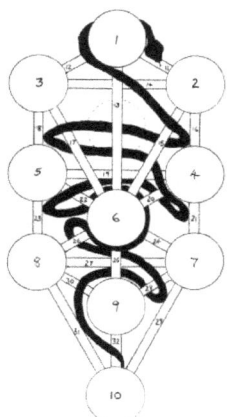

The Tree of Life is also split into three Triads, with Malkuth being left out of these higher regions. The Triads will make more sense once we have knowledge of each Sephiroth.

The Supernal Triad. Spiritual, Creating, Unity undivided.

The Ethical, Governing Triad. Abstract, forces of evolving life, Higher Self, Over-soul, Unity resumed.

The Astral Triad. Magical, Psychological, Functioning, Will, Personality. Unity assumed.

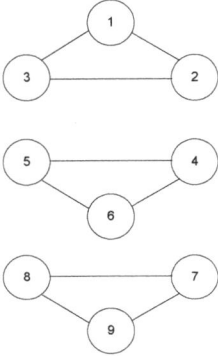

Negative Existence

The tree has three mysterious veils above the crowning Sephiroth symbolising negative existence.

The diagrams below show how negative existence rejoiced in itself, contracted itself, and left behind an emptiness where a monad of pure energy created the first impulses of a concentrated centre, which is Kether, the first of the Sephiroth.

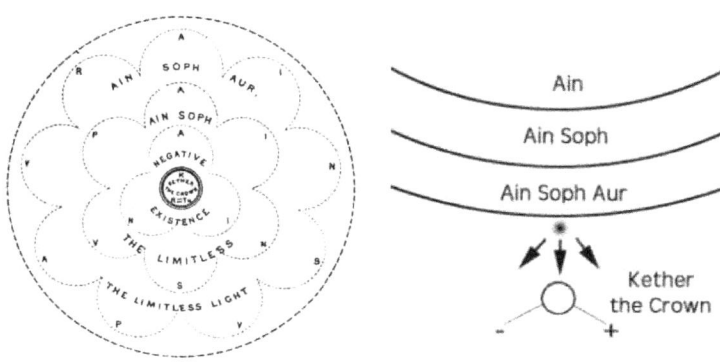

Ain is impossible to know or comprehend, it is zero, negative, no-thing. Ain Soph is of no limits, endlessness, without end. Ain Soph Aur is limitless light.

"First is Nothing, or the Absence of Things, Ain, which does not and cannot mean Negatively Existing (if such an Idea can be said to mean anything). Second is Without Limit Ain Soph E.g. Infinite Space. This is the primal Dualism of Infinity; the infinitely small and the infinitely great. The Clash of these produces a finite positive Idea which happens to be Light, Aur."
Aleistair Crowley, Qabalistic Dogma

Three Ain (the three veils are collectively known as Three Ain) are seen as being behind spirit and will, behind underlying principles, only being the roots of the invisible.

If one comprehends the meaning of Three Ain via a different method other than thought, one can understand the meaning of divine being. If one comprehends the Sephiroth one can understand the meaning of being generally.

The realms of Three Ain enable one to soar much higher within the psyche than that of the Christians whose dizziest height consists of a man with a beard sitting in some clouds.

Three Ain, three triads, three pillars.

The Four Worlds

The Qabalah contains four worlds of emanation where the essence from Three Ain runs through. The four worlds could be looked at as four dimensions, or four states of vibration in the same place. Each world contains a whole Tree of Life, and power diminishes as it descends through the fours world. Emanation bridges the distance between the one and the diversity of existence. Emanation theosophy is also highly evident in Platonism, Gnosticism, and ancient Egypt.

The four worlds are thus:

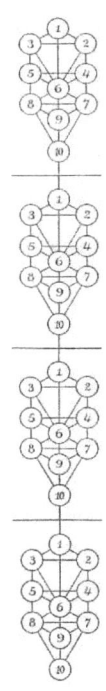

Atziluth, The world of Emanation, Pure spirit. Ten Gods link to each Sephiroth. Other attributes:
The force of Yod י, Fire, South, Leo, Spring, Wands, Absolute. The Macrosrosopus, The Vast Countanance. Divine Thought.

Briah, The World of Creation. Ten Archangels link to each Sephiroth. Other attributes:
The force of Heh ה, Water, West, Scorpio, Summer, Cups. Archetypes, Father & Mother. Moral.

Yetzirah. The World of Formation. Ten Angelic Orders of Intelligence link to each Sephiroth. Other attributes:

The force of Vau ו, Air, East, Aquarius, Autumn, Swords. Microsrosopus, The Lesser Countenance. Reproductive. Symbols, Images.

Assiah. The Material World. Ten planetary bodies link to each Sephiroth. Other attributes:
The force of Heh ה, Earth, North, Taurus, Winter, Pentacles. The Bride. Action. Frequency and Consciousness as Form.

It is pure spirit in Atziluth (the home of Adam Kadmon) which activates all the other worlds becoming. Each lower world contains Sephirothic configuration as the one which proceeded it, each lower level is a lower image of the proceeding World. The ten Sephiroth, the ten archetypal attributes of God, are thus repeated in each World or plane' of existence, thus producing a fractal cosmology wherein each part mirrors the whole.

We can show these worlds another way and add in Three Ain (x1 x2 x3 below). Here we see each of the forty Sephiroth containing all of their lower Sephiroth, ending up at Malkuth in Assiah where physical matter resides.

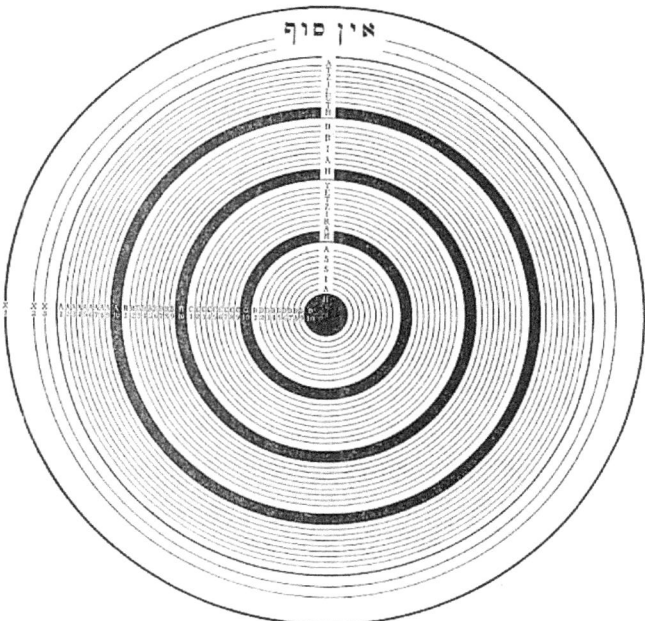

We can link what goes on everyday in our minds to the four worlds. We have an idea born out of potential, the void, (Atziluth), we then give energy to the idea and start mentally creating (Briah). We collect the different parts of the idea, and structurally toy, perfect, and formulate the idea with images (Yetzirah), finally bringing it into manifest physical reality via action (Assiah). What we see in Assiah is the catalyst for a new cycle of creative imagination.

There are two other useful ways of showing the four worlds. Below left shows the Tree as a whole, a complete singular, and the four worlds divided within it. This representation can be used with the fractal knowledge that a whole tree resides in each Sephiroth, as do all four worlds. Below right shows an overlay of the four worlds which conjures much information from its overlapping patterns. This latter way is known as Jacobs ladder due to Jacobs dream in Genesis, "a ladder set up on earth, and the top of it reached to heaven; and behold the angels of God ascending and descending."

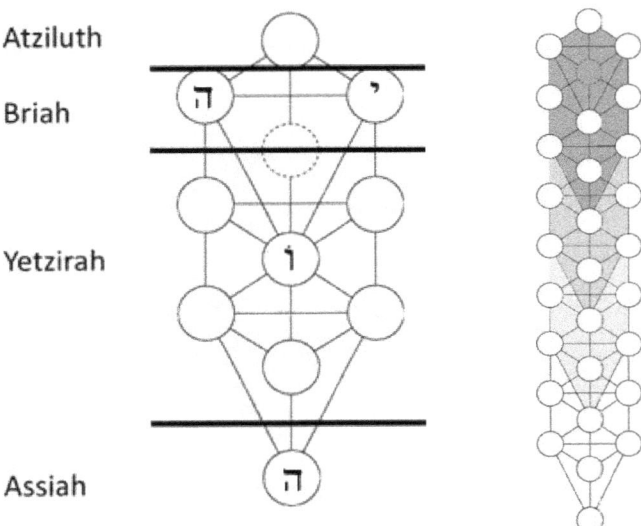

The Tetragrammaton

Unknown to Sunday school teachers is that from the original Hebrew texts that ended up conglomerating the Bible, in over 7,000 places the four letters יהוה (YHVH) were changed to אדני (Adonai, meaning Lord in English), and to אלהים (Elohim). This was to keep secret the four sacred letters that constitute the Tetragrammaton, which itself is from the Greek Tetra and Gramma, meaning four-letters, or four-writings.

The Tetragrammaton is also found in the Dead Sea Scrolls and the The Septuagint, which is a 3rd to 2nd century BC Greek translation of Hebrew Scriptures.

Then more recently, what the Biblical translators started to do was take the vowels from Adonai and mix it with the consonants of YHVH to come up with Jehovah. They only used Jehovah so no one could pronounce the name correctly. There is no "J" in Hebrew and in Hebrew the word "Hovah" means ruin or mischief. I won't go into the Jehovahs Witnesses and their beliefs as it really is not worth the energy, they are so far down a pot of falsity that no rope could claw them back up. Who is harvesting their energy and for what purpose is open to much debate.

In the Jewish Kabbalistic tradition to know the missing letter of The Tetragrammaton enables one to say the true name of God, the secret of secrets within the Arcanum. For thousands of years it is said that only Jewish Priests were allowed to utter the full name when in ritual.

Even though we are on the Hermetic path we still need to cast a net over the mysteries surrounding יהוה without falling into an associated pit of endless complexity that has grabbed whole lives of Jewish mystics.

A letter from יהוה resides in each world, but arguably more importantly is that יהוה also resides on a single tree; Yod in Chokmah, Heh in Binah, Vau in Tipareth, and Heh in Malkuth. This is interesting as to why Kether seems left out.

YHVH is phonetically spoken like four vowels, EE AHH OOOH AAA. (EE + AHH = Yah,) (OOH + AAA = weh). So when you phonetically pronounce the four letters together they sound like Yahweh. Often interpreted as signifying "To Be" or "I am that I am." This has more fuel when we place the letters יהוה on top of each other in their order, and in their related four worlds descending.

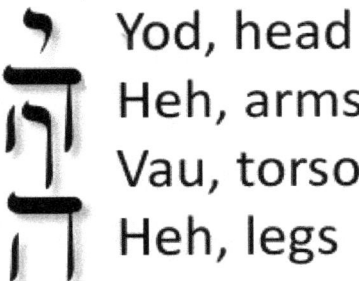

Yod, head
Heh, arms
Vau, torso
Heh, legs

This looks very much like a man, and could be thought of as Adam Kadmon. Is the missing letter the secret of the four elements, the secret of nature that alchemists have whispered for centuries?

If we breath the fifth element (the fire of spirit) into יהוה (archetypal man) via the Mother Hebrew letter ש (Shin; the traditional meaning being Fiery, cosmic, or holy spirit), we end up with יהשוה (YHShH, Yeshuah). The Hebrew Yeshuah literally translates in English to Jesus.

In the first section of this whole book we mentioned Adam Weishaupt for ill reasons, but one of his statements should be shared.

> "No one....has so cleverly concealed the high meaning of his [Jesus] teaching, and no one finally has so surely and easily directed men on the path to freedom, as out great master, Jesus of Nazareth. This secret meaning and natural consequence of his teaching he hid completely, for Jesus had a secret doctrine, as we see in more than one place in scriptures."

Adam Weishaupt, Founder of the Illuminati

Not wishing to go much deeper into Hebrew translations, we should add that the word for "tree" in Hebrew is composed of two letters: ע (Ayin) and צ(Tzadik). ע (Ayin) means "eye" and צ (Tzadik) means the "righteous one." We find in Psalms: "The eye of God is to the righteous."

When we come across יהוה as we progress we are now armed with the foundation information we need. A re-read of some of the Bible with these core ancient truths will yield a very different read and can give plenty of Qabalistic fuel for the tank.

> *"In the beginning was the Word, and the Word was with* ~~Elohim~~ *the Tetragrammaton, and the Word was* ~~Elohim~~ *Tetragrammaton."*
> *Gospel of John, 1:1*

> *And the* ~~LORD God~~ *Tetragrammaton planted a garden eastward in Eden; and there he put <u>the man</u> whom he had formed. And out of the ground made the* ~~LORD God~~ *Tetragramnaton to grow <u>every tree</u> that is pleasant to the sight, and good for food; <u>the tree of life</u> also in the midst of the garden, and the tree of knowledge of good and evil."*
> *Genesis 2:8-9*

Adam's name in Hebrew is יהוה. In Genesis were are told that God removed a rib from the body of Adam to create Eve. Rib is the letter י (Yod), which leaves הוה, meaning Eve. י (Yod) also relatively represents the world of Yetzirah, formation.

One can see how complex it can get, and how only a deep knowledge of Hebrew can open the doors buried deep within the Bible.

We will move on and use the Hebrew letters later in number form as each letter interestingly represents a numerical value.

The Veils

There are two veils actually within the tree, the Veil of Paroketh, and the Veil of the Abyss. Paroketh refers to the four elements, פ Peh water, ר Resh air, כ Kap fire, ת Tau Earth, also the bottom four Sephiroth each relate to an element too. We can only pass through this veil once the soul has initiated itself enough to remember itself, and obtained the powers it needs to overcome the egos inertia. Only then, the veil between soul and ego will gradually disperse. Mastery of the four commands; To Dare, To Know, To Will, and To be Silent will only then allow the soul to have improved enough to draw down the fifth command from spirit....To Go.

The Veil of Paroketh, also known as the Veil of Illusion, sits at Tipareth guarding the entrance to union with ones spirit. If the tree was shown as the four worlds with 40 Sehpiroth, then this veil would sit just at Kether in Yetzirah.

It's portal where consciousness must pass when roaming the tree, separating worldly from archetypal experiences. It represents our forgetfulness of our real identity due our ego and persona living in the false perception of reality below the veil. Our soul resides the other side.

The world of reality and truth can only be perceived behind the veil of illusion, but as one gets near this veil there is what is known as "The Dweller on the Threshold." This head of a leviathon rises out of this veil guarding the crossing, formulating in the inner shapes of archetypal experiences that can petrify and test ones core inner being. This is needed to see how much one wishes to cross, and to ensure one is purified, and has a pristine state of consciousness.

The veil of illusion is itself illusory because there is no real distinction between the physical and spiritual worlds, there are only streams of energy. What we see as a table or floor only appears that way due to how our senses construct the energy streams. We may pass across this veil as easily as passing through a hanging curtain, but first one needs to know how to move the curtain aside. When we start climbing the tree later on this will make much more sense.

***

The more mysterious Veil of the Abyss lies higher up the Tree separating the Supernal Triad from the rest of the Tree.

Crossing of this Abyss is the point when consciousness has a real separation from the I, and the body, and melts into the void. If the tree was shown as the four worlds with forty Sephiroth, then this veil would sit just below Tipareth in Briah.

In 1909 A. Crowley attempted to cross the Abyss, afterwards he made the following comment, "This doctrine is extremely difficult to explain; but it corresponds more or less to the gap in thought between the Real, which is ideal, and the Unreal, which is actual. In the Abyss all things exist, indeed, at least in posse, but are without any possible meaning; for they lack the substratum of spiritual Reality. They are appearances without Law. They are thus Insane Delusions...Now the Abyss being thus the great storehouse of Phenomena, it is the source of all impressions."

This may appear a little dark, but to get through the cracks in the matrix and seriously rise spiritually one often needs to see how much fear one can overcome. One who has failed to learn and incorporate the virtues of the Sephiroth of the Tree of Life will surely be sucked into the Abyss, lured by the promise of endless knowledge.

What is interesting is that the Lightning flash jumps across the Abyss from Binah to Chesed, a leap across the void, across the invisible non-Sephiroth known as Daath. Here we may simply say that Daath as a Sephira, does not exist.

There are five paths crossing the Abyss, and again we see the four elements in the shape of Cancer (Water), Gemini (Air), Aries (Fire), and Taurus (Earth). The fifth path is the moon, signifying the Subconscious and the hidden. The five Major Tarot Trumps on these paths all show large amounts of symmetry too.

The Torah speaks of failed attempts to create the earth, these failed because the pillars were not in equilibrium, and the failed attempts are in the abyss; shattered worlds and dark spirits linger with no time or space.

> "When you look into the Abyss, the Abyss also looks into you." — Nietzsche

Do not fret. One climbing across, or even close to the Veil of Paroketh alone is more than enough to get a glimpse to the true essence of self. After this, higher realms may not be desired, but the inertia created may mean one desires a further leap. The climber decides where on the climbing frame he wishes to climb.

The Temples of the Sephiroth

The Sephiroth are static, objective, natural forces and states. Each Sephirah can be likened to a unique shaped vessel that once full overspills into the next. They are infinite and perfect when Three Ain imparts his fullness to them. Each Sephirah has positive and negative polarity within it allowing us to pinpoint where the balance of our core attributes sit within a Sephirah, and furthermore, between the pillars. We can liken the Sephiroth to nouns and consonants, and the connecting subjective paths to verbs and vowels.

The flow of emanation of the Sephiroth is akin to the paint strokes of creation giving more coats to its masterpiece or even to the footprints of creation getting heavier until they manifest in the material.

> *"The Ten ineffable Sephiroth have ten vast regions bound unto them; boundless in origin and having no ending: an abyss of good and ill, measureless height and depth…"*
> The Sepher Yetzirah, Book of Formation

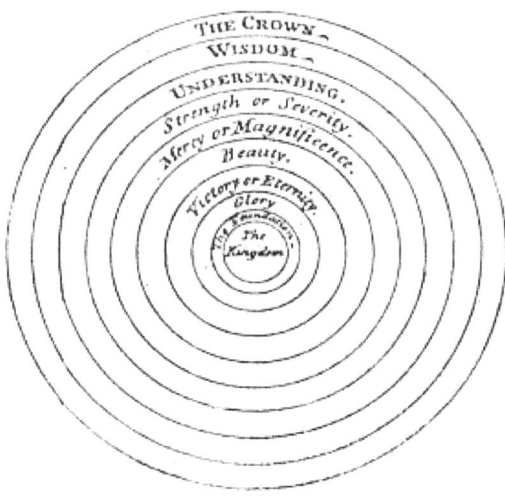

The Sephiroth are evident in the Universe and in man; physically, in his soul and in his personality. Adam Kadmon is the full Tree though some scholars place him covering only the Formative 6 Sephiroth.

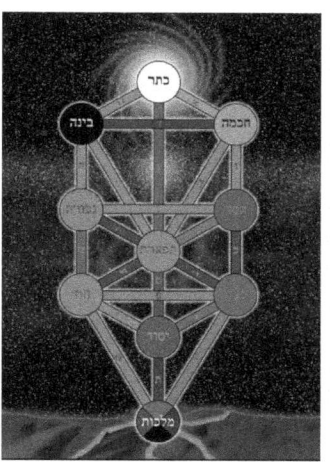 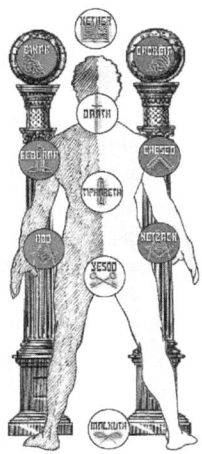

Each Sephirah is akin to a Temple of light, with a host of archetypes and personifications. These provide the handles for one to climb in and get to know a Sephirah intimately. Each Sephirah along with its energy, stories, and symbols, has four hierarchies of archetypal intelligences, or Names of Power. Whether these are natural forces, deep in the psyche, or out there in the upper astral planes I will leave for you to discover. These intelligences definitely guide one around the tree if used correctly. The Vibrational God Name resides in Atziluth underlying all power within the Sephirah. The Archangelic natural forces, or archetypal ideas reside in Briah. The Angelic Order, or intelligences are a group of beings residing in Yetzirah. The Planetary bodies reside in Assiah and represent the celestial object which is the product of the relative Sephiroth, plus a reminder that the human world is bound by the planets.

The word Angel comes from the Hebrew 'messenger,' and meditating within a Sphere gives messages so we will refer to these as Astral Messengers. We will soon show how this is achieved. Remember, we are just looking for fuel, we are not looking to become masters at reciting Qabalistic lore, we just wish to use the handles, and to use them respectfully with grace.

Madam Blavatsky said, "The whole cosmos is guided, controlled, and animated by almost endless series of hierarchies of sentient beings," and that "no such form or shape can possibly enter mans consciousness, or evolve his imagination, which does not exist in prototype as least as an approximation."

Also relevant is a statement from Augusta Heindal, "All of the great hierarchies work in our body constantly."

We are about to step into a deep world of archetypes and we need to explain a little more about this. Symbols and ideas are how the mind works, for instance the letter 'A' is just three lines but it stokes a thought construct in the mind, just as a road sign does. The symbols and archetypes within the Tree of Life are linked with higher parts of the psyche, sub conscious, and core being. It is a proven method for attainment so hang in there if at first glance much of the information presented seems strange. For now kill the intellect and open the subconscious to each Sephirah by contemplating the correspondences, and feeling the energy that resides within. The Sephiroth will become less abstract as we flow down the tree.

1, Kether, The Crown.

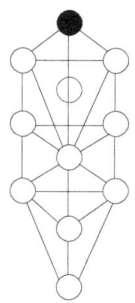

Names: Concealed of the Concealed, Ancient of Days, The Great Countenance, Primordial Point, Macroprosopos, The Most High, The Head which is not, The Smooth Point.

Symbols: Crown, Swastika, Point.

Meditative Image: An ancient bearded king seen in profile (only the right side of his face).

Spiritual Experience: Union with God

Fuel for Meditation: Almond in flower, Diamond, Ambergris.

Vibrational God Name: Eheieh; I Am That I Am. Source of all energy.

Astral Messenger: Metatron; Bright Archangel of Presence. Twin of Sandalphon.

Intelligences: Chaioth Ha Qadesh; Holy living creatures.

Planetary Body: Rashim ha Gilgalim; First Swirlings.

Virtue: Completion of the Great Work.

Vice: -

Sepher Yetzirah Path of Wisdom: 1, Admiral or Hidden Intelligence.

Colours: Atziluth: Brilliance, Briah: Pure White, Yetzirah: Pure White, Assiah: White, flecked gold.

Tarot: The four Aces.

Deities: Ptah, Brahma.

Kether is the point, a monad of pure energy where the unmanifest becomes manifest. A centre crystallising in the midst of non-being to create a space for emanation. The Crown is not of creation, it is the crown above creation, and one could place this upon Adam Kadmon.

It is a raw potential spark of pure being, with no attributes, activity, force, or form, where all opposites are contained in a peaceful union. A state of existence that is unknowable and impossible to comprehend by any created man. A re-created man?

It is the highest point, 1, but let us not forget that Malkuth, 10, is just as holy.

Only being able to see the bearded king in profile signifies that half of Kether is unmanifest, akin to the dark side of the moon. Kether then is only separated from Three Ain due to "the will to will."

Light is the first thing manifest, and in Kether light gives comprehension of itself to itself. Light not as our senses see it, but light as spirit in potential. In Malkuth we see that matter draws down spirit, as well as spirit coming down on its own accord through the emanations.

> "In the beginning there was neither existence nor non existence, all this world was unmanifest energy.....the One breathed, without breath, by its own power Nothing else was there."
> The Hymn of creation, The Rig Veda.

The myths state that the messenger Metatron gave the doctrine of Qabalah to Abraham, not to his vessel in Malkuth but to his spirit in Tipareth.

The Holy Living Creatures are the four sacred animals found in the Biblical tales from Ezekeil and John's Revelation; the bull, lion, eagle, and man. These represent the four elements and the four opposite signs within the Zodiac (Taurus, Leo, Scorpio, and Aquarius). It is interesting to see these creatures reside within Kether in the world of formation, where in turn these creatures can be placed upon the swastika and spun to give birth to the First Swirlings of Rashim ha Gilgalim in Assiah.

These zodiac signs are the four fixed signs, and summing the number of these four signs yields 26, the number of the Tetragrammaton (Taurus 2nd, Leo 5th, Scorpio 8th, Aquarius 11th).

These creatures are ever present in Catholicism, and esoterically also represent the four apostles in mystic Christianity.

2, Chokmah, Wisdom.

Names: Aba, The Supernal Father.
Symbols: The Lingam, The Phallus, Yod, The Inner Robe of Glory, The Straight Line.
Meditative Image: A Bearded man.
Spiritual Experience: Vision of God Face to Face.
Fuel for Meditation: Mistletoe, Ruby, Musk.
Vibrational God Name: YHVH
Astral Messenger: Ratziel; Prince of Knowledge of Hidden Things.
Intelligences: Ophannim; Wheeling forces.
Planetary Body: The Zodiac, Mazzaloth; Inner Intellect.
Virtue: Devotion.
Vice: -
Sepher Yetzirah Path of Wisdom: 2, Illuminating Intelligence.

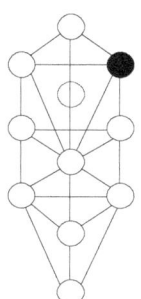

Colours: Atziluth: Soft blue, Briah: Grey, Yetzirah: Pearl-grey, Assiah: White flecked with red, blue, and yellow.
Tarot: The four Twos.
Deities: Janus, Odin, Athena, Nuit.

The source of all in Kether starts to move its way towards denser manifestation. Infinite power in infinite motion in infinite timeless space, Chokmah is the most abstract form of force, whereas Malkuth is the densest form of matter.

Chokmah is undifferentiated force in chaos, whereas Kether is undifferentiated potential. In Chokmah, this potential begins to move, begins to be realised, but unless it is limited in some way, unless it can be contained, nothing may be created, nothing will become manifest. A good analogy for Chokmah is electrical energy; while much is known about electricity, all that we know is known only because we are able to trap its energy by various means.

Chokmah has its pressure equal in all directions, using embryonic functioning laws it is of virile activity, hosting eurekas and stimulus.

A dynamic male thrust and drive of force.

It is the Sephiroth of Gods wisdom with the will to create. The first generation of the one. It is the action of the mind of God in manifestation, the ultimate "let there be light."

It is passive in relation to Kether, but positive and active in relation to Binah, and rests at the head of the positive pillar of mercy.

The virtue of devotion is one way to get up the rungs to attempt to claim the vision of God face to face, but if one actually does there is little chance of coming back. His own manifest universe would pulverise.

The Father of creation; outward, outward, but inner-outward too. Inner creation is Chokmah force, the seeds for life. Male energy at its most abstract level, developing outward from the I AM.

Chokmah is creation on its highest plane, therefore it is the home of the eurekas sought from the Alchemists attempting to create the Philosophers Stone. Eureka moments are themselves fractal singularities with no time or space and result from creating within chaotic force.

The Tetragrammaton rests in this Sephirah in Atziluth, and there are 12 different ways of ordering יהוה creating the 12 Banners of the Mighty Name. This links to the twelve signs in the Zodiac that reside in Chokmah in Assiah.

The phallic symbolism represents the male outpouring of energy. Therefore with sexuality being a means of expression of life force in a human, this act is a fractal of the Chokmah force in play in the cosmos.

The Inner robe of glory signifies the light within us hidden within the flesh.

To experience Chokmah in any way we would need to feel and align with the dynamic rush of cosmic energy, and this is where secrets of The Emerald Tablet will be used later.

3, Binah, Understanding.

Names: Ama, The Supernal Mother, The Great Sea, The Throne, The Chrone, The Mother of Form.
Symbols: The Yoni, The Triangle, The Chalice, The Outer Robe of Glory, The Vesica Piscis, Heh.
Meditative Image: A Mature Women. Matron.
Spiritual Experience: Vision of Sorrow.
Fuel for Meditation: Lotus, Pearl, Myrrh.
Vibrational God Name: JHVH-Elohim
Astral Messenger: Tzaphkiel; Eyes of God.
Intelligences: Aralim; Mighty Ones, Thrones.
Planetary Body: Saturn ♄ , Shabbatha, Outer intellect.
Virtue: Silence.
Vice: Avarice.
Sepher Yetzirah Path of Wisdom: 3, Sanctifying Intelligence. Faith.
Colours: Atziluth: Crimson, Briah: Black, Yetzirah: Dark brown, Assiah: Grey flecked pink.
Tarot: The four Threes.
Deities: Nephthys, Shakti, Mary, Isis.

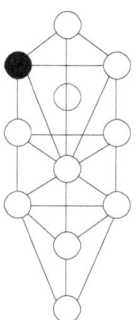

Binah is the womb, the Great Primordial Mother, containing, absorbing, and shaping the chaotic force of Chokmah. She is the roots of form and all that is material.

As she is across the Abyss, it is only the archetypal idea of form; the grabbing of random force into patterns so that the freedom of force becomes conditioned, stabilized, and preserved.

She confines and contains slowly within definite limits, just as a vacuum is confined within the three sides of the two dimensional triangle. The title Understanding signifies that for to understand anything, we must be able to contain it within some frame of reference.

Binah completes the Supernal Triad, and heads up the Pillar of Severity. It may seem strange that a Mother heads up the Pillar of Severity and the Father tops the Pillar of Mercy, but this makes more sense when we realise all life has positives within negatives and negatives within positives. Even in a human partnership we are the positive in a relationship when the other is of a lower potential, and negative in a relationship when the other is of a higher potential. This is a higher arc than the physical vessel polarity of male and female.

The Chokmah Binah relationship completes the Triad that we find in all Theologies, representing the highest Yin and Yang, Shiva and Shakti.

In Assiah we could state that doing things in the world is Chokmah, and coming home to a comfortable home is Binah, the active and the passive, the father and the mother. Our concepts of gender down in Assiah are minute compared to what is playing out in the cosmos.

The womb of Binah contains everything, and through her the remaining Sephiroth are born. The 7 vessels that flow from her womb became known as the 7 days of creation, and important to note here is that on the seventh day God rested. Most dogmatic Christians think this is Sunday but we know that the Sun God worshipping Vatican moved Sabbath from Saturday to 'Sun'day. This commenced in 321AD with Constantine bringing in new civil laws.

The slow absorbing great womb of Binah bears many characteristics as to its planet Saturn. Ruled by the Father of Time, Chronos, Saturn is a restrictive, barren, patient, ageing energy. Saturn has many moons and Binah is the principle behind all moon forces.

The stabilising of forces is what form actually is, and the birth of form is also the beginning of death. This death is the sorrow within Binah, and also sorrow for the fall of man.

The virtue of silence holds true for any adept. Talking about anything dissipates associated energy, it pushes what is only in *your* cloud to the consciousness of others and then they can feed, modify, and take from the cloud. This is amplified within esoteric study and practice.

The Outer robe of glory is form itself, and the Astral Messenger is said to be the keeper of the records of evolution within the great akashic sea of consciousness.

Here we complete the first pairing of polarities within the Tree. The middle pillar Sephiroth (except Kether and Malkuth) have their positive and negative balanced in equilibrium because they are composites of the pair which precede them.

Daath, Knowledge (or Gnosis)

Daath is not a Sephiroth, it is invisible, and due to it being invisible it should not really be placed upon the Tree at all.

It is often not represented at all, but when it is symbolised we find it exactly upon the Abyss below Chokmah and Binah.

Names: The Hole, The Tunnel.
Symbols: The Empty Room, The Cloud Hidden Peak.
Spiritual Experience: Vision across the Abyss.
Astral Messengers: 4 Protectors of the Quadrants.
Intelligences: Caduceus serpents protect entrance.
Planetary Body: Sirius, "Know as I am known."
Virtue: Future confidence.
Vice: Cowardice, Apathy.
Colour: Transparent, invisible.
Deities: Janus, the God who looks both ways.

I am not comfortable with writing about Daath, it is invisible and also a sacred mystery. Much has been incorrectly written about Daath so I will choose words carefully and move on swiftly.

The esoteric secrets of the tree, supreme illumination, and supreme realisation can all come from solving the mystery of the invisible Non-Sephirah. We will lay with care some tiny drops of gasoline when the climbing frame is more complete.

Daath is a point where all knowledge is contained, it is the unity between the Supernal Triad and manifestation.

One could say one needs Wisdom (Chokmah) and Understanding (Binah) to obtain real Knowledge (Daath). In this we could create the example of $E=MC^2$; Chokmah knows the theory, Binah understands what the symbols represent, and Daath knows it all inside and out.

> *"Happy is the man that findeth wisdom, and the man that getteth understanding."*
> *Proverbs, 3:13*

> *"And the spirit of The Tetragrammaton shall rest upon him, the spirit of Wisdom and Understanding, the spirit of counsel and might, the spirit of Knowledge and of the fear of The Tetragrammaton."*
> *Issiah, 11:1*

The Caduceus Rod from ancient Egypt encapsulates the Tree of Life showing the serpent's heads resting upon Daath. This Hermetic alchemical glyph from ancient Egypt is worthy of meditation.

Daath is a gateway, some say to a hidden tree, but one needs momentum from Tipareth to be able to peek behind the veil of Isis.

> "Ten are the Sephiroth out of nothing, and not the number nine, ten and not eleven. Comprehend this great wisdom, understand his knowledge, inquire into it and ponder on it, render it evident and lead the Creator back to His throne again."
> The Sepher Yetzirah
> ***

The following are two choice quotes that will take us forth onto the lower seven Sephiroth.

> "No one knows earthly eden but the little face (seven lower Sephiroth), and no one knows the heavenly Eden but the great face (Supernal Triad)...should the upper eye (Kether) cease looking into the lower eye (Malkuth) the world would perish."

> "Seven Spirits of God sent forth into all the earth."
> Revelation 5:6

4, Chesed, Mercy.

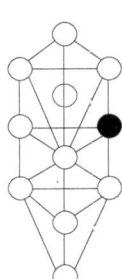

Names: Gedulah, Love, Magnificence, Majestic.
Symbols: The Tetrahedron, Pyramid, Orb, Sceptre, Crook, Equal Armed Cross.
Meditative Image: A Mighty Throned King.
Spiritual Experience: Vision of Love.
Fuel for Meditation: Olive, Amethyst, Cedar.
Vibrational God Name: El; Glory Manifested.
Astral Messenger: Tzadkiel; Benevolence of God.
Intelligences: Chasmalim; Brilliant Ones.
Planetary Body: Jupiter ♃ Tzedek; Justice, Inner Emotions.
Virtue: Obedience, Humility.
Vice: Bigotry, Hypocrisy, Gluttony, Tyranny.
Sepher Yetzirah Path of Wisdom: 4, Cohesive, or Receptive Intelligence.
Colours: Atziluth: Deep violet, Briah: Blue, Yetzirah: Deep purple, Assiah: Deep azure, flecked yellow.
Tarot: The four Fours.
Deities: Indra, Amoun.

Chesed, the first Sepiroth of the Formative World is the beginning of manifestation as we can comprehend it. An apex turns the triangle of Binah into the pyramid, creating the embryo of shape, space, and time.

This sphere is of productive life giving force with purpose. It is the expansion of will of the Supernal Triad. It is still abstract but the limits established in Binah are now at work.

Chesed contains stable firmness, a smooth, soothing order of Royal Splendour. It is a harmonious kingdom ruled by a loving charitable king; a protector, an organiser, a preserver. From his throne he gives fair laws, and creates peace as he guides his people with forward thought. It is the four-square principle of organisation and worldly rule (Jupiter).

When in forward thought one is automatically operating in the Sphere of Chesed for it is the principle of ideas, the building up of abstract archetypal thought. One has to operate well here to be able to master the storehouse of images in Yesod.

All forms within Chesed are really only as dense as forward thought images within our imagination, and we must not fall into the trap that these forms are not real, they are as real as brick and mortar.

Often named Love instead of Mercy, this reminds us that Chesed aligns smoothly with Gods will. "Love is the law, love under will," once said Crowley, and this quote lives within Chesed.

It is deviation from this sphere that causes ill in the world, but that is not to say its balancing counterpart Geburah is not required. Chesed builds up and Geburah tears down, and the balance between both manifests within Tipareth; the perfect equilibrium of the whole tree.

Rulers of groups of people need to claim the virtues of this sphere because when a member of authority starts to identify the self with the ruling principle, the vices always become evident.

Chesed is Chokmah in a lower arc and the sceptre reminds us of this, whereas the equal armed cross represents the four elements in equilibrium, the start of manifestation.

5, Geburah, Severity.

Names: Strength, Justice, Judgment, Destroyer.
Symbols: The Pentagon, The Tudor Rose, the Sword, the Spear, the Scourge, the Chain.
Meditative Image: A Mighty Chariot Warrior.
Spiritual Experience: Vision of Power.
Fuel for Meditation: Oak, Ruby, Tobacco.
Vibrational God Name: Elohim Gebor; Judging, Ruling, Amazing.

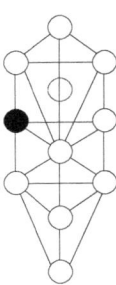

Astral Messenger: Khamael; Flaming Warrior.
Intelligences: Seraphim; Fiery Serpents.
Planetary Body: Mars ♂ Madim; Action, Outer Emotion.
Virtue: Energy, Courage.
Vice: Cruelty, Destruction.
Sepher Yetzirah Path of Wisdom: 5, Radical Intelligence.
Colours: Atziluth: Orange, Briah: Red, Yetzirah: Scarlet, Assiah: Red, flecked with Black.
Tarot: The four Fives.
Deities: Vishnu, Thor.

Geburah is the binding of force to form. It is the slow, steady, preservation of useful form, and the killing of useless limits. Therefore, Geburah tempers, breaks down, and limits the abundance of Chesed.

We could say that the creative will inherent in the manifestation of the universe stops to look at what he has done so far and after careful judging and assessment, it tears away and breaks down what is useless, undesirable, and past its time. It then cuts away with warrior like strength.

Chesed is the expansion of divine will, Geburah is representative of its contraction. This is required as Mercy is life giving power that is never ceasing, and some limits need to be put in place.

Geburah represents the principle of energy in controlled motion for particular purposes. Therefore, the principle is true for such motion at all levels, whether it be the car engine, the revolution of the world on its axis, the power behind galactic motion or that behind human desires, all of which by virtue of Geburah are driven to perform varying kinds of activity.

He protects his kingdom with the sword of justice unlike the orb of Chesed. He is the more active side of rulership with no room for sentiments. He can put the fear of God into us by his awe and wrath to uphold and defend what is right.

The energy upholds the strong hand of good that stands up to oppressors, the ultimate spiritual battle in service. With slow constant vigilance and endurance the watchmen in the watchtower are ready to call the war hungry warriors into action at any time.

This may sound devastating, but it is only destructive to that which is temporary for Geburah lives in the eternal.

In Geburah there is much war like symbolism, and due to this many incorrectly attach fear, anger, fury, and violence to Geburah.

Geburah is a needed energy and even though a vice, destruction is required at times; cutting away cancer, bad habits, toxic people, or unhealthy beliefs. Destructive changes are necessary to evolve the soul, and destruction in our lives always brings an abundance of learning.

It is the Christians fear of destruction that places them in a Qlippotic state within Chesed. They have no swing of rhythm, it is either God or the Devil, and therefore they have no equilibrium. They live in Chesed, and all else is evil. This is limiting and just not true of the Universe and how the realm exists. One needs to smash the coconut to drink its fruit.

We need calm detachment when using Geburah energy, it is your inner law and how aligned to it you are that creates the results. A harsh or unbalanced use of Geburah energy can result in wrecked cities, dead soldiers, and weeping women due to the energy being so severe. Used with the notable movements of Mars wisely, Geburah can become a strong ally in cutting away what does not serve ones reality. Many wars (even recently) have been started in alignment with Mars movements, and this has harnessed extra energy.

Many compassionate people are what one could say, "too Chesed." Nice to everyone, over compassionate, but get walked over and eaten. Spirituality is not sentimentalism. True compassion sees the essence of things, whereas sentimentalism is the attachment to the issue; self indulgent emotionalising, aligning with a victim mentality for the ego payoff. The sword of Geburah cuts this away in one stroke.

But the game is not to be static in the middle between these two Sephiroth all the time, we need to be in a controlled rhythm; to know when to dip into Chesed, and when to dip into Geburah. To know this we must align to a higher will.

The five petaled Tudor Rose gives us a link to Netzach; the Rose is a symbol whose Planetary body is Venus, the counterweight of Mars.

The pentagram is a symbol that can be used to invoke and banish, and represents the regulation of force.

Out of all of the Sephiroth, it is Geburah energy that is needed at this time, to cut away the lies, the masks, and the deceit in the world. Only then can we step up further into love, into the realm of a true orderly harmonious Chesed.

The partnership of Chesed and Geburah (idealism and realism on a lower arc) creates time and space in the universe, and the required combustion that gives birth to Beauty.

Even though Jesus finds his place in Tipareth where all of the sacrificial Sun Gods live, we could say that Jesus is Chesed and Mohammed is Geburah.

6, Tipareth, Beauty.

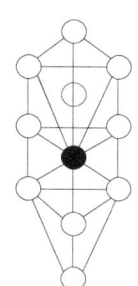

Names: The King, The Son.
Symbols: The Calvary Cross, The Truncated Pyramid, The Cube, The Lamen.
Meditative Image: A King, a Child, a Sacrificed God.
Spiritual Experience: Vision of the Harmony of things, Conversation with Guardian Angel.
Fuel for Meditation: Acacia, Topaz, Coffee.
Vibrational God Name: YHVH Eloah Va Daath; Ruling light, God Manifest in Mind.
Astral Messenger: Raphael; Spirit in the Sun, Healing of God.
Intelligences: Melachim; Elemental Kings.
Planetary Body: Sun ☉ Shemesh; Centre, Heal, Opposites.
Virtue: Devotion to the Great Work.
Vice: Pride.
Sepher Yetzirah Path of Wisdom: 6, Mediating Intelligence.
Colours: Atziluth: Rose-pink, Briah: Yellow, Yetzirah: Salmon-pink, Assiah: Golden amber.
Tarot: The four Sixes.
Deities: Horus, Jesus, Krishna, Rama, Apollo, Addonis, Dionysis, Ra, Osiris.

Tipareth mediates between "above and below," and is the balancing perfect centre and keystone of the whole Tree. It holds all of the other Sephiroth together ensuring all conflicts are resolved.

It receives the abstract forms from Geburah and reflects them as illuminated particles of light in spirit onward to Netzach.

It is a lower Kether and a higher Yesod, with the source of light coming from Kether through the Sun, then reflected onto the Moon in Yesod. On these three Sephiroth we can also place the Father, The Son, and the Holy Ghost respectively, but whereas Kether views Tipareth as a Son, Malkuth views it as the King. If Kether is God unmanifest, then Tipareth is God manifest within us. Tipareth can be viewed as where soul and spirit reside. There are strangely two spiritual experiences in Tipareth, this signifies the veil of Paroketh going through the middle of the Sphere. The conversation with ones guardian angel really means connection to ones true higher self, the merging with ones spirit that resides across the veil. It is only once here in Tipareth that one can really see and feel the harmony of things at a natural electromagnetic level or to understand the mysteries of the crucifiction. It is only here that one can experience true mystical experiences with then Tree.

To reach this sphere of illumination one must have been self initiated in all the lower Sephiroth and Paths, and then one will know that all the lower Sephiroth converge in unity at Tipareth. The lower Sephiroth could be looked at as the lower self, the personality, and the four elements.

Tipareth is the great realisation of the nature of self, this cannot be put into words here but we will try later when we are upon the climbing frame. To achieve the Tiparethic state one needs to make sacrifices. Sacrifice is really transmutating a force to another type of force because no force ever dies or perishes. It is a losing of what one has known to be life.

I have acquaintances who have spent weeks of solitude within this sphere after a tough climb; the whites and sparkle of their eyes, and the light shining from their being is one to behold. It is a very real place.

This Great Work is really about rebirth and regeneration of the soul, hence we find all the sacrificial, redeeming, crucified, and resurrected Gods here. The devotion to the Great Work is devotion to something higher than ourselves, it is devotion to go within and devote time to being accepted to the higher hierarchies within consciousness.

The child symbol is representative of rebirth, and along with the sun shown behind a head, or just the bottom half of the sun, these symbols are evident throughout Catholic churches in Europe.

> "Except ye be converted, and become as little children, ye shall not enter into the kingdom of heaven."
> 18:3 Matthew

Tipareth is the highest point for most religions, it is also the gold that the alchemical philosophers make from base metals using the Philosophers Stone.

The second triad is now complete, the triad of Gods moral power.

Placing The Hexagram around Tipareth yields interesting contemplation. Is it really "The Star of David," or is it two triangles, or even the symbols of the four elements superimposed?

Interestingly, and unknown to most, is that St. Pauls Cathedral in central London designed by astronomer Christopher Wren contains much Tipareth and Tree of life symbolism.

To see the full glare of the Sun within Tipareth is a sight to behold.

7, Netzach, Victory

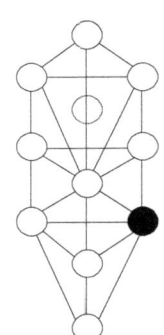

Names: Firmness, Valour.
Symbols: The Girdle, The Lamp, The Rose.
Meditative Image: A Beautiful Naked Women.
Spiritual Experience: Vision of Beauty Triumphant.
Fuel for Meditation: Rose, Emerald, Red Sandal.
Vibrational God Name: YHVH Tseva'oth, Lord of Hosts.
Astral Messenger: Haniel; Power of Love and Harmony.
Intelligences: Elohim; Ideas, Order of Principalities.
Planetary Body: Venus ♀ Nogah; Understand outside thir
Virtue: Unselfishness.
Vice: Lust.
Sepher Yetzirah Path of Wisdom: 7, Occult Intelligence.
Colours: Atziluth: Amber, Briah: Green, Yetzirah: Bright yellowish green, Assiah: Olive flecked with gold.
Tarot: The four Sevens.
Deities: Hathor, Aphrodite, Orpheus.

Netzach is an active masculine energy supporting Chesed from a lower plane, but Netzach is also very feminine. This shows that this is the Sephirah of polarities, polarities on a higher plane than we normally think of them.

The force is still free moving as it comes into Netzach but is now moving into fluid patterns and shapes. Akin to a prism it splits up the love filled rays received from Tipareth into billions of potential life forms, setting the ground plans and blueprints for forms to be able to manifest.

In its essence it is the organising idea behind the first form, and thus begins the astral triad.

The lower four Sephiroth are much more tangible because we are now where normal consciousness applies.

Netzach is the temple that holds in the astral plane; instincts, emotions, feelings, intuition, art, nature, and creative ideas. It is the forces of nature, forces of expression; the raw urges to express and to create. A place where one can find Mother Nature dancing and creating new life.

Sexuality lives in Netzach, not just the physical act, but the essence of the polarity and the force. Aphrodite, Guinevere and Juliet are all of Netzach energy. The cult of Aphrodite were trained in the art of love, and attained to the passions of men not only on a physical level, but on a consciousness level too.

The vice of lust in Netzach is not just sexual either, it is the misplacement of force and expression. The pagan cults knew this, and they entwined nature's elemental energies with sex energy in celebratory ritual often.

The Vision of Beauty can be obtained by learning the victory of the nature of energy, the victory of creating, and the victory of delight in life force.

Netzach is truly an awakening Sephiroth.

The titles of firmness and valor are akin to both pillars being within Netzach. These attributes are a foundation to obtain the self-initiation of Netzach.

To use or invoke higher energy using Qabalah, one must always draw from Netzach, for if one is solely in the ceremonial rigidness of Hod no results will be gleaned. If one cannot use the magik within Netzach, the scepticism of the scientist in Hod will cease all proceedings. These two Sephiroth are inseparable. We need Hod though as feelings unchecked by reason often equate to disaster in many areas of life.

The lamp is a related symbol because it is used in magik regarding fire, and Netzach is the fire element of the lower four Sephiroth. This fire is the fire of the animal instinct, and links Netzach to Mars, the lover of Venus, in Geburah.

Being in a forest creating ideas with the sun shining through the trees is Netzach in its lowest possible arc. The Trees being themselves creative thought forms when flowing through Netzach is it upon its highest arc.

All feelings and emotions in Netzach stimulate thoughts, and all thoughts reside in Hod, the next Sephirah.

8, Hod, Splendour

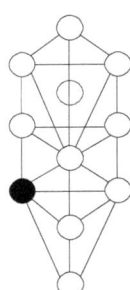

Names: Glory.
Symbols: Names and Versicles, the Apron.
Meditative Image: A Hermaphrodite.
Spiritual Experience: Vision of Splendour.
Fuel for Meditation: Moly, Fire Opal, Storax.
Vibrational God Name: Elohim Tseva'oth, God of Hosts.
Astral Messenger: Michael; Transmutation, Protection, Wisdom.
Intelligences: Bene Elohim; Order of Archangels.
Planetary Body: Mercury ☿ Kokvah; Intellect, Understands Inner Things.
Virtue: Truthfulness.
Vice: Dishonesty.
Sepher Yetzirah Path of Wisdom: 8, Absolute, Perfect Intelligence.
Colours: Atziluyh: Violet purple, Briah: Orange, Yetzirah: Russet red, Assiah: Yellowish black flecked with white.
Tarot: The four Eights.
Deities: Hermes, Hanuman, Anubis, Thoth.

Now differentiated parts of the manifestation of spirit originating in Kether begin to become autonomous. In Hod they are given the vital energies which are necessary for them to become finally expressed in Malkuth. Hod gives a means of communication between the parts, establishing potential relationships for all forms of life.

Being the Sephirah of the Air element, it is the sphere of the intellectual and rational mind; therefore we find in Hod all science, learning, writing, communication, and the Mercury powered Hermetic Philosophy. This pillar is the Hermetic path, whereas the middle pillar could be seen as the devotional path, and the far pillar as the natural mysticism path. The Hermetic Ray comes through the mind, and Hermes was the Priest of pure reason and truth.

In Greek mythology, Mercury, the winged messenger was also called Mercury the psychopomp (guide of the soul and afterlife). He was one of only a few deities who could traverse between the upper and lower worlds.

Hod is home to all esoteric philosophy, occult knowledge, and magik. In magik we are really talking about mental forms and images being created, formulated, and ensouled. A trained will and imagination can bring these to life upon the astral plane.

But in Hod these are just thought forms, one needs to draw from the natural forces in Netzach using soft imaginative, emotional, loving empathy to ensoul the forms. Form is a limitation, but with the force of Netzach one can create the dynamics. Hod and Netzach are only then fully effective when carried into their equilibrium in Yesod. Hod could be looked at as Hermetic magik, and Netzach as Nature Magik.

Hods visual images are different from the treasurehouse of images in Yesod because in Hod they are created by the mind and intention. Therefore in Hod we find all the images of personified polytheistic deity from the Egyptians, Assyrians, and Greeks.

Hod is a reflection of Binah through Chesed, meaning that force from high can be drawn down, and this is the Vision of Splendor; the high divine power manifest in the lower realms.

Michael is the astral messenger, and as a protector he is seen throughout Catholicism, especially in Southern Italy.

The Apron is a Masonic symbol representing the craftsmen of the mysteries, the makers of forms.

Language and the power of words are symbolised by the Versicles. Hod being just below the warrior's sword of Geburah, can cut just as deep with literature, mantras, and magikal phrases. There actually very little difference between magikal phrases and modern day auto suggestion science within Natural Linguistic Programming (NLP).

Einstein was of a Hod persuasion, he was extremely logical and he created experiments within his mind about the speed of light. Most people heavy with Air astrological signs within their astrological chart also live more in Hod, as do those trying to attain spiritually by solely reading and ingesting theory in a logical way.

The fact is that knowledge is required to attain mastery of energy because knowledge will always seek out knowledge, and then open more and more doorways.

9, Yesod, Foundation.

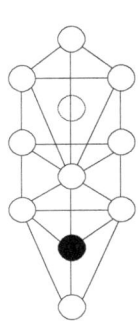

Names: Treasure House of Images.
Symbols: Perfume, Sandals, Incense.
Meditative Image: A Beautiful Strong Naked Man.
Spiritual Experience: Vision of the Machinery of the Universe.
Fuel for Meditation: Ginseng, Quartz, Jasmine.
Vibrational God Name: Shaddai El Chai; Almighty Living God.
Astral Messenger: Gabriel; Hero of God.
Intelligences: Kerubim; Strong Guards.
Planetary Body: Moon ☾ Levanah; Rules the Hidden.
Virtue: Independence.
Vice: Idleness.
Sepher Yetzirah Path of Wisdom: 9, Pure Intelligence.
Colours: Atziluth: Indigo, Briah: Violet, Yetzirah: Dark purple, Assiah: Citrine flecked with azure.
Tarot: The four Nines.
Deities: Diana, Ganesha, Hecate, Isis.

Yesod is the foundation of all forms and physical existence. Its lunar waters swirl to organise the forms designed in Hod, finally breaking the unity.

It is the etheric substance and the astral plane. Where the fleeting, illusory, cyclic, and pulsing activities create the framework of how particles will be meshed together into separate forms.

It purifies all of the emanations and activates the four elements in Malkuth, and in Malkuth we find the fifth element Ether, above in Yesod.

Yesod is the power plant of the universe, it is the motivating principle and the home of all auras, etheric, and astral bodies that are connected to all in Malkuth.

All electromagnetic and astral energies underlying the material world are in this power plant, it is the soup of electromagnetics that we cannot see with our five senses, but still a soup that is mentally malleable. This energy is the raw source of images upon the astral plane.

The storehouse of images in Yesod holds all that exists, and mystics and yogis who can change their physiology visit Yesod to change the corresponding images. These images and others live behind our conscious experience, and are a mix of beautiful, petrifying, future, past, and discovery.

All dreams, unconscious thought, out of body experiences, and even the workings of Homeopathy are in the Sphere of Yesod. The experience and use of the astral plane is not evil as Christian declare, it is a very real part of our consciousness and is a healthy, rewarding, meditative discipline.

All work upon the Paths and Sephiroth will draw from the images stored in Yesod. But once a connection to Yesod has been gleaned it by no means will stay forever, constant discipline in dreams and meditation are needed to keep the connection which will gift the querent much information, awareness, and experience.

Yesod stabilises the opposites, and works with charge, discharge, attraction, repelling, and compensating. So it is of little wonder that the moon is the body of Yesod. The moon waxes, wanes, and handles the machinery of tides, menstruation, and the rise and fall in astral light. Much like Yesod, the moon has no light of its own and reflects light from the sun. We cannot look directly at the sun, so we look to the moon to learn.

The moon is a symbol of fertility of the mind as well as of the loins, and Yesod is linked to the reproductive organs not only to represent regeneration, but to represent electromagnetic charge in energy. This symbolism is added to when on the Sixth day of creation (Yesod is the sixth Sephiroth below the Abyss) Adam and Eve were evident.

An interesting point to make here is that the Merovingians worshipped the Moon Goddess Diana, and in the very same underground tunnel where their rituals were once held, the recent Princess Diana died in questionable circumstances.

When sparks of feelings rooted in intuition fly at us like a thunderbolt, this thunderbolt of images comes from Yesod. But it has zig-zagged from Netzach and Hod, and even sometimes from Tipareth if one is deep along the path. This reminds us that Yesod also has paths coming straight down from Tipareth, reflecting from Kether, the highest.

The image of a strong man could be deemed as the archetype, Atlas, who finds himself in many Hermetic Alchemical Diagrams.

The Yesodic use of herbal smells and incense work subtly upon the subconscious mind, and the sandals symbolise work within mystic circles.

Yesod is the place the adept must first rise to but only after crossing the daunting thirty second path beforehand. Only after further penetrating into Tipareth can one come back into Yesod and truly claim the Vision of the Machinery of the Universe, which is very similar to the vision of Harmony within Tipareth.

10, Malkuth, Kingdom.

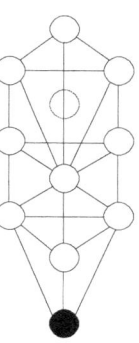

Names: The Gate, The Inferior Mother, The Bride, The Door to the Secret Garden.
Symbols: The Altar of the Double Cube, The Equal Armed Cross, The Magik Circle.
Meditative Image: A Young Women Crowned and Throned.
Spiritual Experience: Vision of Guardian Angel.
Fuel for Meditation: Willow, Rock Crystal, Dittany.
Vibrational God Name: Adonia Malekh; Lord who is King, Adonai Ha Aretz; Lord of Earth.
Astral Messenger: Sandalphon; Twin of Metatron, Ma
Intelligences: Ishim; Souls of fire.
Planetary Body: The Four Elements, Olahm Ha Yesodoth; Sphere of Elements.
Virtue: Discrimination.
Vice: Avarice, Inertia.
Sepher Yetzirah Path of Wisdom: 10, Resplendent Intelligence.
Colours: Atziluth: Yellow, Briah: Citrine, Olive, Russet, Black, Yetzirah: Citrine, Olive, Russet, and Black flecked with gold, Assiah: Black, rayed with yellow.
Tarot: The Four Tens.
Deities: Lakshmi, Sphinx, Demeter, Persephone.

All the emanations finish with material manifestation in the Kingdom of Malkuth. The sphere of mans fall.

It is the outer garments or shells of that conjured within Yesod, classified and arranged in Hod, differentiated in Netzach, given independent life in Tipareth, based on controlled drives from Geburah following the ground plan of Chesed, which is contained within the framework of such a plan by the limiting action of

Binah, which regulates the undifferentiated energies of Chokmah, derived from the need of Spirit in Kether to become manifest.

Malkuth is still subtle, it is the earth soul and the Salamanders, Undines, Sylphs, and Gnomes that in archetype are the four elements. Make no mistake, the four elements are subtle, strong, protecting, and obedient energies when harnessed properly. Paracelsus stated that each of the four elements consisted of a vaporous principle and a gross corporeal substance, and Huxley said that protoplasm is the formal basis of all life, being the clay of the potter. In modern day, science has different words for these elements but the essence has not changed; nitrogen, hydrogen, oxygen, and carbon, or active, receptive, mediating, and material. The ancient world through all continents recorded elementals in myth stating that they live between the flesh and spirit worlds. The different traditions meet at the core truth that four elements have an extremely subtle characteristic energy held in a higher plane than physical manifestation. The Druidic pagan rituals that still flourish in corners of Britain still stoke up ones higher regard for the elementals, and for centuries Qabalah and the work of the Alchemical Philosophers have both been firmly based upon the four elements.

Fire ▲   Water ▼   Air ▲   Earth ▼

The dense flesh is still a temple of the highest and we need to function in Malkuth and learn the lessons here to evolve. We need to have our roots deep into the earth to soar high upon the planes, and it is only after learning and implementing the lessons of Malkuth that we can begin to look up to the higher spheres, and then all we do in the higher spheres is come back in service of light.

Most of our species live the lives only in Malkuth with unconscious fleeting visits to Hod and Netzach. Due to the trick of the five senses most only perceive dense matter, and an objective physical environment even though modern science waves the signs of energy and electromagnetics. Not to worry though as one day the serpent lying coiled at the base of the tree will drive the whole species back to its home.

Malkuth is called the Bride, and it is said of the Bride that she has to be redeemed. With the idea that the messenger is a twin of that in

Kether we can say Malkuth is Kether on a lower arc, and that Kether is the Malkuth of the unmanifest. Malkuth is the seed that has the potential for the tree, and the tree has that potential expressed within the manifestation.

The inferior mother in Malkuth has a place upon the throne of Binah where the Supernal Mother awaits.

The Gate refers to ways through the cracks in the Malkuth Matrix via shamanism, dreams, and death of the shadow self.

The Altar of the Double Cube signifies above and below, and the equal armed cross again represents the four elements in equilibrium.

In Malkuth, Yesodic energy is very strong in crystals, metals and chemicals, but the best conductor of Yesodic energy is an actual person. To move energy within the Tree one must start and end in Malkuth to earth properly or one will face the consequences.

All that is above is manifest in man, and all of nature is manifest in man too. Man has the characteristics of all the animal kingdom; the brave lion, the loyal dog, the treacherous cat, the slippery fish, and so on. All the Zodiac qualities, and therefore the whole universe exists in man too.

Malkuth is where the real work and service lies, and any climb up the tree must only be to come back improved, renewed, and with fresh ideas.

> "We live on earth to celebrate our life in unison with the universe."

***

The Sephiroth are all a part of ourselves in constant activity, and we need to project ourselves into each Sephiroth to know our deep inner world more intimately.

The Sephiroth can be imagined as the internal psychic organs of God. Once they have come into existence, they cannot be separated from Him. They are Him, a good analogy being the veins, arteries and nerves in our earthly bodies, which in their own way, are representative of us. As the divine power of the light passes through these vessels, His light takes on different hues. It is this distinction which is referred to by mystics who speak of the light of God and the light of nature.

Sephirothic emanation, though of course archetypal, is a way of looking at manifestation in a much more real, energetic, scientific, logical sense. It is from the view that mind came before matter.

All pantheons, myths, and theologies find their way onto the relevant stages just showing how fit for purpose the tree is. So many other tales, objects, myths, smells, and attributes fit onto each Sephiroth but I only wish to give enough fuel without the pretentious ramblings found in other publications. It does not matter what you are into, the story of Qabalistic emanation is a very decent way of explaining reality that has lasted scores of centuries.

From a lineage going back centuries I was shown a very real way of raising ones being into Tipareth. I have never been a member of any religion, nor ever will, but this is a sacred science, a science that works in the light, and the glory in Tipareth is one to behold.

A re-read of the Bible knowing the words attached to each Sephiroth yields a truer read, and Genesis, Daniel, Ezekiel, The Menora, and Revelations all contain much Qabalah within them. The Bible is at its heart an allegorical, Qabalistic, moral, poetic doctrine, but has been received by the unthinking masses as literal history.

The Qlippoth

The Qlippoth means shells, form without force, and is deemed by many to be another tree that hangs off the black quarter of Malkuth, in an underworld of sorts. This is not strictly true because the Qlippoth is within each Sephirah. The Sephirah are spherical with an equator, and we can slip past this equator into the Qlippoth. This may sound dark, but each of us has Qlippotic qualities within us, it is all a question of polarity. In the Qlippoth there are demonic forces and intelligences holding different names of power, this is the realm of the black lodges and dark occultist, and dare I say, those sitting behind globalisation at present.

The Qlippotic forces were created naturally by the period of imbalance between the establishment from one Sephirah to the next, and by the sin of the fall of man. We must reiterate that evil does not exist, there exists just balanced and imbalanced force, which are both part of the one.

To slip past the equator in any of the Sephirah into the Qlippoth, darker energies will come and leech one deeper into the Qlippoth, akin to a shoplifter getting grander ideas of theft, or a drug addict looking for a bigger hit.

The vices of each Sephirah are a sure way to fall over to the dark side, along with the following traits:

Chesed - False Ideology
Geburah - Anger, Temper, Rage
Tipareth - Hollowness
Netzach - Routine, Toxic Habits
Hod - Rigid Order, conscious lying
Yesod - Zombeism
Malkuth - Stasis

It needs to be said that too much extreme energy of the virtues in an uncontrolled way easily slips one into the Qlippotic. We need to use the opposite pillar to pull us back from any Qlippotic tendencies or face the energies we have invoked.

Paths Reference

Each of the ten spheres are connected by at least three of the 22 subjective paths. Each of the paths is identified with A) a letter in the Hebrew alphabet, B) one of the 22 major Tarot trumps, C) a Zodiacal sign or body, and D) any number of other mnemonic triggers, like fragrances, metals, gems, magical weapons, animals, Egyptian, Nordic, or Greek Gods. The paths start at 11 continuing on from Malkuth at 10, in total making up the full 32 paths of wisdom in the Sepher Yetzirah.

The following sections will go deeper into the paths attributes, but first we will present a corresponding reference.

	Hebrew	Tarot	Astrology
Path 11:	א Aleph, 1, Ox	Fool (0)	Air
Path 12:	ב Beth, 2, House	Magus (1)	☿ Mercury
Path 13:	ג Gimel, 3, Camel	High Priestess (2)	☽ Moon
Path 14:	ד Daleth, 4, Door	Empress (3)	♀ Venus
Path 15:	ה Heh, 5, Window	Emperor (4)	♈ Aries
Path 16:	ו Vau, 6, Hook	Hierophant (5)	♉ Taurus
Path 17:	ז Zain, 7, Sword	Lovers (6)	♊ Gemini
Path 18:	ח Cheth, 8, Hedge	Chariot (7)	♋ Cancer
Path 19:	ט Teth, 9, Serpent	Strength (8)	♌ Leo
Path 20:	י Yod, 10, Hand	Hermit (9)	♍ Virgo
Path 21:	כ Kaph, 20, Palm	Wheel of Fortune (10)	♃ Jupiter
Path 22:	ל Lamed, 30, Ox-goad	Justice (11)	♎ Libra
Path 23:	מ Mem, 40, Water	Hanged Man (12)	Water
Path 24:	נ Nun, 50, Fish	Death (13)	♏ Scorpio
Path 25:	ס Samekh, 60, Pillar	Temperance (14)	♐ Sagittarius
Path 26:	ע Ayin, 70, Eye	Devil (15)	♑ Capricorn
Path 27:	פ Peh, 80, Mouth	Tower (16)	♂ Mars
Path 28:	צ Tzaddi, 90, Fish-hook	Star (17)	♒ Aquarius
Path 29:	ק Qoph, 100, Back-head	Moon (18)	♓ Pisces
Path 30:	ר Resh, 200, Face	Sun (19)	☉ Sun
Path 31:	ש Shin, 300, Tooth	Judgment (20)	Fire
Path 32:	ת Tau, 400, Cross	Universe (21)	♄ Saturn

Note1: Hebrew: Symbol, Hebrew name, value, brief meaning that can be elaborated.
Note2: Some Qabalists remove the Fool and place the Magus at Path11. This shifts the Trumps and astrology (not the Hebrew) up one leaving Path32 near clear. After having worked both ways and undertaken much research, I advise using the above order.

Numbers & Gematria

> *"Number is all."*
> Pythagoras

Esoteric Numerical Symbols

What exactly are numbers? They are symbols, and they mathematically and geometrically make up the fabric of reality. The Pythagorean schools looked at numbers very differently to the modern day western schools, and we should note that Pythagoras was initiated in Syrian, Egyptian, Babylonian, and Phoenician mysteries. The mystery schools know that the virtue of discrimination is what enables us to see the different meanings between the symbols 1 and 2, and that by allowing our language of concepts to have meaning, this enables numbers to have meaning.

The following esoteric look at numbers from 1 to 10 will not only enable one to delve into the Sephiroth and Tarot more deeply, it will enable one to view life with more depth. Numbers in 2010 seem to be nothing more than a "count of quantities," but as the western schools are preparing to churn out tax-paying worker ants, this is the way it will be for a little while longer.

0 . Zero is space without frontiers, negative, unmanifest, the circle where one cannot see where it begins or ends.

1 . One is principle, some-thing, positive, unity. It creates all other numbers, and from 1 we can multiply to the infinite. It is the same essence reproduced and copied; we call 2, 2, but really it is 1 and 1. It is the first spark from the source, an Aries type energy.

2 . Two is polarity, duality, opposites, sharing, Yin and Yang. It is 1 looking at itself. It is the mate of man and the mother of society. It provokes reaction, and resists, denies, and clarifies. 2 is static.

3 . Three is the integration of 1 and 2, the triad, the trinity, the number of creation. It is the Magician and High Priestess giving birth to the soul within the Pregnant Empress. 3 is the core essence of all that is, the cohesion that binds.

At times we cannot see the 3 but it is everywhere; the love in a partnership or the idea between the painter and the canvas. It is the energies within each element; the fixed, mutable, and cardinal, and it is also the mind, body, and soul.

3.5 Three and a half has mystical value due to being half of 7, this decimal value appears many times in the Bible.

4 . Four is stable and even, the physical plane, achievement of the 1st cycle. It is the square, the tetrad, the base of a pyramid. It is the cross + vertical in spirit, horizontal in material. A circle around this cross creates the symbol of Malkuth. 4 is the moon phases, cardinal points, the elements, and the aspects of man; physical, mental, emotional, and spiritual. 1+2+3+4 = 10 which is The Tetractys symbol held most sacredly within the Pythagorean schools. It contains the key to harmony; 4:3 = The Fourth, 3:2 = The Fifth, 2:1 The Octave. The symbols were and are always displayed with dots because Pythagoras taught that the dot symbolised the power of the number 1.

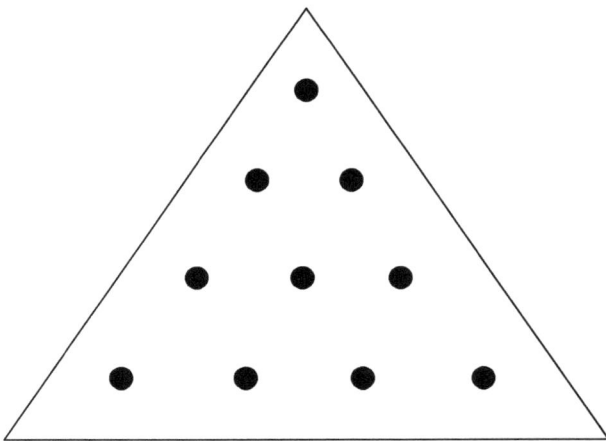

5 . Five is the Pentad, the initiator of changes, the breaking of what is already established and the starting something new. Halfway in the path of 1 and 10, it unites the female 2 and the male 3. The 5 pointed Pentagram is the union of the 4 elements and ether; upright representing consciousness over material, but reversed instincts are overpowering consciousness. The centre of the pen-

tagram is a pentagon, and there is irony as to why the world's military headquarters is of this shape and name. In every multiplication, 5 restores itself.

6 . Six is the Hexad, The Star of David, male and female, above and below, the call to evolve upwards. It is the number of equilibrium. The hexagram is created by cutting the circumference of a circle 6 times with its radius. 6 is the number of time and space as it is the amount of directions within any volume. Pythagoreans named it "The Perfection of Parts." 6 multiplied into itself always remains as a unit within the result. On the 6th day man was created and on the 6th day of the week Jesus died on the cross. 6x60 = 360, the degrees of a circle.

7 . Seven is the Heptad, it is of perfection and sacredness. 7 is found in the rainbow, the chakras, the days of the week, the sins, the main internal organs, and in the harmonic scale in music. It is the 3 of divine spirit and the 4 of material matter combining to represent God in the physical. 7 is the phenomena of growth, and multiples of 7 are all steps of growth, especially in human solar years. The moon passes through 7 days of waxing, full, waning, and renewal, and Plato stated in his "Timaeus" that the number 7 came from the soul of the world (Anima Mundana, or Adam Kadmon). The 7 ancient planets are linked to the 7 alchemical metals and the 7 days of the week (the names of which are derived from Latin). See how the numbers look like the astrological symbols, plus how following the line of the geometry gives us the order of the days of the week.

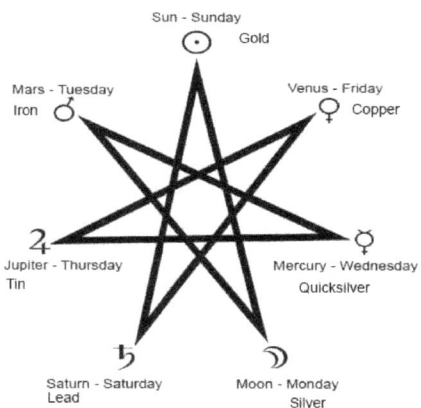

8 . Eight Is the Ocdoad, it is evolution and justice when one understands the laws of cause and effect. It is the infinity symbol and constantly moving. Hermes was "Master of the city of 8." The fertilised ovum links to the Egyptian text that declares, "I am 1, who becomes 2, who becomes 4, who becomes 8, and then I am 1 again.

9 . Nine is the Ennead. It is initiation, the last of the single digits. 0 and 1 are now together and are not separated. Now initiated, there is no need to follow anyone else. It is the prophet and also the Hermit Trump; stop relying on outsiders to guide, listen to inside then one can't be blown off course. It is the months of gestation, a bridge, a transition. 9 is the mystical Enneagram symbol that Gurdjieff stated removed the need for all books and libraries. Any multiplication of 9 reproduces itself, e.g. 9x17=153 = 1+5+3 = 9.

10 . Ten is the Decad, 0 and 9 are now separated to show the end of initiation. We are now back to 0 and 1 on a new octave; a new beginning, ready to start again. The word Decad derives from 'Dechomia,' meaning to receive. 10 is complete, it contains all the numbers, it is infinite and called "the fountain of eternal nature" because all within give the same result; 1+9, 2+8, 3+7, 4+6, 5+5. 10 is when the invisible becomes visible, the manifest of the unmanifest in perfection. It is 1 on a different level. Only 10 makes It possible to see the invisible (zero). The word "ten" in Hebrew was used instead of "a large number," and all Hebrew letters equate to 10 in gematria.

10 is the apple of a Tree, inside it is a seed, a potential for another. The apple is the in between state.

Hebrew and Gematria

The Sepher Yetzirah states that the universe was created when divinity arranged the 22 Hebrew letters in their particular order; a triad, heptad, and a dodecad.

When the meaning of each letter is meditated upon and understood, one can as a mantra make the sound of each letter in order whilst activating the relevant "state of being." This soon yields an intitation related to the flow of creation but the depths of this excersise are not in the scope of this book.

The three Mother letters, Aleph, Mem, and Shin are the foundation of the alphabet, the prime trinity, representing Air, Water, and Fire.

From the trinity all nature took form in the seven Double letters; Beth, Gimel, Daleth, Kaph, Peh, Resh and Tau each expressing a double significance, and representing the seven Planets and other septenaries.

The fabric of space in which the seven double letters evolved was divided into twelve parts, which are the twelve remaining letters; Heh, Vau, Zain, Cheth, Teth, Yod, Lamed, Nun, Samekh, Ayin, Tzaddi, and Qoph. These twelve letters symbolise the twelve directions in space, human body parts, and the twelve signs of the zodiac.

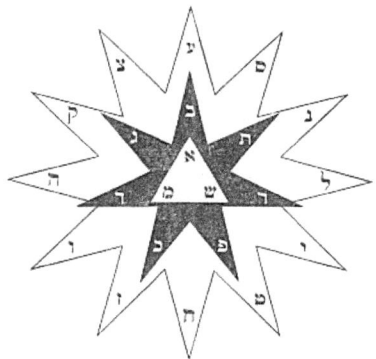

ת Tau, being the last and twenty second letter is the perfection of creation, it is summary of everything in everything, it is the mystery that reveals itself directly to the soul. ת is also the symbol for the furthest development of creation, and the sign which the Lord told the people of Jerusalem to mark upon their foreheads, as related by the Prophet Ezekiel.

ש Shin has a shape referring it to the Trinity. Composed of three ו Vau's placed next to each other giving the number 666. This is the number of the Sun, of man, and also of the Beast in Revelations. It is not evil as often thought, but for some theorists if you add it to the year 1346, when the Black Plague (the Great Mortality) occurred then you achieve the year 2012.

The Hebrew words for "love" and "unity" both have the numerical value of 13. This fact is held to indicate that "the nature of unity is love." This also reiterates the intrinsic relation between 1 (Unity) and 3 (Trinity) which is the divine basis for the triad. Also, with hvhy = 26 = 2 x 13, we can see that "hvhy is Unity and love manifested in Duality." 13 also represents being able to transmute above the influence of the 12 zodiac signs, it is only deemed unlucky due to the date when the Knights Templars were persecuted.

The Hebrew word for "mother" is 41, "father" is 3, and added result in 44, the value for the word "child."

The Garden of Eden is 144 and the tree of knowledge is 233. 144 and 233 are numbers found in the spiraling Golden Phi Fibonacci sequence.

This can go very deep, and Qabalistic gematria is also evident within the Great Seal of America as well as other modern day events that most would just not believe without a deep research into Freemasonry beforehand.

> "...To Jewish mystics, every letter in the Hebrew alphabet was a channel to the life force of God and possessed of sacred meaning. Hebrew numbers were also represented by letters so that names and words had numerical values. Finding associations of words with the same value revealed a complex series of hidden meanings beneath the text of the Torah, the book of law attributed to Moses. In fact, the entire Torah can be considered to be a single long word spelling out one of the names of God. The significance of the name of God goes back to ancient Egypt where knowing the name of a God allowed one to gain power over that God."
> MacGregor Mathers, Co-founder of the Order of the Golden Dawn

Qabalistic Numbers

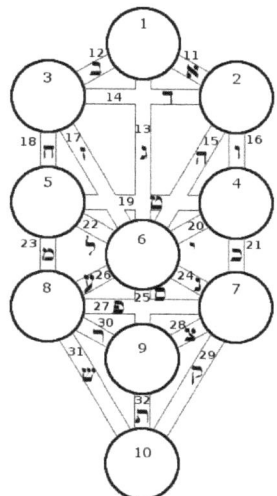

Above we see the numbers of the Sepher Yetzirah 32 paths of wisdom upon the Tree of Life, along with the Hebrew letters. The roots of the Sepher Yetzirah are lost to antiquity, but the Hebrew people associate it to Enoch or Abraham, the Greeks to Hermes, and the Egyptians to Thoth. The 32 paths of wisdom hold some keys to unlocking the secrets of the Qabalah, but it is not a necessity by any means, these can also be unlocked by using other toys in the toybox.

> "….for by a secret system of arranging them [the letter and numbers on the Tree of Life] the mysteries of creation are revealed."
> Manly P Hall referring to the 32 paths of wisdom.

This secret is concealed within the penultimate 32nd degree of Freemasonry, and it's interesting to note that there are 32 spinal segments to the temple (skull), and 32 mentions of God in Genesis.

We have already shared the related intelligences for the Sephiroth, and now we will do so for the Paths (Note that the Sepher Yetzirah gives one or two elaborative and meditative sentences for each Path of Wisdom).

Path11: Scintillating Intelligence, 12: Intelligence of Transparency, 13: Uniting Intelligence, 14: Illuminating Intelligence, 15: Constituting Intelligence, 16: Triumphal or Eternal Intelligence, 17: Disposing Intelligence, 18: House of Influence, 19: Intelligence of the Secret of all the Activities of the Spirit, 20: Intelligence of Will, 21: Intelligence of Conciliation and Reward, 22: Faithful Intelligence, 23: Stable Intelligence, 24: Imaginative Intelligence, 25: Intelligence of Probation or Temptation, 26: Renewing Intelligence, 27: Active or Exciting Intelligence, 28: Natural Intelligence, 29: Corporeal Intelligence, 30: Collective Intelligence, 31: Perpetual Intelligence, 32: Administrative Intelligence.

A Qabalistic number one may come across is Qabalistic Pi, which is 3.142857. If one divides a Sephirah's degrees into 7 (360/7) one achieves 51.42857, and if one does the same with 21 one achieves 17.142857. This 142857 can keep cropping up, and the sum of which is 27, which inverted is 72, another Qabalistic number (also Mayan, and Processional).

In Exodus, verses 3:19,20,21 each have 72 letters, and if placed on top of one another so that the 72 letters appear in columns, one can see the 72 names of God. Some Jewish mystics claim the hidden name of God is a 216 letter name in 72 parts only to be found using an algorithm. It should be added here that יהוה placed in The Tetractys also yields the number 72.

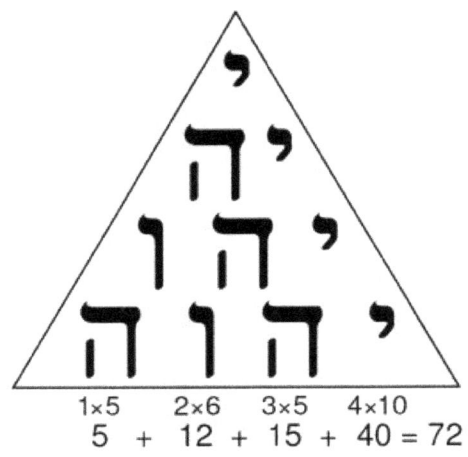

In the earlier sections you may have remembered the number 21 cropping up often. 21 is often the amount of days that retreats around the world contain, this is because it takes 21 days for ones physiology to really change, and of course it is the number before t Tau, 22, completion. But it works as a fractal, one can meditate for 21 minutes and be aligned with the energy, and also after 21 or 42 days of a retreat things will really speed up on a higher octave. 22 is a hexagonal pyramidal and a pentagonal number, it is a door, a gate.

21 is also the sum of 777, a number used much in occult literature. 777 is also a fractal within 21 because after each 7 one can feel an octave jump, whether it be seconds, minutes, days, or years. 777 is also the sum of the value of the Hebrew letters the lightning flash crosses on its ways down to Malkuth.

Some main Qabalistic numbers are 3, 4, 7, 21, 22, 32, 50, 72, 144, 216, 231, 244, 360, 720, 777, 1440.

This is just a tiny skim across the surface of Hebrew numerology and Qabalistic numbers. If interested in this route, the firm content within Liber 500 and Liber LVIII are unrivaled. I know someone who spent a hundred days living within the realm of Qabalistic numbers armed with only a pen, some paper, a meditation stool, and a yoga mat. He flew to a very special place and came back a very special being.

We can use numerology when we come across numbers or words in poignant times, or when and where we feel open to signs. We can then place the resulting number upon the Tree plus look at that numbers core meaning. For example:

Mark = Mem(40), Aleph(1), Resh(200), Kaph(20) = 261 = 9.

Using numerology and Hebrew one can also devise personal mantras.

Elements & Astrology

The Four Elements

Using and getting to know the four elements is fundamental to work upon the Tree of Life, the knowledge will also give more substance to ones relationship with nature too. The elements are not abstract symbols or archetypes, they are actual subtle forces of energy and also the foundations that underlie Qabalah, Astrology and Occult science. The elements interweave and make up all form and matter, making them the building blocks of the physical universe. When the life spark leaves a human upon death, the elements then dissociate and return to their primal state.

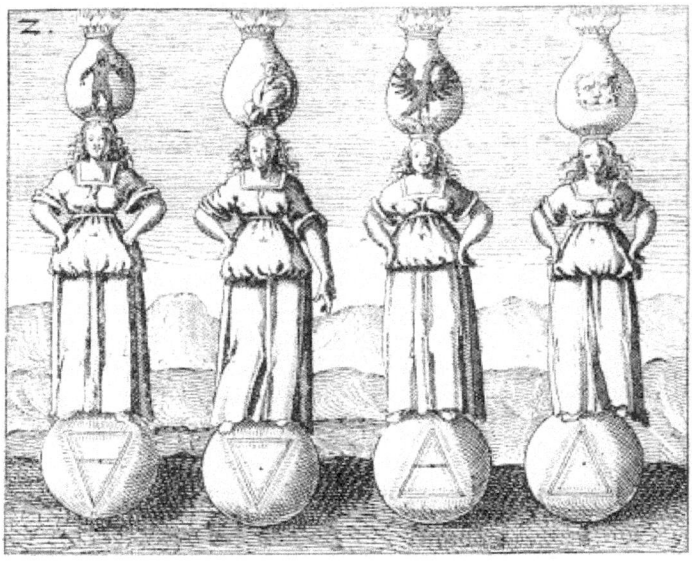

Modern objects in the western world disconnect people from the true source of things; Chemical shampoos, chemical weed killers, chemical bleaches, televisions, and an absurd overuse of plastic. Everything seems to be synthetic and cheap, therefore we are removed from our planets original materials and no longer in respect of their origin - the four elements.

We have already covered an introduction to the elements within their rightful home in Malkuth, but we need to go deeper. The ancients all around the world looked sacredly towards the elements; in China, Tibet, Greece, India, Japan, and Sumer, and the oldest case arguably coming from India were the Sanskrit terms were, Akasha (Ether), Tejas (Fire), Waju (Air), Apas (Water), and Prithivi (Earth).

Various traditions view Fire and Water as coming from Ether with Air mediating between these two, for all three then solidify to create Earth. Other traditions link Fire closely with Air, and Water with Earth. This is all worthy of meditation.

Let us look at the attributes which make up each element:

Fire

Energy, action, motivation, dynamism, initiative, inspiration, will, courage, creativity, passion, self, communication, improvement, leadership, firmness, risk, confidence, adventure, outward energy, enthusiasm, passionate involvement, optimism. Impatience, impulsiveness, bluntness, jealousy, irritableness, egotistical, consuming, domineering, anger.

Wands tarot Suit, South, Spring, Male, Atziluth, Kings.

Water

Feelings, depth, modesty, compassion, tenderness, receptivity, privacy, reflection, empathy, subconscious, intuition, forgiveness, tranquility, emotions, fluidity, relationships, inward energy, sensitivity, reflection. Mood swings, oversensitive, boredom, apathy, dependence, secrecy.

Cups tarot suit, West, Summer, Feminine, Briah, Queens.

Air

Mental activity, clarity, rational thinking, decisions, reasoning, aspiration, intellectual pursuit, ideas, ethics, diligence, curiosity, communication, kindness, optimism, need for sociability. Conflict and struggle, craftiness, pain and restriction, uncaring, gossip, fickleness, lacking endurance.

Swords tarot suit, East, Autumn, Male, Yetzirah, Knights.

Earth

Endurance, stability, material, practicality, senses, roots, respect, caution, thoroughness, punctuality, work, crafts, responsibility, the body, the home, security, nature, protection, wealth, comfort, acquisition. Over conventional, perfectionist, stubborn, uncreative, predictable.

Pentacles tarot suit, North, Winter, Feminine, Assiah, Pages.

It is beneficial to look at ones own character and record honestly where the above positive and negative attributes are evident or missing (a soul mirror). This allows one to see which elements are imbalanced or lacking, and due to each astrological zodiac sign being related to an element, this character study will be in tune with ones astrological birth chart. The western astrological birth chart gives much information regarding the balance and weight of the elements that ones manifested expression is consciously attuned to. Viewing astrology from the view of the elements gives a much more holistic view.

When one can see what traits in which elements are imbalanced, one can use will, the ingestion of intention fueled water and food, plus pore breathing to become "the positive opposite," or to "deny the negative."

The most harmonious of couples, partnerships, and friendships balance out the elements together, for if two lovers are both heavy in the fire element it really does become a powder keg. The negative qualities listed above arise from too much energy of that element. If an element is lacking in someone all together, then the positive traits of the corresponding element will be in small amounts, or even non-existent.

Furthermore, the elements each have three vibrations; cardinal, fixed, and mutable, as we will soon see.

Here are two base exercises in meditation one can perform to align closer to the elements. Will, intent and imagination are required.

- Pore-breathe inwards seven times the whole of the Earth element. Imagine that the whole universe is a brown or yellow, dense, heavy, gravity with you at its centre. On out breaths relax and still be in that Earth centre.
- Pore-breathe inwards seven times the whole of the Water element. Imagine that the whole universe is a cool green-blue water fluidic ocean with you at its centre.
- Pore-breathe inwards seven times the whole of the Air element. Imagine that the whole universe is a light blue feeling of space, expansion, and lightness with you at its centre.
- Pore-breathe inwards seven times the whole of the Fire element. Imagine that the whole universe is a warm red flamed fire with you at its centre.
- End with four strong out breaths, blowing each element out in reverse.
- In one long inward breathe, bring in Earth to the feet, legs, and thighs, Water from the thighs to the high abdomen, Air up to the top of the neck, and Fire into the head. Blow out in reverse whenever ready. (This is a great way to open and close meditations).

Note: Some may have noticed that Qabalah orders the elements Fire, Water, Air, then Earth, whereas occult teachings tend to use Fire, Air, Water, and then Earth. There is a place for both, neither is incorrect.

In just a few days of performing these exercises one will know about it for sure. These are just a base and one can experiment as long as they keep each element in balance, and start with Earth each time.

The Chaioth Ha Qadesh in the Yetzirah world of Kether remind us that the elements are higher forces and to be respected.

The Zodiac & Planetary Bodies

The cosmos of stars and nearby planets act as a complex machine of clockwork and gears, forever in motion, constantly enabling different characteristics in human births. It is akin to a giant engine with different energy values, every second allowing more human diversity in addition to the karmic and genetic fractal attributes. Due to these astrological bodies, all humans are a whole and unique expression of universal principles, patterns, and energies.

We all know that our sun and moon give us large amounts of energy but skeptics seem to refuse any other cosmic body affecting us. Oh the folly in man, most think they are just dead lifeless objects.

Planets are fundamental life forces, and if we are not aware of them we are at the mercy of them. Each planet resonates at a frequency by velocity, proportions and make up, therefore has a conscious core, and this energy reflects a part of the psyche of man. Simply, we could say that the planetary archetypal energy resides in man too, as above, so below. The planetary bodies are the most tangible and ultimate talismans, and this was known by the Chaldeans.

Astrology, like travel, can be looked at as an appreciation for the cosmic symphony of synchronicity. Each week I look at the planets movements and re-order criteria in my week to fit better, this is pure science, as too is a study of astrological birth charts. The world elite in 2010 make modern day astrology look silly deliberately via the mainstream media, but they are masters at using the planetary bodies themselves. Even Carl Jung used astrology on top of psychology with his clients, and even though astronomers only seem to see light and gas, the wise always notice landmarks of universal will.

> "As long as you still experience the stars as something above you, you will lack a viewpoint of knowledge"
> Friedrich Nietzsche."

> "In contemporary astrology, it is generally thought that planetary phenomena cause or are reflected in events on Earth. However, the magikal tradition takes this concept one step further by harnessing or co-creating with the planetary phenomena. Many Hermeticists feel that these acts even comprise a spiritual practice because by working with the planets, they come closer to the one."
> Warnock, Hermetic Gnosis.

Uranus, Neptune, and Pluto, plus the houses and aspects we will shun as these are all relatively modern and have no place within Qabalah.

The Table below shows the 12 signs plus their element, their energy of element, their ruling planet, and their order within the solar year.

Each element is in the state of Cardinal, Fixed, or Mutable. Cardinal is an initiating, outpouring of energy, an acting upon goals. Fixed is a persistent, organising, rigid energy that builds on what is already in place. Mutable is a changing, adapting, renewing energy, it is flowing, open, and able to replace things.

After reading the rest of this section it is important to commit to memory the understanding of this table and its symbols.

	Cardinal	Fixed	Mutable
△	1 ♈ ♂	5 ♌ ☉	9 ♐ ♃
▽	4 ♋ ☽	8 ♏ ♂	12 ♓ ♃
△ (air)	7 ♎ ♀	11 ♒ ♄	3 ♊ ☿
▽ (earth)	10 ♑ ♄	2 ♉ ♀	6 ♍ ☿

Saturn ♄

Slow, creates obstacles, gives limitations, contraction, effort, endurance, perseverance, stability, introspection, discipline, focus.
Seriousness, routine, enemy of progress, death, inaction.

Jupiter ♃

Improvements to self, elevate consciousness, protects, inspires, wisdom, generosity, joy, wealth, goodness, optimism, faith, justice.
Dishonesty, service for recognition and pride, harm oneself, over confidence.

Mars ♂

God of war, active, outgoing, dynamic energy. The arrow is the will guiding spirit. Leadership, initiative, determined, valor, risks, decisive.
Violence, vengeance, lack of sensitivity, tactless, impatience, impulsive.

Sun ☉

Vitality, radiating, transformative, life giving, confidence, creative, sustaining.
Pride, arrogance, desire to be special.

Venus ♀

Attraction, harmony, beauty, desire to please, gentleness, tact, grace, harmony, art, sociable, aesthetic awareness, sensual.
Self indulgent, emotional demands.

Mercury ☿

Hermes, intellect, reason, communication, skill, logic, analytical, flexible, verbal and written expression, quick understanding.
Hypercritical, cynical, anxiety.

Moon ☽

Mystery of what is hidden, subconscious, reflection, esoteric study, receptive, contemplative.
Moody, secrets, lack of discipline, insecurity.

Aries ♈ The Ram   "I am"

First to charge, leads, potential manifested, advance, courageous, active, enthusiastic, strong willed, frank, joy of being, decisive.

Impulsive, jumps into things, bully, overpowering, blunt.

Taurus ♉ The Bull   "I have"

Reliable, conservative, care for people and projects, brings what needs to be brought, enjoys luxury, sensual, routine, enduring.
Possessive, insecure, lazy, sees red.

Gemini ♊ The Twins   "I Think"

Open minded, flexible, restless, intelligence, sees both sides, changes, spontaneous, witty, learning, creativity.

Fickle, too many projects at once, rarely touches down.

Cancer ♋ The Crab   "I feel"

Strong subconscious, cold untrusting outside and a soft vulnerable inside, just like the crab. Resourceful, strong intuition, good solutions, inner world very strong, caring, imaginative.

Can be difficult to connect to outer world, fragile, secretive.

Leo ♌ The Lion   "I will"

Can see big picture, centre of attention, leads the show like the sun. Need to do from heart, need a calling. Beauty, love and energy to those close. Loyal, perseverance, determined, ambitious, strong willed, creative, enthused, leadership.

Pride, bossy, patronising, intolerant, vanity, temper.

Virgo ♍ The Virgin   "I analyse"

Practical, rational, intellectual, practical as Taurus but more free from material and more adaptable. Gather facts and details, investigating, orderly, methodical, modest, reserved, helpful, service.

Trouble seeing the big picture, perfectionists, conformity, finicky, critical, hard to please, easily worried, take themselves too seriously.

Libra ♎ The Scales   "I balance"

Strong mind but mellowed by Venus, iron hand in the velvet glove. Strong will, express smoothly. Brings balance, beauty, peace, and harmony to people and actions. Focus on others, loves people and family home. Justice, tolerant, idealistic, diplomatic, kind.

Fear of conflict, no opinion, sit on fence, gullible, argumentative, flirty, compromising.

Scorpio ♏ The Scorpion   "I desire"

Phoenix, eagle, snake, scorpion. Inner conflict, water and mars. Strong energy, strong emotion, rises from ashes, can go deep into dark side of self and things. Transformation gifts, magnetic, piercing, passionate, intense, skilled, big subconscious, tenacious, psychic.

Unstable, secretive, self destruction, can sting, jealousy, resentful.

Sagittarius ♐ The Archer   "I see"

Half man and half horse. Control over lower instincts, arrow to the stars shows high aspirations. See what is beyond, motivates others to do the same. Likes freedom, good travelers, philosophers, independent, protecting, inspiring, open mind, jovial.

Lack of perseverance, inconsistent, take easy path, arrogant.

Capricorn ♑ The Goat   "I use"

Ambitious, earthy, goes for summit, can accomplish all. Saturn patience, determined and willful. Prepare and plan well, can withdraw from a flow to wait for a better one more conducive to path or project. Long term views, endurance, caution, thoughtful, practical, efficient, reflective, reserved, reliable, proud.

Cold, rigid, over conventional, slow, lack of trust.

Aquarius ♒ The Water Bearer   "I know"

Share information and knowledge, good teachers, communicative and expressive. Happier in groups than individuals, strong sense of community, humanitarian. Act from intellect rather than inner knowing, inventive, foresight, freedom, visionary, unconventional.

Stubborn, keep to preconceived ideas, unruly, loves controversy.

Pisces ♓ The Fish   "I believe"

Open, absorb all from environment like a fish. Fluid, slippery, trouble separating from others. Strong deep emotions, impressionable, sensitive to outside influences, connected to all. Intuition over logic, compassionate, receptive, merciful, humble, self sacrifice easy.

Vague, indecisive, overly compliant, lack of motivation to start projects, passive, vulnerable, easily influenced, fuzzy boundaries.

***

We have now covered the core energy of the signs and planets for the purpose of knowing the Tree of Life more intimately. If one is interested in astrology readings for people then one should be aware that just knowing ones sun sign will not yield too much information.

The ascendant, moon sign, balance of elements, and planetary locations are all major keys in any true interpretation.

Below is the Tree of Life with just the astrological energies placed upon it. The next section regarding Tarot will fit this section like a glove and also build up more of the Tree, another coat of paint so to speak.

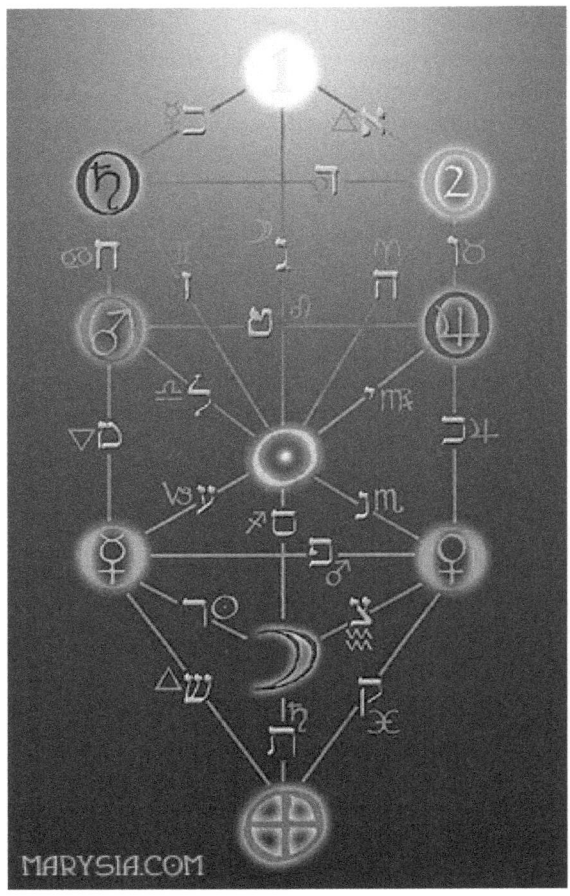

Note: Malkuth is often displayed with a cross representing the four elements. The four elements combine on earth, therefore it is correct astrologically to place the earth symbol in Malkuth. The + at the bottom of the diagram is earth

Tarot

"A prisoner devoid of books, had he only a Tarot of which he knew how to make use, could in a few years acquire a universal science, and converse with an unequalled doctrine and inexhaustible eloquence."
Eliphas Levi, 19th Century Qabalist and scholar

Many believe the cards are only a few centuries old, but the cards real source was the Egyptian mystery schools where they were known as "The Book of Thoth." It was the gypsies (with Egyptian roots) and the contact with Saracens by the Knights Templar during the crusades that brought the cards into medieval Europe.

The Tarot consists of seventy eight cards; four suits of ten each with four court cards, plus twenty-two "Trumps" which make up the Major Arcana. The word has meaning too, the Egyptian words, "Tar" and "Ro" together mean Royal Road, and ROTA (TARO reversed) means wheel.

There are many different decks, but the main Portuguese, French, Arthur-Waite, and Crowley decks all contain similar core symbolism, archetypes, stories, and meanings. I advise using the Arthur-Waite deck as it has much symbolism matching the Tree of Life.

All modern playing cards derive from the Tarot, and even chess has esoteric roots when we look at its symbolism and history deeply enough.

Anyone seriously using Tarot with no knowledge of the Tree of Life will be working with large holes within their art for sure. The Tree and Tarot complement each other and fit so well that it is hard for anyone to state that this design is by chance.

Major Arcana

If we digest the Levi statement or study the Tarot in any serious way we soon find that Tarot is not predominantly a book of divination, but that it *can* be used for divination. The Major Arcana is really predominantly a story, a plan, a blueprint, a spiritual adventure that shows where one is along the way.

The Major Arcana are also strong forces and energies coming from the realm of the spirit and the higher self. They are archetypes that represent powerful forces influencing our lives.

The Major Arcana shows The Fool (0), the soul, embarking upon a great quest of spiritual attainment and the energies it encounters along the way. The Fool is an archetype that many humans never even realise as their souls are shut down, it is an archetype for realising one is a soul confined within a material vessel, and then seeking to go on the journey of attainment, the journey back home.

				0 The Fool			
I The Magician	II The High Priestess	III The Empress	IV The Emperor	V The Hierophant	VI The Lovers	VII The Chariot
VIII Strength	IX The Hermit	X The Wheel of Fortune	XI Justice	XII The Hanged Man	XIII Death	XIV Temperance
XIV The Devil	XVI The Tower	XVII The Star	XVIII The Moon	XIX The Sun	XX Temperance	XXI The World

We see 777 again with The Fool sitting above ready to start his quest. Below we will look at the supreme journey walking though all the Trumps, adding some words about the energy of each Trump and a meditative question to get to know the Trump and its relations to the Tree of Life better. Every colour and symbol has a meaning and the relations to the Tree of Life are abundant, alas, this would take hundreds of pages and I only wish to give a core base.

The Fool (0)
Journey: No more self judging, the soul arrives at the border ready to change form, the bag holds the wisdom that is always with us. Curiosity and innocence on the new beginning of realising one is an infinite spirit.
Energy: New beginnings, idealistic, no experience, folly.
Question: What does the dog mean?

The Magician (1) Egyptian Root: The Magus
Journey: The beginning of consciousness, will, and inner transformation. The alchemist bringing spirit down; the priest prays, but the magician attracts.
Energy: One arm in Binah and one in Netzach. Skill, will, faculties, manifestation, craft, occult intelligence, manipulation of the material.
Question: Why are the four elements not completely visible?

The High Priestess (2) Egyptian Root: Isis Veiled
Journey: The opening of sub consciousness, the beginning to seek answers from the mysteries. The scroll has the mystery of creation; the key of the Tree of Life. She is the guardian, Isis veiled. The pillars are those of the Tree. The hidden book with the full truth is not revealed to uninitiated.
Energy: Moon Goddess, spiritual bridge, secrets, mysteries, ask deep questions to subconscious.
Question: What is behind the veil?

The Empress (3) Egyptian Root: Isis Unveiled
Journey: The process is fertilised, creative energy, go forth, permitting growth and advancement. The mother of creation, Isis unveiled, out of whose body the initiate is born again.
Energy: Creativity, reproduction, receptivity, love, Venus.
Question: What are the 12 stars on her crown representing?

The Emperor (4) Egyptian Root: The Sovereign

Journey: Stability, knowledge, self control, discipline, authority from higher. Strength, half the process of the first victory (3.5).
Energy: Father of creation, king, authority, law, energy, power.
Question: What does his wand represent?

The Hierophant (5)   Egyptian Root: The Hierophant
Journey: A new station. Master of the mysteries. Continue the Magicians work. He sees if you have enough knowledge to continue, may need a teacher.
Energy: Advice from traditions, conformity, inspiration, wisdom.
Question: Why are the keys crossed?

The Lovers (6)   Egyptian Root: The Two Paths
Journey: Netzach and Hod lovers, in union. Harmony in relations between consciousness (male) and sub consciousness (female). Looking for blessings from super consciousness (archangel). Can only get to super consciousness from the subconscious (the man looking at the women, who in turn is looking up). The Tree of knowledge in the background shows that it must be balanced or the Hierophant will not permit one to continue.
Energy: Harmony, union, attraction, love.
Question: Why four fruits on the tree?

The Chariot (7)   Egyptian Root: The Conqueror
Journey: The first victory, the motors are started, need to keep control of the reigns of both pillars or one will crash. Patience and desires are purified by the new soul. Have to control emotions and thoughts to understand the light from The Hermit. The Fool can now drive. The man is rising, not standing, showing ascension.
Energy: Triumph, self control, conquer. Knowledge about creation.
Question: What does the winged orb represent?

Strength (8)   Egyptian Root: The Balance
Journey: Need to control the Kundalini energy with will and grace. The lion is the spiritual fire energy invoked, it must be tamed.
Energy: Spiritual strength, dominion of material situation. Patience with balance. Will and intention controls desires.
Question: What does the infinity symbol represent?

The Hermit (9) Egyptian Root: The Sage
Journey: The Hermit carries the light and truth and waits for serious students. He knows the path and the way. Illumination is within.
Energy: Prudence, advice, wisdom, guide, concealing.
Question: What does the Star of David in the lamp represent?

The Wheel of Fortune (10) Egyptian Root: The Wheel
Journey: Karma must be balanced and processed. The knowledge of life and its rules.
Energy: Evolution, laws, destiny, karma, fortune. Anubis and Typhon show good and evil.
Question: Why do the four sacred animals hold books?

Justice (11) Egyptian Root: The Enchantress
Journey: Halfway point, 3.5. Judgment of the soul in the hall of Osiris, Only balanced forces can endure. The sword has two edges; construction and destruction. Must have perfect balance in the law of karma, justice from non-justice. The sword of Geburah can strike to bring balance.
Energy: Justice, balance, treaties, law, decisions.
Question: Why does she wear a crown?

The Hanged Man (12) Egyptian Root: The Martyr
Journey: A change of direction in the journey, need to be tranquil in these times. Bound to the cross but in peace. Accepting transmutation and sacrifice.
Energy: Surrender, things clearer upside down.
Question: Why is he an inverted symbol of Sulpher?

Death (13) Egyptian Root: The Reaper
Journey: Personality must die, inner death, big change. Transmutation to allow for new energy. All things die to make way for the new. Past life visions and energies.
Energy: Death and rebirth. Death destroys form but not life. Change voluntary or involuntary but leading to the new.
Question: Why two towers with the sun between?

Temperance (14) Egyptian Root: The Alchemist
Journey: Second Victory. Integrate and understand tests, visions and signs. Perfect relations between conscious and sub conscious. Need a lot of Temperance in the Chariot to drive through the Devils high speed curves that are coming. One foot in water and one on earth showing the bridge between Assiah and Briah.
Energy: Control of self, temptation tests, spiritual bridge, realisation. Life pours from the invisible to the visible and vice versa.
Question: Why square with yellow triangle on the chest?

The Devil (15) Egyptian Root: The Black Magician
Journey: One will be tested with fear, how much fear can one take? The Devil will attach to those who permit. Use intellect and courage. Devil only has power if you give it to him.
Energy: Divine forces are reflected in an inverted state. Torch is false light which guides unillumined souls to their own undoing. Material temptation, all that is separate from the light, attachments.
Question: Why do the people stay even though the chains are loose?

The Tower (16) The Lightning
Journey: Destruction of inner world that's not true or important. Destroy all that's no help in ones evolution. The tower of the ego blasted from the lightning and crown of Kether. If you leave Assiah the tower of beliefs must go too.
Energy: Sudden destruction. Similar to Death Trump but unexpected.
Question: Why twenty two Yods falling?

The Star (17) Egyptian Root: The Star
Journey: Very fast now, perfect temperance on a higher octave, the feminine energy of creation is now aligned. Spiritual support. 8 pointed star as now transcended the 7. The Hermetic Ibis shows intellectual clarity.
Energy: Intuition, focused energy, inspiration, faith, unexpected help. The star is Sirius.
Question: Why is she naked?

The Moon (18)
Journey: Middle of the journey, 3.5. Deep into the subconscious world. Now two dogs, one came with you, and one is from the highest. Above and below is a mirror, and here true reality emerges from the waters of illusion. The two towers are the Abyss.
Energy: Imagination, psychic faculties, light reflected, listen to the subconscious.
Question: Why fifteen Yods?

The Sun (19) Egyptian Root: The Sun
Journey: The Fool is returning home, spiritual victory, the operation of the sun. Someone now ready to do for humanity what the sun does for the earth. Reborn in the light of Tipareth from riding the horse of Kether. The light of truth.
Energy: Success, happiness, goals realized. The flowers are not following the sun, they are following the rebirth and success.
Question: What is the link to the horse in the book of revelations?

Judgment (20) Egyptian Root: The Sarcophagus
Journey: Resurrection, birth of super consciousness, the super soul. One will be judged and then the books may be opened.
Energy: Renovation, awakening. Spirit, body, and soul in harmony. Free from judging.
Question: Why the red cross?

The Universe (21) Egyptian Root: The Materialist
Journey: The Fools journey is complete, through the door of infinity, all knowledge, akasha. Door, gate to a hidden garden. The process of evolution and the wheel of Samshara has now stopped. Comprehension of cosmic travel. The Gate is Tau.
Energy: Happy endings, freedom, arrive to another consciousness. The wreath is the Oroborous symbol linked up in infinity. The crystalisation of the whole matter.
Question: Why is The Fool holding two wands?

Performing the quest to start the motors of the Chariot is more than enough to really make a mark within your electromagnetic field for years to come , and to achieve Temperance or beyond will give ones soul a real jolt for at least a few carnations.

Each of the Major Arcana Trumps are assigned to a path, and each resembles a part of the psyche of man, the archetypal forces deep inside us. The Trumps also have their archetypes within the astral plane that can be contacted, or they may even come and contact you if you attract them correctly.

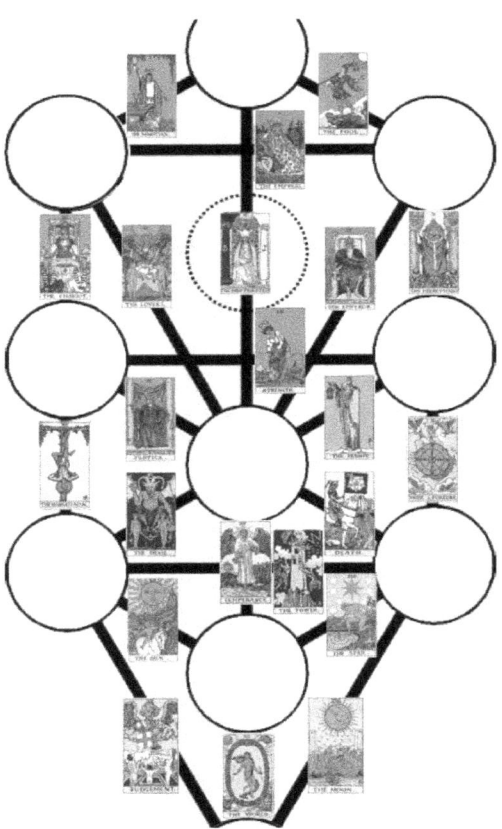

As we can see, the journey we just looked at appears to be reversed on the Tree of Life. This is because the tree has systems within systems, and this can be looked at as the journey of a soul into manifestation coming down. The tree works well this way, the Trumps display energies linking the Sephiroth, and we can also work the Tarot in reverse going up. For instance, from Malkuth we awaken, look to our subconscious, and go through a door of sorts, and these three are the simplified attributes within the bottom three paths and trumps. We will be looking at the paths more deeply soon.

Minor Arcana

Playing cards have their root in the minor arcana, the clubs come from wands, hearts from cups, spades from swords, and the diamonds from the pentacles.

In medieval times pictures were added to the minor arcana and as we wish to use the core of Qabalah we will leave all of these pictures alone.

The Minor Arcana relate more to experiences than higher energies. They consist of four suits linking to the four worlds and the four elements, plus each suit links to the ten numbers and the ten Sephiroth. Therefore, we have more than enough information from just the suit and number to get the information we need. Just place the card upon the Tree, for example:

3 of Cups - Binah, Briah, Water. An absorbing understanding creative energy. Tzaphkiel.

10 of Swords - Malkuth, Yetzirah, Air. A completing, mental, and formative energy. Ishim.

5 of Pentacles - Geburah, Assiah, Earth. A change, challenge, or cutting away in the material physical realm. Madim.

The Aces each reside in Kether and represent the whole root of the energy of the suit, therefore a beginning (1) and all of the corresponding element and world (unity).

Many link the minor arcana to the astrological decans too, I advise against this because in astral the strength of the cards link to the Sephiroth and their relative Names of Power is much stronger.

A great exercise is to lay out all of the minor arcana in the shape of the Tree with four cards at each Sephiroth, this yields a good understanding of the Tree, numbers, worlds, elements, and overall flow.

Court Cards

The Court Cards sit outside the tree residing in Three Ain. They are creators of worlds and can represent archetypal guides and creators.

The Kings and Queens are protectors and advisors that help. The Knights are those that bring changes and the Pages are messengers.

We can see in the Court Cards YHVH within each world and within each Court. Therefore for example, the Knight of Cups is the Air of Water and the Vau of the world of Briah.

		Y	H	V	H
Y		King of Wands	Queen of Wands	Knight of Wands	Page of Wands
H		King of Cups	Queen of Cups	Knight of Cups	Page of Cups
V		King of Swords	Queen of Swords	Knight of Swords	Page of Swords
H		King of Pentacles	Queen of Pentacles	Knight of Pentacles	Page of Pentacles

Divination

To use Tarot we will need to be laying cards so we need to cover a little about divination. The main point here is not to read too many books on the Tarot, many are fluffy, and most have conflicting material. To get to know the cards better, study the Tree, and lay just one or two cards a day and soon they will manifest into your universe if you are laying them correctly. The Tarot is a very real way of allowing us to eavesdrop on the pictorial subconscious mind.

Some rules with laying cards.

- Make sure you use a new deck which is only for your use.
- Keep the deck wrapped in a cloth, somewhere with little energy movement.
- Perform a few minutes of meditation before laying cards, a candle and incense will both help.
- Open up to your intuition, you are performing a ritual of sorts, imagine a circle being drawn around you, focus.
- Ask the Tarot respectfully to give you guidance in what you are asking (invoke the Tarot group soul so to speak), and set a time frame regarding your request.
- Shuffle the deck still focusing on the parts of your subconscious you wish to glimpse.
- When closing, thank the energies and close the circle.

A great simple spread to use that will align you with energies of the Tree and the Tarot is shown below.

Throw the cards in the order shown, and then turn them up in the following order, 1,3,4,5, and then 2.

This spread will present information from the physical, intellectual, emotional, and spiritual (from across the veil), and then all information will converge within Yesod.

After a while one may be able to work out what Yesod is from using the other cards numbers, worlds, Sephiroth, and intuition. This is a great exercise and gives amazing results.

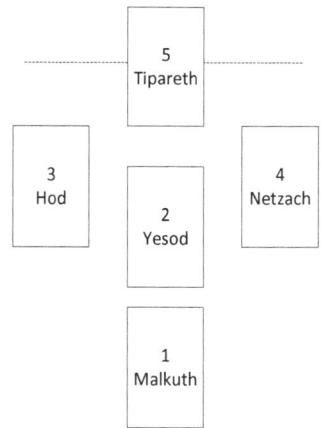

The Tarot is a core element of the Tree of Life, it will yield deep clicks in understanding, climbing, and receiving. When asking the Tarot for guidance we shouldn't use yes or no questions, it works more with surrounding energies of a situation or thought construct. Here are some examples of how we pose our questions:

- What is there for me to learn or benefit from……..
- What are the surrounding energies regarding……..
- Throw three cards for each option regarding a decision, a viewing each of the three cards as a whole.

We are not going to cover divination for other people as this is more about the art of psychic perception and less about the science.

The whole crux of Hermetic Qabalah is to use symbols to link "archetypal symbols and images to archetypal energies," and then linking the results to archetypes deep in the psyche of the self, and then up onto higher spheres. The Tarot is a very important part of the climbing frame.

The Chariot of Osiris from an Egyptian deck.

Dreams & Astral

The Astral Plane

We will take a short break from Qabalah and look at some required tools that will help our upcoming climb upon the Tree. We have mentioned the word "astral" many times so far, but what actually does this mean?

Astral could be thought of as the (lower) fourth dimension, a dense spirit plane that is close to ours. All life, colour, thoughts, and physical objects have an astral body (or signature) that lives upon the astral plane, a plane that resides a level up from the etheric, or auric plane. Our astral body is a duplicate body to which the physical body owes its continued existence and persistence.

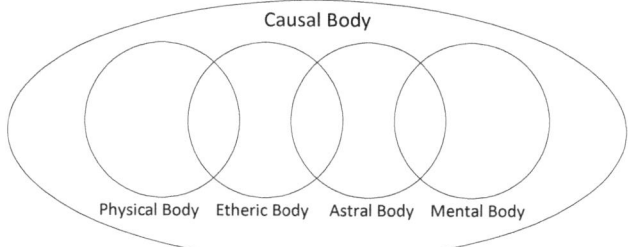

Our astral body when excited and expanded can become a subtle body of its own, but normally and for the length of our life here, the astral body is firmly connected to our physical vessel by an electromagnetic fluid. Death as we know it is really just the disconnection of this fluid, and then the transmutation of core consciousness moving upwards towards a more subtle plane.

The astral plane has many realms and levels and each resides within the universe we live in, but within dimensions that our five senses and core design are normally cut off from. The lower astral realms contain an energetic shadow of all that is in the physical. The higher realms that vibrate faster have no concept of space or time, and consist of other, more remote energies and archetypes.

To sum up, the astral plane is Yesod, and Yesod is the astral plane, and to have a mental grasp regarding astral, one needs to understand the Law of Correspondence as well as the Sphere of Yesod.

Many look at astral travel as something they could never do but every single human has the ability lying dormant within them, it just takes practice and will. Others look at the astral plane as something unbelievable but most of us go there every single night via dreams. Ever woken up from a big dream with your heart beating quickly? Ever woken up with a jolt after a short dream? These are both a form of lower astral travel, and the faster we are vibrating within our auric egg, the more the doors to the astral plane will present themselves.

In parts of India one can feel the crackle of astral light in the air sweeping down from the Himalayas. The legends, myths, and continuous devotion and worship for millennia have built up a strong reservoir close to the physical. On full moons one can feel this crackle too.

> "People like us, who believe in physics, know that the distinction between past, present, future is only a stubborn, persistent illusion."
> Einstein

Near death experiences, out of body experiences (OBE), many abduction tales, and all shamanic experiences are all a form of astral travel. Basically, an astral journey is the separating of the astral body from the physical body and the secretion of DMT in the brain. Many people who have done yoga or spiritual retreats have experienced an OBE involuntarily solely down to the Kundalini energy rising so fast. For instance, if you live in tick-tock and then leave the office after years and then sit up a mountain meditating, practicing yoga and eating green sludge for weeks, for sure, something mystical is very likely to happen.

Astral experience has always been the key to the mystery schools and secret societies. They have always taught that what we can see touch and feel presents us with only a relative reality, and beyond that which is considered 'real' by most people are worlds of an even greater reality which every individual has the ability to explore. The mystery traditions promote the emergence from darkness of a limited sense reality and thought framework into a larger consciousness.

Whether you believe this or not, it is what has been taught in secret all the way back to Osiris, and who was Osiris? A deity of the resurrection of the soul, and what was the coiled cobra worn at the third eye of the Pharaohs symbolising? It was for sure representing the darting out of the body through the stimulated inner eye. There are also many de-classified documents displaying the use of 'remote viewing' within the military since the 1940's, it is all very real, but don't take my word for it, do your own research.

Many initiatic ceremonies within Orders and Secret Societies are designed to induce an out of body experience using sensory deprivation and even fear. Initiates are shown first hand that one's spirit can live out of the body and be a spirit amongst spirits, able to return to the material world reborn, carrying new perceptions and abilities.

Why perform astral travelling? For fun? Am I just crazy and just wish to escape the 'real' world? (That answer is another book all unto itself, as is what actually is 'the real world'). The answer is that it is imperative for the human race to update its view on "how the world actually is" and to look with new eyes at "the way things are." Revising and seeing it all differently is how many scientific breakthroughs such as DNA and gravity were manifested. So those who look at astral travel as nonsense are really detached from true history, plus evolutions main events. A dimension close to us is attainable and in corners of this place lurks the past, future, and many answers.

Before we try and launch ourselves out of our heavy parasitical bodies, there are some techniques that will help pave the way.

Lucid Dreaming

Lucid dreaming, or even just a good level dream awareness can really give one a fuller more self empowered existence with much more information and experience. Lucid dreaming and dream awareness will also enable one to go deeper into the Qabalah. All of the people I have gone deep into the Tree of Life with have each had the Tree come to them within dreams and do amazing things.

Most humans look at dreams as unreal or unimportant, but the blatant truth is that dreams are a very real part of our existence and we spend around a quarter of our lives asleep (where our brain waves are nearly as active as during waking life). We might as well use this time! In dreams (Yesod) we can receive clues, clicks, clarity, signs and messages, saving time for the plane of physical causality to present these within our linear time carnation (Malkuth). Would you rather learn a lesson in a dream or have to spend a year in a toxic relationship? The sort of information we can receive is; what is lacking, what to divulge from the day, what is coming, how you really feel, what you really wish for, core fears, how to approach an issue or person, your deepest love, memories and events to process and learn from, and so much more.

> "We dream 24 hours a day, when brain is awake and when brain is asleep. The difference is that when the brain is awake, there is a material frame that makes us perceive things in a linear way. When we go to sleep we do not have that frame, and the dream has a tendency to change constantly."
> Don Miguel Ruiz, Toltec Wisdom.

The first thing to learn is dream awareness. The fact is that we all dream many times every single night, but we only remember the dreams that we wake up during. If just before sleep we perform the affirmation, "I will remember my dreams," with exactly the same intent we have the night before having to awaken early for a flight or similar, we will be firing the correct neurons in the brain.

Upon waking up the following is extremely helpful in dream recollection:

- Don't move or open your eyes or feel your physical location.
- Gently try and recall images and feelings. If this is difficult move slowly back into the position you were when you were asleep (if you actually have moved).
- Move back slowly through the dream in rewind, then from the start work forwards. Replay parts and search for more details; feelings, colours, people, moods, and actions.
- When you have dug up all you can, write some keywords down in a journal.
- Later in the day during meditation, go back into the dream to see what else is there for you to see.

Once this has been performed for a lunar month you will see your dreams flow in accordance with the moon. Most people have big dreams around the new or full moon and other periods of lighter dreams. When this is known one will know when to really concentrate upon dreams. Amethyst and quartz crystals near a clean bed, and minimal networks and electricity in the bedroom all help too.

Achieving lucidity within dreams is something many people do sporadically or have done before. Lucidity is being able to be conscious in ones dream; to choose to fly, choose to ask questions, or to change the environment with the mind. There are some set techniques that can help this occur.

Work to induce a lucid dreaming is mainly performed during the normal waking day, we can do the following with some Geburah style intent, discipline, and will:

- Look at your hands and habitually really ask them, "am I dreaming?" This will soon be done in a dream and you will see that your hands are just colours of energy, and this will trigger lucidity.
- Habitually touch a door or a wall and ask, really ask, "am I dreaming?" In dreams walls and doors are spongy.
- Before sleep, affirm, "I will have a lucid dream and I will remember it."
- Study your dreams and look for signs that show you where dreaming, this could be strange animals, a far away location, or someone doing something that's impossible. These are all triggers to becoming conscious within a dream.

We need to improve our ability "to remember to remember," so we can create triggers in the normal day where we remember to ask ourselves "am I dreaming?" It could be crossing a road, hearing a laugh, or using a key, it's up to you. Sooner or later in a dream we will see something and realise we are dreaming, then we can become conscious and explore the subconscious mind. There is a tale of one man who studied lucid dreams who hopped like a frog everywhere for a few days, then in his dream could leap for miles.

If you do become lucid and keep waking up in the physical after a very short time, try spinning in your dream, this will create a vortex of sorts and hold your energy within the lower astral plane.

Some people have difficulty in becoming conscious within dreams no matter what happens and in this case we can use an old Tibetan technique. When you wake up and can recall a dream, hold the dream in mind and "go back into it" staying conscious. Mentally place yourself back in the location of your dream, surround yourself with the same people and feelings and gently go back in but keeping a point in your third eye fully conscious. Soon the dream environment you are holding in mind will change upon its own accord and you will know you are within a lucid dream.

All lucid dream work should be done during times of REM (Rapid Eye Movement), the science of which is shown on the following page.

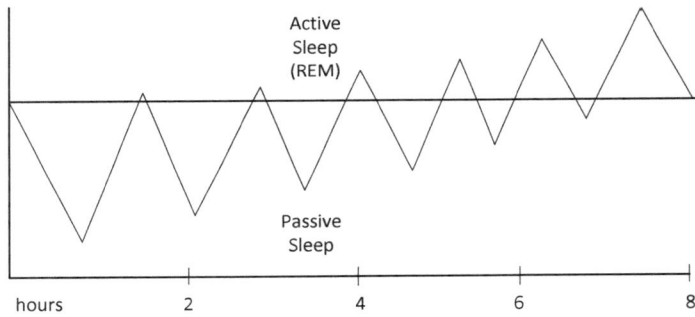

The diagram shows that we can only really attempt lucid dreaming after six hours of sleep, as it is only then that REM is sufficient enough and all of the deep sleep of repair is out of the way. A great method is to set your alarm at six hours of sleep, and then eat a little cheese or nutmeg or drink some mugwort tea before going back to sleep. Another trick is to have a quiet alarm that beeps just a few times every twenty one minutes between the hours of six and eight. This will keep one on the periphery of sleep and waking realms and here is where one can induce lucid dreams. It is important to not "wake up" or move when the beeps come.

Using these methods can induce up to five clear recallable dreams in a single hour, so even if lucidity is not reached, much information from the subconscious mind will be gleaned.

Another trick is for when you first realise you are waking up; when this happens put all of your consciousness into your third eye for at least a minute and relax passively, this can induce an array of different experiences, including geometrical tunnels hosting symbols.

Within your dream journal it is also good to record the level of lucidity you achieved along with the dream signs that enabled you to become conscious. The recording of this will soon form patterns and/or regular handles. You will probably find after a while some reoccurring dreams and these are important messages from the subconscious. Aiming to work out the core meaning of these will save a lot of time and effort in the physical realm.

If you dream consciously you are on your way to moving around the spirit worlds communicating freely and you may even learn about the future which in other ways are blocked. This can lead onto astral travel to view other parts of the universe in other dimensions.

16th century initiate Paracelsus who was the father of much medicine and homeopathy claimed to have been able to visit people in dreams. I had someone do this to me when I was being taught these methods, and she knew what she had done in the dream too.

> *"If we listen patiently to our dreams and the messages they contain they will eventually lead us to health . . . how much better to take advice from the other half of yourself than from another person."*
>
> Dr. Ann Faraday

We will be working more deeply with dreams later on when we work with The Emerald Tablet upon our Merkaba Chariot.

Mental Travelling

We can be visualising, contemplating, or meditating in our homes but be mentally far away....which reality is real? Just enter an internet café and everyone has their consciousness elsewhere, where exactly is their electromagnetic energy located?

Imaginary journeys are as old as the human race, and when a scientist makes a thought experiment and speculates on the nature of the universe there is little difference to that of the mystic. Einstein imagined and visualised himself riding a light beam and discovered the theory of relativity. He discovered that matter, gravity and density bend space-time, and that the greater the curvature the slower time goes. He concluded that the only absolute of nature was the speed of light. The universe is about eighteen billion years old but it shouldn't be thought of as time flowing like a river, time is not a physical thing we can examine, it's just a dimension of space. These facts are proven to this day but we are fooled into the dogma of linear time via our senses. Astral travel is possible simply because it is aligned with many truths.

Going back to thought experiments, they are virtual experiences in a mental reality, and we all do them to a level but place them simply into the "thinking" box.

Mental journeys are how we train the imagination and will, they are the gymnasium for the imagination, and they are a sure fire way of loosening the astral body, sharpening the third eye, and raising concentration to a level that is required. Trained day dreams and daily meditations are the big keys that unlock the astral doors, and these keys have been taught in India, Tibet, and Persia for millennia.

I don't wish to go too much into mental travel here as we will do this Qabalistically in the next chapter, but here are a few foundation techniques for the imagination to allow us to roam around in our 'mental bodies.'

- After meditating yourself into a good zone, mentally imagine you are sitting opposite yourself, use the conviction of your will to keep you there, look at your vessel as separate from your consciousness.

- Imagine you are in the first house you ever lived in, be there, you are there, summon all your will, walk around and notice objects and feelings. Go through all of the houses you ever lived in.
- Imagine you are at a friend or relatives house, picture them, what are they doing, how do they feel? Often this can glean information that is actually true if our abilities in mental travel are of a good standard.
- Walking down the road imagine an animal walking with you, it could be a tiger, or an animal of fantasy, imagine it walking in front of you, around you, up to other people, climbing trees.

These are just a base, and the only limit is your imagination. The most important words here are sincere, intent, and will.

Astral Travelling

If you are finding the achieving of a lucid dream difficult then this may be a bridge too far, and I suggest sticking first with dreams and mental travel until some levels of progress come your way. This is not a rule, it's just usually the way progress is made.

There are scores of books providing techniques on how to project out of the body so I will only share a small sample that I know yield results.

Do not try this unless you are determined, enthralled, and enthused. Also remember the knowledge that it may take weeks before a true projection really happens.

- Wake up with an alarm after six or seven hours sleep, get up and have a little stretch, a little nutmeg and a small amount of honey or sugar will be good too (it helps with the visuals). Massage your head and third eye and go back to bed.
- We require no outside noise so earplugs can help, also a small fluorite crystal on the third eye can help too, as will the removal of metal jewellery.
- Lay on your back, palms up, with the arm a few inches away from the body and the legs slightly apart.

- On an in breathe tense all of the muscles; face, toes, fists, everything, and upon the out breathe relax everything. Repeat a few times.
- Relax into deep yogic breaths.
- Imagine you are hovering a few inches above your body and hold this feeling with relaxed willed focus for a few moments.
- Then twist yourself (conscious mental self) so that your head is at your feet and your feet are at your head, hold this with your imagination for a few breaths (the mental self is shown in the lighter shade).

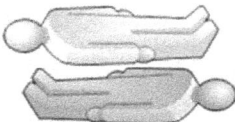

- When firmly in this position, on an in breath pivot yourself to standing up, and on the out breath pivot yourself more so that your third eye is hovering just above your physical third eye.

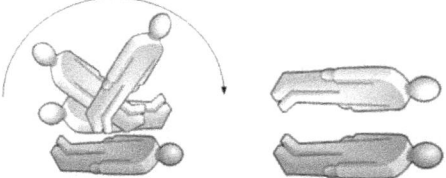

- Now on each round of in and out breathes, pivot back and forth.

- Only when you really feel like you are a hundred percent the consciousness of the moving subtle body can you move on to the next ex-

ercise. If you lose your concentration don't worry, just go back to the relaxed breaths and start again.
- With your third eyes facing each other, on an in breath move up towards the ceiling, on the out breath move back down so that the third eyes are near each other. Increase the distance between you 'both' and even go out of the top of the roof.

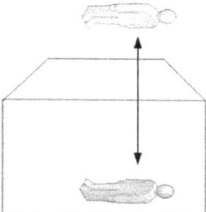

- Now move around the room (mental body) in a circle facing outwards taking in your surroundings, then stop and stare at yourself and perform a crazy dance; flap your arms and legs around, this will help loosen the astral body. Remember like goes to like, and the more astral we make our consciousness and astral body, the more astral they will become.
- Now you can go back to the pivot or raising technique or even just the hovering above the physical body. Keep your consciousness away from thoughts, keep it upon a single thread in the third eye and keep breathing relaxed.
- Focus on what you can hear in your consciousness, focus on the vibration in your 'astral head,' magnify this noise or sensation; imagine it coming out of speakers. Focus on your third eye and the noise with more intensity (staying relaxed).
- After enough practice, some vibrations should come, these are often in the arms, especially the forearms and elbows. Also you may here some whooshing or interference type noises. These are the signs that we are now ready to project.
- There are many ways at this stage to initiate the projection, here are a few:
    - Imagine a rope out of the solar plexus, start climbing it at a steady pace, then faster and faster.

- - Stare at your physical body and will the astral body to come out and merge with your mental body.
  - Start running, and when sprinting take a giant leap.
  - Calmly rise up and up in full lotus using the command "I will."
- Once in the astral plane, the world is *your* oyster, and only your fear and lack of imagination can hinder you. The stories of silver chords and possible death are nonsense, ignore them.
- If the above techniques are not working for you, you can try something in the evening; as you are falling to sleep as per normal, put all of your consciousness into a pinpoint in your third eye, you are hiding there until the body falls asleep. Do not think, just help ease the body to sleep with relaxed breathing. Soon your body will be in paralysis signalling the time to project out. The lure of actually going to sleep is strong but use will and intent.

Launching any kind of projection with all of your will when you are not vibrating enough will knock you out of kilt for a few hours, you will feel fuzzy. If this does happen use cold water, heavy food, or obsidian or tourmaline crystals. Also pressing hard on the balls of your feet will help. Hang in there, I know how it feels, keep trying.

The astral realm (especially the lower astral realm) looks to deceive and scare newcomers away. In astral sitting in full lotus plus the use of blue flaming pentagrams is a great way of protecting yourself. A flaming pentagram can shrink large entities, and if not it is probably a lofty being to be respected and loved. If things get scary just remember that love is greater and bigger than any fear, and that dark cannot exist where there is light. Your astral body assumed the form of any powerful thought which you consciousness invokes.

If you suspect that images from your memory are influencing your vision, trace the letter t (Tau) in white light (Saturn, memory), and if you suspect images are from your imagination and not from astral, trace b (Kaph, Jupiter, clarity).

Upon return, align with your physical body and slowly wiggle your toes and fingers whilst relaxing for a further few minutes. Journal your experiences as patterns will emerge.

In astral karma is still effect, so be wary about what you are doing and what it affects in Malkuth. Be brave and respectful and always try and bring something back. If you need grounding afterwards, you can stand on some grass bare footed and imagine vines rising up from the centre of the earth and twisting around your feet, legs and hips, pulling you down with the feminine nurturing energy of Gaia.

Pathworking & Skrying

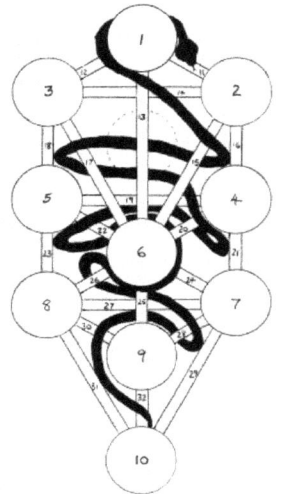

"Let the disciple seize hold of the tail of the serpent of wisdom, and having with firmness grasped it, let him follow it into the deepest centre of the hall of wisdom."
The old commentary.

"Imagination can be trained to grasp higher realities than the materialism being peddled by the apostles of common sense."

"It is better to conquer yourself than to win a thousand battles. Then the victory is yours. It cannot be taken from you."

Introduction

Pathworking is also known as Skrying which comes from the word "descry," meaning "to see." Both words are linked to seeing, traveling, and rising upon the Tree mentally (and/or astrally) within the Paths and Sephiroth. Pathworking is essentially the use of active imaginative meditations to roam the Tree of Life.

Pathworking is not hard, we sort of do it daily in day dreams, it could be just as simple as sitting in front of a Tarot Trump and stepping *into* it via the imagination. Pathworking alleviates the stagnation some people meet in meditation by giving us a journey, an adventure, an excursion. Though the symbolic scenery of the 22 subjective Paths and the 10 objective Sephiroth we can turn archetypal knowledge into very real, tangible, implementable knowledge.

The Paths are subjective because they are representations of deep parts of our unique psyche. Traits, experiences, and emotions are within, and therefore everyone will Skry the Paths differently. The subconsious contains a great deal of expereince that you absorbed without knowing anything about it, and Pahworking will present this information to you.

Pathworking could be deemed a form of self hypnosis using symbols to change consciousness, a catalyst that opens up ones psychic abilities and raises ones soul up to a higher plane. Upon this journey, bodily, mental, spiritual, and emotional tensions from the past can come back and appear amplified. When this happens we can look at the associated karma, story, point of view, belief, and action, and fix these inner blockages and stories.

The only purpose for working the Paths is to understand our true nature and that of the world around us. By travelling the Paths we can absorb the intimate experiences and lessons learned there and grow from a mundane, clouded awareness, to a more spiritual clarity. This clarity is the result of a progressively deeper understanding of our own complex nature with all its moods, facets and characteristics. The order in which the Paths are traversed and the order in which the three symbols are encountered in each path guide one through a systematic progression of understanding, making more and more sense of our complexity.

Through the journey it is possible that we can pass from the world of illusion through the veil of illusion into the world of spiritual reality. But this world of the spirit as we see it is an illusion too, the reality is certain enough but our minds can only comprehend it in terms of our own mental capacity. This is why we comprehend our incursions into the spirit world in terms of encounters with angels and demons, or journeys through the heavens in fiery chariots. The spiritual universe contains angels and demons only because we have labelled certain energy constructs in this manner. In just the same way, the physical universe only contains the concept of "table" or "floor" because we happen to perceive certain energy constructs in a particular way.

"The universe is a projection of ourselves; an image as unreal as that of our faces in a mirror, yet, like that face, it only changes if we change ourselves. In that light, therefore, all that we do is to discover ourselves by means of a sequence of hieroglyphics and the changes which we apparently operate are in an objective

sense illusions....It enables us to see ourselves, and therefore to aid us to initiate ourselves by showing us what we are doing."
Aleistair Crowley

How to Skry upon the Tree

"Imagination is more important than knowledge."
Albert Einstein

The imagination is the crux of Pathworking, it is all based upon training the imagination and will a little at a time. It could all be looked at as a Western version (and more exciting version) of the Eastern Tattva symbol meditations, where again controlled day dreams train the imagination to become in touch with subtle realms.

Sound like delusion daydreaming? Well, I ask you how many of the one billion plus Shiva worshipers on this planet have actually seen a blue destroyer God? None, not one! They are ALL using their imaginations to feed an archetype! This archetype then has so much harnessed force it lives in the astral plane able to return energy. This is how Pathworking works, and due to the many Magus and Skryers having trod these paths for centuries, the energies exist upon the astral plane. This paragraph is worthy of meditation for this is also how all deities, reiki symbols, mantras, sigils, and almost all esoteric occultism works.

The mystery traditions held this science long before the array of personified polytheistic Gods were "created" in ancient Egypt.

"Earthly things must be known to be loved; divine things must be loved to be known."
Pascal

All forms in our mind are physical, mental, or astral by a difference of level. Usually we can only see parts of our subconscious mind through dreams, intuition, Tarot, and the like, but with training the will and imagination this internal veil (which can also be linked to the Veil of Paroketh) moves higher and higher.

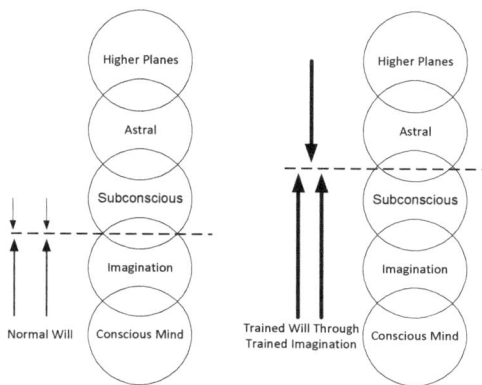

"Faith must confirm the imagination, for faith establishes the will."
Paracelsus

Now there are some safeguards to Pathworking so one does not become what Francis King called an "astral junkie" or what Israel Regardie called a "cosmic foofoo." We need to be getting feedback from our Pathworkings after a short amount of time or we can slip into the realm of illusions and delusions. In this there is a small risk of becoming ungrounded and losing touch and disassociating from the 'real' world. Always remember we are Pathworking to gain and to receive, not to play in fantasy.

The safeguard is simply to know the nature, attributes, and symbols of the Sphere and Paths extremely well, because with thought altering techniques such as archetypes and archetypal Gods, proven conceptual models and paradigms need to be embraced or we veer off course.

Don't let this small risk put you off, there is too much to gain, we have inbuilt protective mechanisms anyway and Pathworking is pretty much harmless and something to be enjoyed (try telling that to the ultra serious societies in robes). You have already Pathworked in 'real life' many of the energies already, we are just now doing it in meditation and maybe in astral too, each of which will bring more benefits to your core being.

All of the Qabalistic God forms and archetypes are in the imagination, but the force around them is real and active in astral. When visualising an archetype within the Tree, you are working from the Treasure House of Images in Yesod and creating a form for the force to come down into, the force that will animate the picture. Soon we should be receiving messages, feedback, and possibly even teachings.

When we have the realisation in Pathworking, "I didn't put that there, the Path is changing" we know we are on the right track. Often when Pathworking around a particular Sphere or Path the real world can simultaneously give us synchronistical clicks, memories, realisations, and tests associated to the Pathworking we have been performing. When this test or realisation is implemented into your core being for good, then one will have been (self) initiated into that Sphere or Path. This is hard to explain, but you will know when it happens. Often these self-initiations can come on a physical, mental, astral, and soul level all at once and they can be strong.

There is no need to belong to a group or have a 'leader' wearing robes telling you that you are initiated.

When the Paths are worked upon new information regarding the nearby Sephiroth will also come, and this will also give more information about the Paths, and vice versa, it is a spiral of sorts, and this is an attribute to the voyage of self discovery.

There are many different ways to Pathwork, I will share some tips and a good solid base, but find the way that suits you, if it feels right to you and you are getting feedback, go with it! The most important things to remember are that more dedication equals more results, and that the warrior with the most concentrated imagination is the one who climbs the highest.

Tips and prerequisites:

- If ingesting alcohol or toxins regularly, do not Pathwork.
- Mediatate for at least ten minutes before any Pathworking.
- Always start in Malkuth, (even fleetingly for advanced Skryers).
- Only one main Path or Sphere at a time for beginners.
- It is better for beginners to have trodden the bottom three Paths before heading to Yesod, Hod, or Netzach.
- Always try and use a relevant object (gemstone, scent, plant, colour) for your destination Path and/or Sphere, this will help harness and focus energy from Malkuth where you are 'earthed'.

- Having the four elements in the room will help too as they will keep you linked to Malkuth and protected throughout.
- Be a warrior, enjoy it, and remember we are not the pursuer but the pursued, nor the protector but the protected.

A Pathworking base:

- When in a good meditative zone, say internally the four Names of Power for the Sphere you wish to enter.
- Imagine coming towards a large Sphere and going through a membrane of sorts, there you find a gateway to the Temple.
- Imagine you are in a large and complex Temple, one that perfectly resembles the Sephirah on an energetic and symbolic level.
- There should not be one thing out of harmony. Use the imagination to build it up.
- Invoke the intelligences or astral messenger, or just have a look around (the astral messenger will probably come and find you anyway).
- Build up the Temple with your imagination each time you come, layer upon layer. How does the Astral Messenger look to you? What stories are in this Temple for you? What feelings are stirring? Test your surroundings via colours, symbols, names, and energies.
- The Temples represent an energy we must explore. They each show us by example one of the ways we must try to see our world. They show us by example a role we can learn to play as we apply that point of view in our lives.
- Orient yourself as to which Paths come off which cardinal points and move towards one until you find a gateway with the corresponding Hebrew letter on it.
- Spend time looking through the gateway into the Path before stepping into it.
- Step out of the temple into the beginning of the Path, when you step out of the Temple you should strongly affirm that the Temple is behind you.
- You are now inside the three-dimensional Tarot Trump. Build up the image, what can you see and feel? How does the Temple you were just in combine with this energy? Are there animals or archetypes you

can converse with? The Trump has symbolism offering instruction for finding the gateway to that Path in your life.
- In the middle of the Path is the Hebrew letter, shining in white light, it is the key to the Path. It seems left there deliberately to show us what to watch for, what to watch out for, what to study further and how to deal with the changes that come from the experience.
- Near the end of the Path is the Astrology sign which is the spiritual significance of the Path. Though at the end of the Path near the gateway to the next Temple, the energy of the sign is evident within all of the Path.
- Before leaving, what is the point of view of the whole Path, when have you trodden this path in real life?
- When finished dissolve all the images and close out your meditation clearing your space with intent (by closing the circle or putting out the candle etc).

Upon returning to any Sphere or Path, you will realise you have already built up some images, you can then keep adding new coats of paint, more detail. Sooner or later, the archetypes on the other side of the veil will come and add to the painting too, this is the point when you know you are on the right track. Do not force it, it is meditative, and remember that the mind grows with what you feed it.

The Paths and Spheres

To be honest, with what we already know about the Paths we can start meditating into them right away. There are many books on Pathworking and they all support just how subjective the Paths are by all being different!

This section is just to set a base for the Paths and provide some correspondence. I will give larger bases regarding the lower sections of the Tree because as you rise up the tantric road map you will form your own unique Pathworking universe. This section will help start you off and I will present the Paths in an order that is very workable, and also include the lowest two Sephiroth.

Remember, just like a child who half heartedly learns to ride a bike and falls, Pathworking is the same, you must really go for it with your will fuelled imagination and really do it. This is the only way for your higher self on the other side of the veil to sit up and take notice.

Malkuth

Affirmation: "I am made in the image of the divine."

Uses: To balance out the elements, to ground, to realise dreams.

Trip: You see all around you rolling olive-green fields and feel that this is the realm that you will learn of the existence of other things, things other than earth. To the north is the large palace of Adonai Ha Aretz, and to the south, east, and west, are other Palaces where tests related to the elements and elementals will need to be passed to leave this Sphere. The north holds fire and karma, the east water and desire, the south air and inertia, the west earth and its restrictive forces. Supportive and hindering elementals such as gnomes and orcs lurk in these palaces so tread carefully.

Sandalphon will be seen roaming around the palace to the north or in the nearby meadows, she is a tall brunette princess energy who resides over all of your dreams. She is usually seen with a pet sphinx that knows many secrets of the tree. Only she will allow you passage to the Paths, and she may request a symbol or even one day give you some esoteric tools to use higher up the Tree.

In a chamber in the same palace resides the Ishim dancing around the Temple fire. They appear similar to embers but are in fact souls of humans that once danced in the light.

The rich diversity of the earth plane interpenetrates this whole Sphere making Malkuth a large magical wonderland of things to do and see. This rich dynamic base coupled with your own human wants, desires, fears, and lacks makes your wanderings here in Malkuth an adventure and a half. Take your time with this sphere and enjoy it. There is a wealth of opportunity here that you should not miss.

Once more experienced in Skrying, Sandalphon may continue to give tests in Malkuth to keep you connected to this Sphere, she will also know all about what you get up to in other Paths and Spheres so look at her as a comforting base. She may even take you to see Adonia Ha Aretz if something important is happening.

Path 32 Malkuth – Yesod

The Universe (21) ת Tau. Saturn
Affirmation: I am the end and I am just beginning.
Colour: Indigo.
Fuel for Meditation: Crocodile, Ash, Nightshade, Salt
Meditative Image: Malediction.
Title: The Great One of the Night of Time.

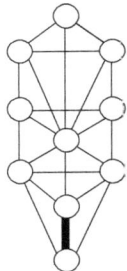

This is a dangerous Path of introspection, a tunnel to
the underworld from leaving earth. One can be fooled on this Path so it is wise to deal with personal phantoms before looking at how to embark upon ones first steps to mystical awareness.
This Path can be trod both ways, and the Goddess within the Trump may often ask why one is here. The Saturn energy restricts and slows you down and the Path will only let past those who understand the meanings and symbolism behind the four sacred animals.

Note: Only the Atziluth colour is given because the Paths are usually only shown in this world and the colours fit the energies so very well.

Path 31 Malkuth – Hod

Judgement (20) ש Shin . Fire
Affirmation: The divine flame burns within my soul.
Colour: Orange Scarlet
Fuel for Meditation: Lion, Nitrates, Fire Opal, Hibiscus.
Meditative Image: Pyromancy.
Title: Spirit of the Primal Fire.

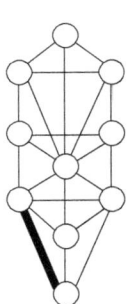

This Path asks the soul to wake up out of its tomb,
to burn away all that is not true within the lower personality. By connecting the body in Malkuth with the rational mind in Hod we can use our intellect to see what in our lives are instinct and what is reason. We can look to books and core doctrine to understand the fire we are aiming to ignite.

All fire Gods live in this Path as they seek to awaken the spiritual fire in the Pathworker and awaken the spiritual will. The Archangel with the Trumpet seeks to change physiology and judge personality.

Path 29 Malkuth – Netzach

The Moon (18)   ק Qoph . Pisces
Affirmation: I will evolve to be a worthy vessel of God
Colour: Crimson.
Fuel for Meditation: Fish, Pearl, Ambergris.
Meditative Image: Illusions.
Title: Ruler of Flux and Reflux.

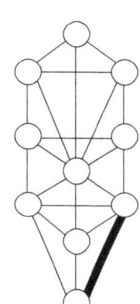

This is the Path of the opened subconscious mind,
a victory over the material into feeling, evolving intuition, and the great unknown.

It is a victory over animal instincts and environmental imprints, a control over the primitive and savage.

The animals in the path scavenge over the dead and heed to the cycles of ebb and flow.

This Path is a stepping out into the realm of nature mysticism, paganism, and a love of nature, a stepping into the subconscious and noticing the dream worlds and true inner feelings.

The murky waters of the moon hide important memories that are attached to the soul for reasons that need to be known.

Yesod

Affirmation: I will uphold the universe.

Uses: To evolve psychic skills, to see images from visions, memories and dreams. To align with electromagnetic truths.

Trip: An ethereal, almost transparent temple awaits, the central chamber has the shape of a nine sided polygon where Gabriel is often quietly conversing with the four Kerubim, the four forces of YHVH. Incense adds to the ethereal feel as the moon shines through the open roof onto the violet misty walls.

Winged Gabriel is often seen with a tortoise and often asks what images from the treasurehouse, what parts of the machinery of the universe, or which memory do you wish to see and learn from? He shows you that Yesod is the place where you can observe the cycle of all things, like life and death, summer and winter, beginnings and endings. He knows how you can become fully aware of the cyclic nature of the Universe itself.

You can sense and touch the energy in Yesod that feels like there is a plan, and that you and the universe are a part of this plan.

Path 30 Yesod – Hod

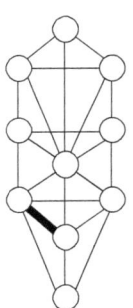

The Sun (19)   ר Resh . Sun
Affirmation: My thoughts are on awareness of God.
Colour: Orange.
Fuel for Meditation: Leopard, Sunflower, Cinnamon
Meditative Image: Wealth.
Title: Lord of the Fire of the World.

This is a warm and light path mainly linked to the head (Resh), and the higher rational thought and intellect within.

This Path is a conduit of higher intellectual energy that further fine tunes the lower personality, ensuring we endeavour to see real truth by growing and rejuvenating.

Being an opposite of Path 28, it can help if one is lost in an emotional net , one can tread here and use reason to get out of it, similar to the Hod and Netzach relationship.

We must be wary though that the Sun, just like reason can make things wither and die if shone too much. We can start to understand the limits of the intellect and start to connect the personality to an inner and higher light. We can see where we have run away from the light and hidden in the intellect.

The Path prompts us to become initiates of the sun, meaning that we can do for humanity what the sun does for the planet.

Path 28 Yesod – Netzach

The Star (17)   Tzaddi . Aquarius
Affirmation: Separateness is an illusion.
Colour: Violet.
Fuel for Meditation: Peacock, Galbanum, Coconut.
Meditative Image: Astrology.
Title: Daughter of Firmament: Dweller between Waters.

This is an artistic, inspiring Path of nature, creativity and intuition.

Linking the astral of Yesod with the emotions of Netzach this Path is deeply meditative. Instead of trying in meditation or focusing on a subject, we cast out the fish-hook of Tzaddi and allow ourselves to be meditated, for our sub conscious to come and find us.

The lady at the lake is always interested in where we are focusing our energies, she makes sure we are meditating fully when making decisions about where our energy is being used. She knows our highest ideals and fullest potentials and is eager for us to step into these by focusing energy. She is in control of her energies as she has one foot in Assiah and one in Briah, and is working between them smoothly and with full faculties.

This Path also reminds us that all below the Sun is natural; all forces, magik, expression, and phenomena. We can see here our wishes fulfilled, and we can learn to live more abundantly and expressively.

Is in this Path that we can find loving tales and characters such as Cinderella, romantic princes, and fair maidens.

Notice the Tree of Knowledge in this Path too, and the Hermetic Ibis, these can give one more depth to the Path of nature and meditation.

Path 27 Hod – Netzach

The Tower (16)   Peh ♂ Mars
Affirmation: The word of God will sustain me.
Colour: Scarlet.
Fuel for Meditation: Bear, Ruby, Pepper,
Meditative Image: Wrath and Vengeance.

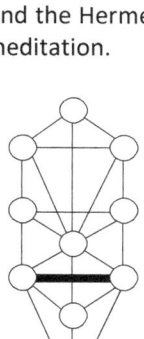

Title: Lord of the Hosts of the Mighty.

This Path is the main beam of the personality.

A highly charge Path due to being upon the lightning strike, it links Netzach and Hod aiming at creating balance between creative emotional power and concrete rational thought.

The King and Queen falling represent the inner male and female, they will fall unless united in harmony between the pillars and this can only happen if many parts of the personality are sacrificed. Too much Hod and the fire from Tipareth will smash the rigid tower to penetrate, and too much Netzach will ensure the Tower is flimsy and unstable when the fire penetrates.

The divine fire comes from beyond the crown (Kether) but lower down we need to balance, harmonise, and create a secure foundation at the level of the personality by destroying all that is not true.

The Tower Trump is appropriate as it is sudden shock that changes the personality; a bereavement, a relationship split, a change of career, and this path is this very force. The bear can be seen full of this force roaming the tower throwing things out of the windows he no longer needs.

Peh means mouth and it is through this organ that we give speech and intake food, the main attributes as to what gives the lower personality its existence.

The Mars energy helps us to break down the old to make way for the new, to cut away parts of the false ego. The whole Path lets us know that the spiritual quest is not all sweetness and light, it is work.

The Paths until here are really related to the personality, the next few Paths are more related to the individuality.

Path 26 Hod – Tipareth

The Devil (15) Ayin . Capricorn
Affirmation: I will distinguish between truth and illusion.
Colour: Indigo.
Fuel for Meditation: Goat, Black Diamond, Musk.
Meditative Image: The Evil Eye.
Title: Lord of the Gates of Matter.

This Path is one of the hardest to tred.

Here we need to go beyond the teachings we received in Hod to see the light of Tipareth, we need to enter spiritual consciousness from realizing which are our deluded misconceptions of reality.

The devil is the supreme manifest, the master of the material, and the falling for illusion. When have you fallen so low you sought drugs, items, or sex to appease an unhealthy hunger? When have you lied for these things? When has your desire for an object come first? Have you been involuntarily slaved by anger, by faith in a dogma, by a physical desire? All of these are the illusory devil. Orgasm is an indicator of the power of God, but minds cannot conceive this.

The Trump shows Baphomet, a deity that the Knights Templar worshipped. This may add weight to the rumour that they achieved enlightenment through supervised disciplined collection of too much materialism and sensuality, in the aim to flip around the other side, a reverse Qlippoth action so to speak. For most, this method slips into degeneration of the soul and lack, and this is where much of the species is today. Just go to Barcelona, many are trying to look beautiful, to have sex, to take drugs; this whole city *is* Path 26.

The devil does not show us that matter is evil, he just shows us it is an illusion and that many of our mental views upon matter are Qlippotic. We need to define our mental concepts on the material realm here to climb any higher up the Tree. This Path, along with 25 and 24 each give supreme tests that enable us to purify the soul before stepping into Tipareth, they are each Paths of self sacrifice.

The Capricorn energy here tells us to tread this path perfectly and slowly to be able to gain the lofty heights and succeed. The eye shows us that true inner vision cannot be fooled by the material realm like the five sense eyes can be.

When you can laugh at the material, you conquer the devil.

Path 24 Netzach – Tipareth

Death (13)   נ Nun . Scorpio
Affirmation: Change brings me growth.
Colour: Green blue.
Fuel for Meditation: Scorpion, Snakestone, Cactus.
Meditative Image: Necromancy.
Title: Child of the Great Transformers.

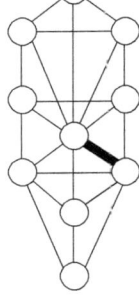

This Path is one of inner death and rebirth where we create emptiness to push ahead the purification with gratitude.

Here we let go of the desires found in Netzach as we seek a higher consciousness, knowing that an inner death has to be accepted before the rebirth into a higher consciousness.

Death is birth and birth is death, and everything lives and dies; our evolution, personality, relationships, and this Path helps us accept these deaths with the knowledge that there is no way back.

The personality is not the true you and only when you realise this will you begin to hold your own within this Path.

Many think they need the personality but names, labels, identities, likes, and character traits, are all impermanent. They are illusions and nothing to do with the real you. You only need truth.

This Path also helps us let go and kill unfulfilled desires that come in dreams, the killing of guilt that hangs onto us like leeches. This path is deep work, but the transmutation abilities in here are powerful, hence why it has the Scorpio energy; higher forces working in lower levels as the Scorpio sign represents.

I remember an Ashram in India where a girl was asking the Swami why it was wrong for her to desire her boyfriend physically, he replied that it was not wrong but that it was an illusion and a short term material pleasure. This Path agrees with the Swami and makes sure that to enter Tipareth the scythe is swung where needed.

The fish is what is sought by Tzaddi, and also resembles the inner workings of the subconscious waters where the truth of what needs to go resides.

On this Path we can seek out our true will, and if found we need to painfully change the inner parts that do not serve this truth.

Path 25 Yesod – Tipareth

Temperance (14) ס Samekh . Sagittarius
Affirmation: I will overcome adversities.
Colour: Blue.
Fuel for Meditation: Horse, Jacinth, Aloe.
Meditative Image: Transmutations.
Title: Daughter of the Reconcilers.

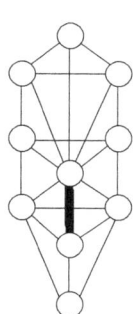

This Path is one of ultimate tests.

Here we lift from personality to individual mystic consciousness.

The Archangel is Raphael from Tipareth guarding the entrance, looking to see what one needs to do to be ready, he knows how far into the inner worlds you have gone and knows what changes you have made.

This Path will raise the following questions; have you shown enough faith? Is the flow between conscious and subconscious minds fused enough? Are you implementing dream messages?

By administering tests of temptation, the Path will see our truths and falsehoods, and where our spiritual beliefs currently are.

Final blocks such as guilt, family, and relationships will need to be purified, and our dedication to the great work will be put under scrutiny, just how much faith and enthusiasm does one have?

The soul has to enter the dark night within, maybe a retreat of solitude is needed, or a fast. Have we purged enough? What is lacking in the will? What is needed to be added or removed from the intellect? What memories need to be processed? Which lower Sephiroth can you visit to purify and find the answers? Interestingly the lowest three paths letters, ק, ו, and ת spell the Hebrew word for bow, and this links to the Sagittarius energy within this Path that holds the bow and arrow.

The Archangel is conversing with your higher self on the other side of the veil so knows what you need, heed the lessons as many mystical experiences are lying in wait. He pours the waters of spirit between the gold and silver vases, signifying Tipareth and Yesod, the higher self, and the fused conscious and subconscious minds.

This Path prompts the soul to turn back or go further on, it creates the last hurdles before divine light fills the vessel, and only when ready can we shoot the bow of the archer upwards. On Path 25 the following quote is relevant.

> "It is through blackened glasses that we can alone gaze on the sun; looked at through a clear glass, it seems to us black, and blinds us. God is for us as a sun; we must walk by his light with lowered eyes; if one tries to gaze fixedly on Him our sight fails."
> Eliphas Levi

Entry to Tipareth

There are some things we need to mention at this point as everyone will approach Tipareth at a different level, a different layer. Tipareth can of course be visited in Pathworking even though ones "consciousness" is not yet of Tiparethic nature.

One can Pathwork into this Sphere and wallow in the blazing light, and seek Raphael for healing and balancing, but this does not mean one is across the veil yet, but this in turn does not mean one will not benefit from Pathworking here.

The Tree is all things to all people, so if one works nine to five in tick-tock and is finding the Tree useful for an hour a week, then that's all good but this person will not be able to raise consciousness to Tipareth within this sort of lifestyle. That is okay too for one can use the Tree how they wish, and if any benefit is gleaned it is worthwhile.

But I know there are some warriors reading, and there is some information that will help around this area. The clue is in Temperance, he is in the wilderness in front of the Sun, the same wilderness that the apostles spent forty days retreating and experiencing mystical visions.

As you approach the veil, a fast, shamanic experience, or holistic therapy will all help you pass some the tests of Path 25. What will be needed is some solitude, this could be three days, five, twenty one, or fifty, it's all up to you, you will know where you are at and where you wish to go to. You will also know when you are across the veil I can assure you with all of my being.

I know a place that for years has given the canvas for a standard forty days in silence with only fluids for food. With this backdrop about forty percent of people arrived to Tipareth consciousness so this gives you some plane of reference.

Truly approaching this veil you will have messages from nature, synchronicities, and dreams all converging in a point of sorts, and much information from this mystical ball will seem more topsy-turvy (Trump 12) the close you get to the veil.

But is there a veil of Paroketh? An obstacle to our progress at this point on the Tree of Life? Yes, there is, but the obstacle is of our own making. Part of the problem is the Tower path; where our own particular belief systems, and particularly the attempt to express our own particular belief system in any kind of human language may lock us into a pattern of perception. Where we are unable to transcend the veil and see clearly what lies beyond it.

But a deeper problem is that our expectations of what we will find beyond the veil are so clear and well defined that we may build up a mental image of it that is so strong that we can convince ourselves that we have been there, when in fact we have not.

So should we dismiss all images and expectations of what we will findwhen we approach the world of Tipareth? Ideally, yes (Trump 12), but this is not a practical way of working for most thinking, feeling, human beings. Instead we try to develop the image through familiarisation, repeated travel on the paths approaching Tipareth, while recognising that this is a journey of the imagination only. Then suddenly, one day, a certain flash of enlightenment will come to us; we will realise that we are actually in Tipareth, and the veil of illusion will finally drop away, and drop away forever.

So from this point of view, the veil of illusion conceals from our everyday senses a greater illusion beyond. The veil of Paroketh is itself illusory because there is no real division between the physical and the spiritual worlds. We may pass between one and the other as easily as passing through a hanging curtain. Of course, first one needs to know how to move the curtain aside, but this is something that has been given to us by many avatars in the past. At Christ's crucifixion it was said, "And the veil of the Temple was rent from the top to the bottom." This means that Christ's teachings gave us the means to see through to the other side of the veil by our own efforts; no longer do we need the intercession of a priest before we are able to approach "God's kingdom."

Many get stuck at Temperance for a time and this can create 'divine anger' which is linked to the letter Samekh. But the more we brew in Temperance, the more we stretch the archers bow back and take an accurate perfect aim, the faster and smoother we will fly through the veil. Is the speed of light fast enough for you? There's some particle physics to back this up later.

Just remember the greatest darkness is just before dawn, and a journey to true Tipareth consciousness is not to be gained easily, the virtue of Tipareth must be gained. Don't worry for now, this will all be covered in more depth later on when we are within the practical work of Merkaba.

"Though we inevitably fail and fall time and time again, there are hours and minutes of delight and joy when the angels of the heights begin to wear again in our sights their ancient aspects of glory, and we are melted in the heat and fire of ecstasy and gladness and gratitude, knowing that we, the dead for centuries and long ages, may yet rise again."

For those close to the Veil of Paroketh it is likely you are experiencing strong energies around your dream and meditation spaces. Below are two exercises that will invoke, banish, clear and protect. Each require movement, visualisation, and mantra, and it is all of these combined that can eject the coarser cells and monadic atoms from consciousness allowing for a spiritually finer, more subtle matter to be attracted in.

Middle Pillar Exercise:

- Stand up straight and imagine Kether as a sphere of light above your head, mentally or orally chant Eheieh until it fills your consciousness (I Am).
- Imagine the light moving down to your neck and throat area and Daath as a sphere of light. Mentally or orally chant YHVH Elohim until it fills your consciousness (Lord God).

- Imagine the light moving down to your heart area and Tipareth as a sphere of light. Mentally or orally chant YHVH Eloah V'Daath until it fills your consciousness (Lord God of Knowledge).
- Imagine the light moving down to your genital area and Yesod as a sphere of light. Mentally or orally chant Shaddai El Chai until it fills your consciousness (Almighty Living God).
- Imagine the light moving down to your feet and ankles and Malkuth as a sphere of light. Mentally or orally chant Adonai ha-Aretz until it fills your consciousness (Lord of Earth).
- Now Imagine light coming up from Malkuth through the middle pillar up to Kether, when at Kether the light turns comes out like a fountain and descends in a spiral.
- Imagine your aura with a hard edge about a metre around you, then stamp a foot to complete and come back.

Flaming Pentagrams:
- Stand facing east, and use the two forefingers of your right hand to draw a pentagram in the air starting at the top and moving to the lower-left. You are drawing a blue flame pentagram into the astral plane full of vitality, you have to make it real with your will and imagination.
- Move your fingers from the finished-top and jab the middle of the pentagram mentally or orally chanting YVHV.
- With your arm still outstretched rotate to the south and do the same but chant Adonia.
- With your arm still outstretched rotate to the west and do the same but chant Eheieh.
- With your arm still outstretched rotate to the north and do the same but chant Agla.
- Rotate back to the east to complete the blue circle of fire.
- Say mentally or orally, "In front of me Raphael, behind me Gabriel, to my right Michael, to my left Uriel," and imagine the archangels of the directions facing you.
- Say mentally or orally, "about me flames the pentagrams, and above me in the column shines the six rayed star." Now imagine the scene with all your will and imagination.

- The above opens space for work, to close space do the same but start your pentagrams at the lower left and then to the top, plus imagine the archangels facing outwards.

Do not be worried if you forget a few things the first few times, there are no dangers and the benefits are astounding, especially if near the veil of Paroketh.

***

We will now go back to the Paths, and as we climb higher up the Tree the Paths and Spheres are so subjective that they become more feelings than images, more meditative intuition than mental travelling. The higher we go we realise the Paths point the way toward concepts which the mind cannot otherwise grasp. Therefore, we will only supply brief information from now on, but again if one wishes to Pathwork straight into Chesed to connect to the energies of mercy and love, or even merge into EL himself then one does not need any rules. Just remember that the more roots you have lower in the Tree, the more fruit the Tree will yield higher up.

Path 23 Hod – Geburah

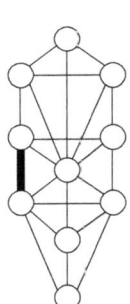

The Hanged Man (12) מ Mem . Water
Affirmation: I am willing to make sacrifices for what I believe in.
Colour: Deep blue.
Fuel for Meditation: Snake, Water Plants, Aquamarine.
Meditative Image: Talismans, Crystals.
Title: Spirit of the Mighty Waters.

Hod expands and Geburah restricts and this Path
leads us to sacrifice the Hod like limitations of knowing, of being in control, of normal consciousness.
On one level it tells us to make the mind a clear, fluid receiving vessel without prejudice, taboos, or local imprints. On another level it tells us that when all appears confusing near the veil just to chill out, "it is what it is."

This Path is the ultimate Zen, sacrifice, and even martyrdom. The suspension of reacting and chasing as is the normal folly of man.

Path 21 Netzach – Chesed

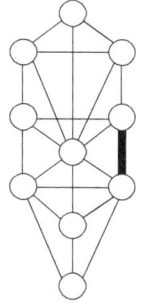

The Wheel of Fortune (10)   כ Kaph . Jupiter
Affirmation: Perseverance in the great work will be rewarded.
Colour: Violet.
Fuel for Meditation: Eagle, Oak, Amethyst.
Meditative Image: Ascendancy.
Title: Lord of the Forces of Life.

This Path holds the forces of karma, destiny, and the rules and cycles of life. If you cross the veil how will your evolving destiny unfold?   Kaph means palm and this is related to palm divination and also to the nailing to the cross; the sacrifice to find ones true destiny.

The wheel spins two ways much like a gyroscope.

Path 22 Tipareth – Geburah

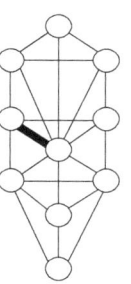

Justice (11) ל Lamed . Libra
Affirmation: I will strive to be just and fair.
Colour: Emerald.
Fuel for Meditation: Elephant, Aloe, Emerald.
Meditative Image: Equilibrium.
Title: Daughter of the Lords of Truth.

Adhere to the Divine laws.

Path 20 Tipareth – Chesed

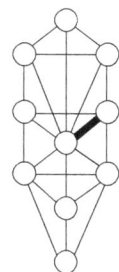

The Hermit (9) י Yod . Virgo
Affirmation: The path of the mystic is lonely, but God will provide.
Colour: Yellow, greenish.
Fuel for Meditation: Rhino, Lily, Peridot.
Meditative Image: Invisibility, Initiation.
Title: Prophet of the Eternal.

The quest does not end in Tiparath, the source is from Kether.

Path 19 Geburah – Chesed

Strength (8) ט Teth . Leo
Affirmation: The union of opposites powers the universe.
Colour: Green, yellowish.
Fuel for Meditation: Lion, Sunflower, Catseye.
Meditative Image: Taming Wild Beasts.
Title: Daughter of the Flaming Sword.

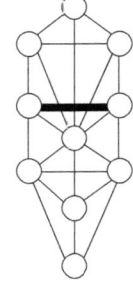

Control opposing forces by harnessing and becoming the spiritual fire.

Path 17 Tipareth – Binah

The Lover (6) ז Zain . Gemini
Affirmation: Seperateness is an illusion.
Colour: Orange pale mauve.
Fuel for Meditation: Lion, Sunflower, Catseye.
Meditative Image: Two places at once.
Title: Children of the Voice.

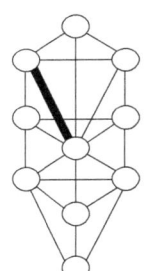

The soul returns to Eden through the Royal Chemical Marriage.

Path 15 Tipareth – Chokmah

The Emperor (4) ה Heh . Aries
Affirmation: Divine energy brings growth and order.
Colour: Scarlet.
Fuel for Meditation: Owl, Geranium, Ruby.
Meditative Image: Power of Consecrating Things.
Title: Chief Among the Mighty.

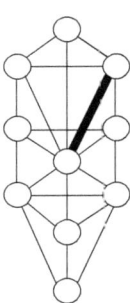

Authority from the Father.

Path 18 Geburah – Binah

The Chariot (7) ח Cheth . Cancer
Affirmation: The spirit of God dwells within me
Colour: Amber.
Fuel for Meditation: Sphinx, Watercress, Amber.
Meditative Image: Power of Casting Enchantments.
Title: Lord of the Triumph of Light.

Conqueror of all the planes. Cheth, the fence, provides the enclosure for the spirit to rise.

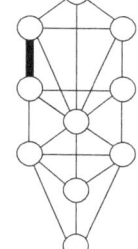

Path 16 Chesed – Chokmah

The Heirophant (5) ו Vau . Taurus
Affirmation: The higher self is the great initiator.
Colour: Red-orange.
Fuel for Meditation: Bull, Sugar, Topaz.
Meditative Image: Secret of Physical Strength.
Title: Magus of the Eternal.

Accurate traditional stubborn teachings show the way.

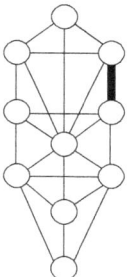

Path 13 Tipareth –Kether

The High Priestess (2) ג Gimel . Moon
Affirmation: A unified consciousness reflects the purity of God.
Colour: Blue.
Fuel for Meditation: Camel, Mugwort, Star Sapphire.
Meditative Image: Clairvoyance, Divination by Dreams.
Title: Priestess of the Silver Star.

The long path across the desert to the secret church where one can face the reality behind the veil of Isis.

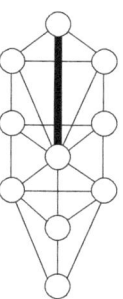

Path 14 Chokmah – Binah

The Empress (3) ד Daleth . Venus
Affirmation: Love and awareness provide a door to initiation.
Colour: Emerald Green.
Fuel for Meditation: Dove, Sandalwood, Turquoise.
Meditative Image: Love.
Title: Daughter of the Mighty Ones.

The universal womb of the supreme Isis.

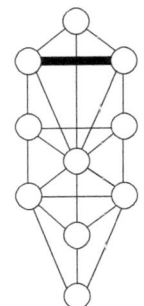

Path 12 Binah – Kether

The Magician (1) ב Beth . Mercury
Affirmation: Those who dwell in the house of God see with clarity.
Colour: Yellow.
Fuel for Meditation: Ibis, Lime, Agate.
Meditative Image: Knowledge of Science.
Title: Magus of Power.

God creates the universe by thought, we do the same on a lower arc.

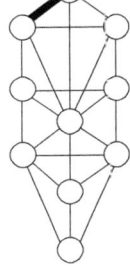

Path 12 Chokmah – Kether

The Fool (0) א Aleph . Air
Affirmation: Gods thoughts shine with perfection.
Colour: Bright pale yellow.
Fuel for Meditation: Man, Peppermint, Topaz.
Meditative Image: Divination.
Title: Spirit of Ether.

Primal creation energy acting upon itself to create the cosmos. From nothingness comes the potential for thought, then thought appears and emanates mind.

Deity Yoga

The Tree and Pathworking can also be used for deity yoga. Deity yoga is mainly known from Buddhism where one can meditate (using visual imagination stoked with will) upon a deity of choice and merge into it, creating and becoming the energy of the deity.

The true Hermetic can perform this style of yoga on the Tree of Life, or with Shiva, Tara, or Ishtar. It doesn't matter because it is all the same egg. The science is that we are riding astral energy of an archetype,

and the folly of religions and dogma has no part to play in our alignment with core truths. Even if we see a shrine to Mary in the Spanish countryside we can summon its roots regarding Isis and harness that energy with love. We are looking for root energy and looking to surf it with sincerity.

To live a human life believing in one deity that creates fear and guilt is mind control, it is negative hypnosis, pure and simple, and though that is not worth our thought, it is worth our dismay.

There are many archetypes upon the Tree and we will give one example using EL within Chesed.

Within the harmonious kingdom of Chesed you notice the crystal clear blue atmosphere. The colour blue with specks of twinkling silver surrounds you. You take a deep breath and see silvery blue enter your nostrils.

Suddenly on the side of a tree a few feet in front of you see the words "EL, God the mighty one," engraved in the tree. The words are etched deeply into the wall of the tree and you call out inwardly the name "EL." Your inner voice echos throughout the universe "EL, God the Almighty One, cover me with your mercy."

From the corner of your eye, you see a large Archangel settle into a spot close to you. You turn to the Angel and call out in acknowledgment "Tzadkiel, prince of mercy." You feel hundreds of Angels enter and you inwardly allow your voice to echo " Has Maleem, Brilliant ones."

You see a Mighty Crowned King in the distance, you watch him in amazement as he approaches you. There's a cup in his hand and the King stands before you and offers you a drink from his cup.

You take the cup and drink the sweet liquid. The King turns and places his back against your chest and you feel his warmth. You feel him merge and melt into you, you realize he has just become one with you. You feel wonderful for the King is you and you are the King. Now slowly open your eyes, and when you do, know that the King is still there as a part of you. You now have all His attributes and have now inherited all of his abundance. Keep this mind set for as long as you can and remember and acknowledge you two are one.

Only your imagination can hinder you.

***

"Know the self, know man, know everyone."

The goal of Pathworking is to evolve and learn about the self. Self study is self observation, it brings things up so we can observe deep feelings, impulses and emotions. We study inputs, beliefs, and how we have reacted in the past, and see what would have been the best way of reacting. We look at patterns, dislikes, impatience, judgments, habits, addictions, compulsions, opinions, and then we harmonise and integrate.

Observing imagination is an important way of self study, it allows us to struggle against the 'normal' self.

> "Thou then who hast trials and troubles, rejoice because of them, for in them is Strength, and by their means is a pathway opened unto that Light."
> Aleister Crowley, Liber Librae

When a man sees that the way he has lived up until now is really not the right way, when he sees all that his life has been made up of in clarity and decides to work, he must decide how far he is willing to go and what sacrifices he is willing to hand over. "Whatever it takes" is the best ploy.

"Withdraw into yourself and look; and if you do not find yourself beautiful yet, do as the sculptor of a statue...cut away all that is excessive, straighten all that is crooked...bring light to all that is shadowed....do not cease until there shall shine out of you the Godlike Splendour of Beauty; until you see temperance surely established in the stainless shrine."
Plotinus

The Unwritten Qabalah

"Wisdom becomes knowledge when it becomes your personal experience."

Introduction

Pathworking should, at the least, help balance your inner world and align you to the energies within the Tree. Now we are going to come back out to the whole and use some rocket fuel from the unwritten Qabalah to align us to some very real forces in our realm. We may possibly even enter 'the mystical spiral' but first one must adhere to the following quote:

> *"The Tree of Life must be learnt by heart; you must know it backwards, forwards, sideways, upside down; it must become the automatic background to all your thinking. You must keep hanging everything that comes your way upon its proper bough."*
> Aleistair Crowley

There is a certain truth in our being that cannot be found via words or text, but it can be found by going there and feeling it with consciousness. The unwritten Qabalah is such a vehicle for taking us there. The unwritten Qabalah could be described as the invisible initiatic system, the initiations that are evident as one rises up to the veil through Pathworking, or from contemplating the content in this section.

In the Tarot 777 system we are now at The Lovers Trump, inner union and balance from Pathworking, but now we need to start the motors of The Chariot.

Things will come slowly, in flashes, and then more, this is the motor of The Chariot firing up. If one starts with a broken engine one is sure for a crash and would need more work upon the Tree's Paths.

If you enter the spiral, many unexplainable mystic experiences can occur, just remember it is not 'you,' don't bring the ego into it, it is just happening and allow it to happen. Be the observer.

Just a touch of the unwritten Qabalah can leave one hungry, and once one can feel the treasures in there then one has to feed this hunger. If hungry enough there is a real chance to create a new way of being, an improved one, one away from the cultural design but aligned with the cosmic design.

Many things can be seen with our third eye that we don't see with our physical eyes, remember yourself, you are a pure essence, so see with the eyes of the soul.

Spiral Rocket Fuel

Contemplation of this section can be done in many ways; in meditation, in retreat, on a train, in a lucid dream, but solitude in nature is the best way to start the motors. In the Merkaba section we will need solitude as a prerequisite and will explain how to go about a retreat later. At the least you need to be working deep in the psyche, between the near fused conscious and subconscious minds.

These questions are not for the intellect, no written book holds the answers except the book deep inside You. Far too many clues have already been given.

- There is an objective Key within the Tree. The creators of the Tree left it there as they knew man was curious. Fruits will fall from the Tree without the Key but the Key can be used to look at the Tree differently and allow the opening of a door, a door that can lead towards an experience known as the Philosophers Stone. It can only be found with cleansed emotions and humility. The Key is in creation.
- What is the true structure of the Tree? The Tree as we always see it is a snapshot so to speak, but it is not idle. Does it move, twist, flow, or pulse in any way?
- Who is, or What is, the role of the Invisible? There is an invisible Sephirah upon the Tree, if it is invisible how can it be shown? When you see the invisible, you cannot say it.
- Why 10 Sephiroth? Why 3 and 7 above and below the Abyss?
- Who is Three Ayin, or What is the role of Three Ayin?

If you find one of the answers to these, the rest will fall quickly into place like massive eureka dominos. But if you get close to one eureka and don't solve it, create more mini eurekas as this builds up the energy. To find the answers to these one must align with the creators of the Tree. What are the creators of the Tree trying to tell or show us?

The Qabalistic Tree of Life is a giant puzzle but the answers are all within it and within the self. Many of the archetypes within Pathworking can help, especially within lucid dreams so invoke them!

Other subsidiary questions that are for sure Spiral Rocket Fuel are:

- Think of when a seed falls from a tree branch in nature and the exact moment the seed touches the soil. What Sephirah or Sephiroth is this? How can the Tree show this?
- Why does Tipareth have the word Daath within the Atziluth Name of Power?
- What is the true base of the Tree?
- Why 22 Paths? Why can we see no Paths diagonally across the Abyss?
- Why are the Tarot Court Cards placed in Three Ain?
- Why do some call Malkuth The Hidden Garden?
- What is the number within the Tree that can help you understand The Book of Revelations?
- Imagine you are in a massive hall, every baby being born in the world now is happening around you, and every member of the elderly that is dying now is all around you too. Think of a fountain, feel it, what is happening? Apply the tree to this visualisation, what does it look like?
- How does creation appear and manifest?
- What is the invisible force that makes things desire to grow, renew, survive, and multiply?
- How does a pyramid give one a clue to enter the Tree?

Be the seeds, the fruits, the roots. Our world is visible to our eyes but that does not mean that the invisible is not inside. Place your awareness in the innocent eyes of your curious, courageous soul.

See the invisible bridge to the invisible Tree, the Tree is not complete, the logic tree is not all there is. See behind, find the essence.

All people see the sun and everyone perceives it differently but the essence is the same.

Go in nature, feel nature, but not with the intellect, use the heart. Feel how life comes from decay in nature.

> "Tear away the shroud of obscurity from nature, there lies the divine of all mysteries."

> "Nature contains nature, nature rejoices her own nature, nature amends nature."

Diagrams

We can work with the Tree as we know that it's not really idle. Meditate upon the following diagrams, and create your own concepts of the true structure of the Tree. Some of the diagrams below are red-herrings but some can lead somewhere special. All show examples of how one can work with the Tree to find the true structure.

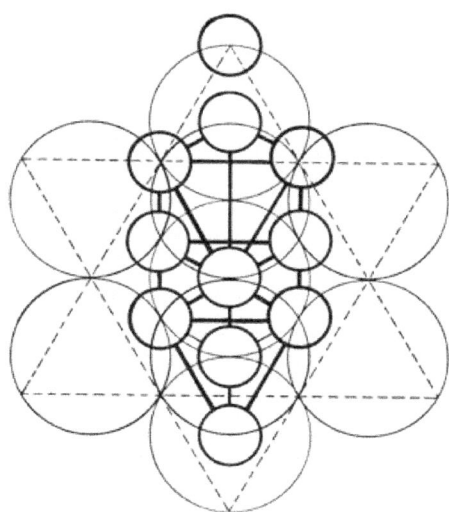

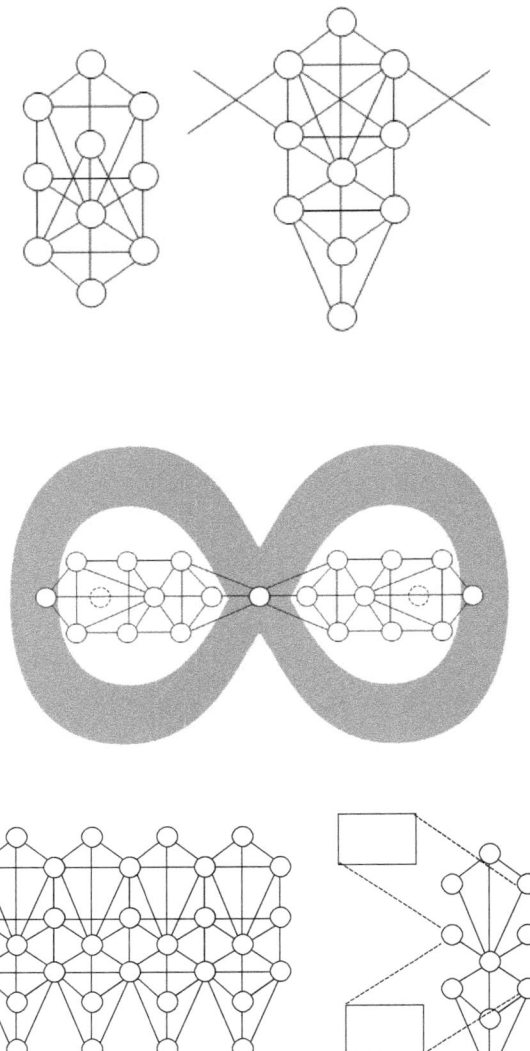

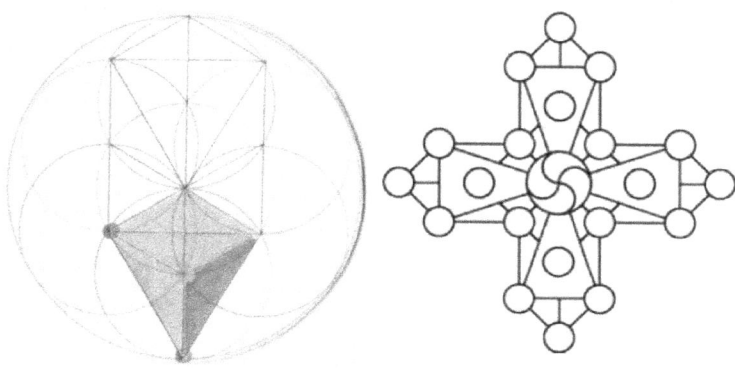

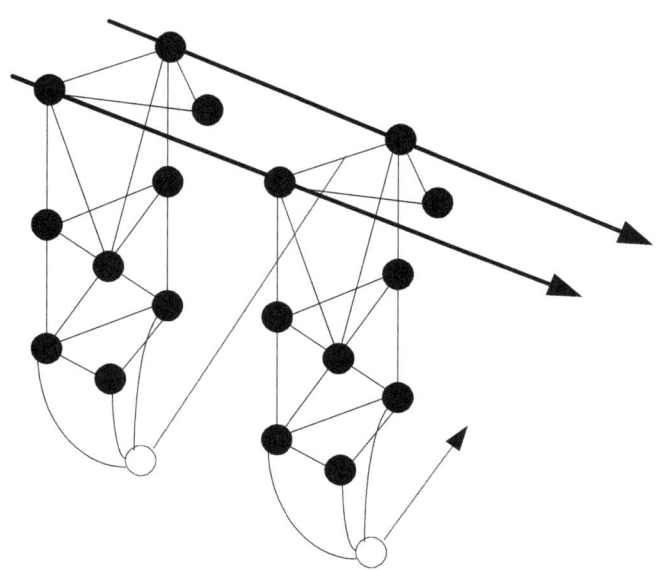

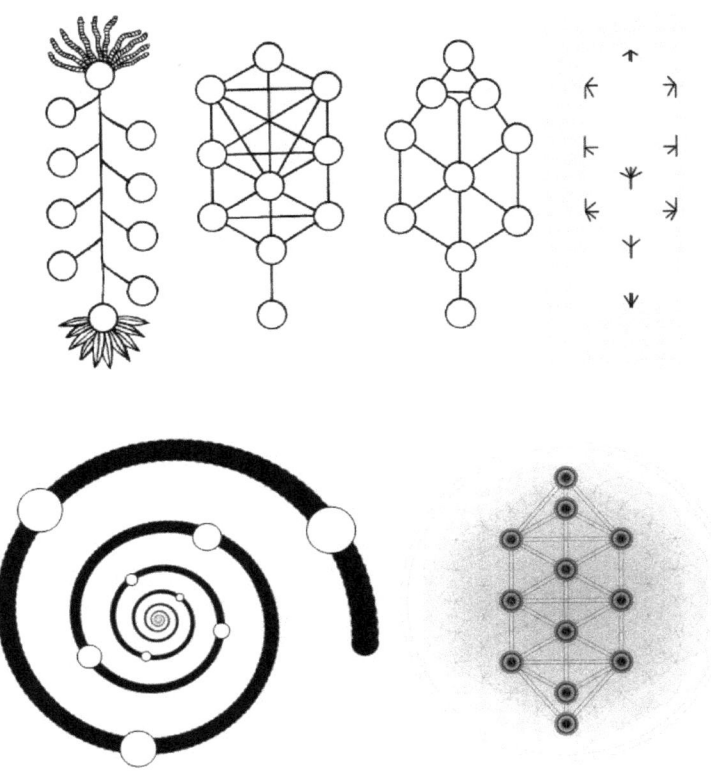

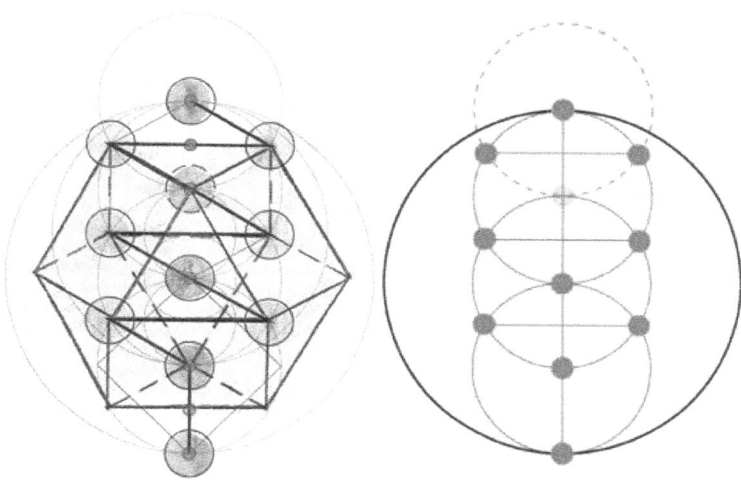

*"And he looked up [the **blind** man], and said, I see men as Trees, walking……he was restored, he saw man clearly."*
The Gospel according to Mark, 8:24,25

Compared to other Qabalah books, I have not ventured deeply into the 32 Paths of Wisdom within the Sepher Yetzirah. This is because it is not set in stone that they relate to the 10 Sephiroth and 22 Paths in the standard 'mainstream' order we have briefly presented in recent sections.

The Paths of Wisdom were added to the Sepher Yetzirah at a later date and in the 16th century the three mother letters were often placed upon the three horizontal Paths, the seven double letters upon the vertical Paths, and the remaining twelve simple letters upon the remaining diagonal Paths.

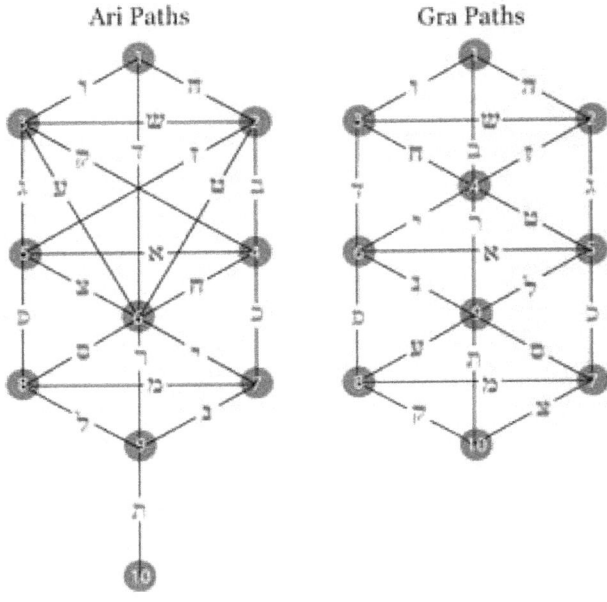

Proverbs 24:3 states that with Wisdom the House (Beth) is built, does this refer to the Ari Paths?

There is another interesting way to look at the Paths of Wisdom when we overlap the four Worlds at each relevant Tipareth with the next worlds Kether, and include Three Ayin above Atziluth. This presents us

with 32 points and 10 large circles which we will deem "The Major Sephiroth." When reading the attributes of the thirty-two Paths of Wisdom on top of this model we yield new information in contemplation.

Trinity of Wisdom

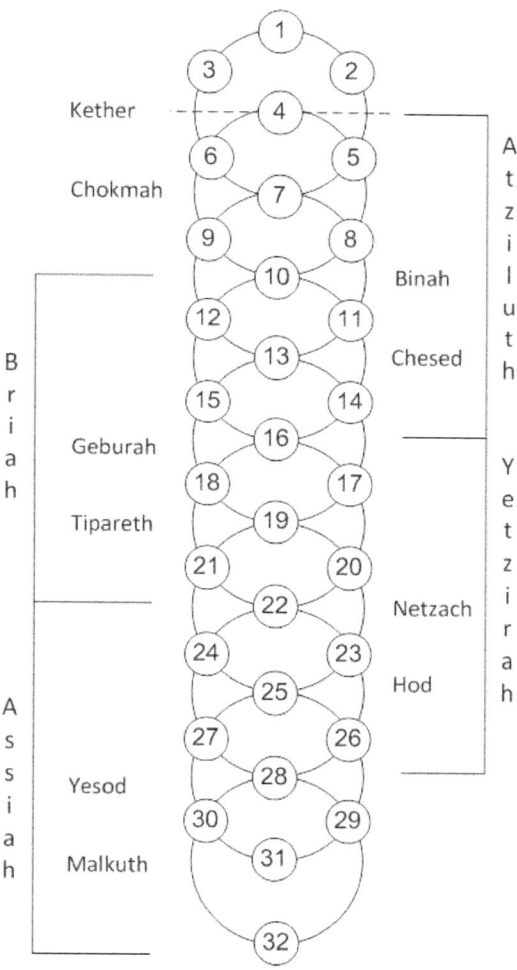

Maybe this look at the 32 Paths of Wisdom has some relation to the floor maps at the Temple of Luxor and Glastonbury Abbey?

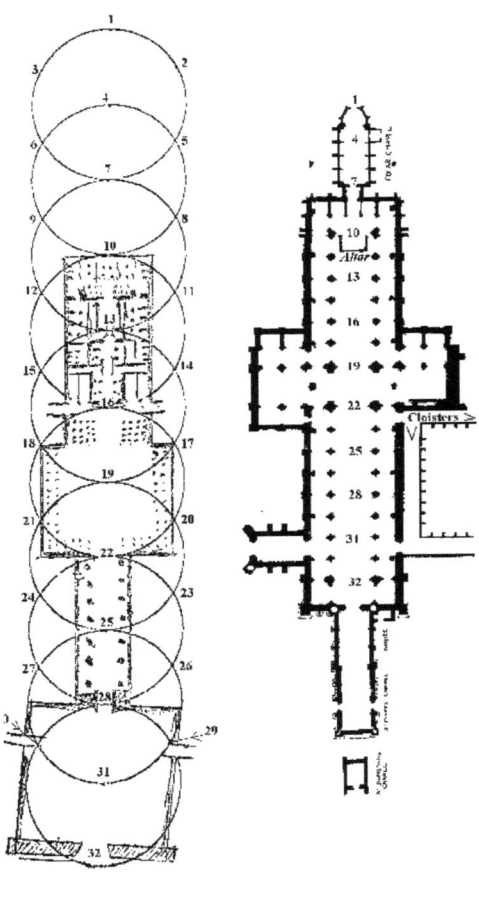

***

For those working within a retreat environment don't use the intellect for any of this material, be the Hanged Man. The spiral will come to you when your physiology is ready. If you are actually within the spiral and your vibration lowers, do some more work within the questions to push you back up. If your rocket starts descending, come down for more fuel.

I entered into the unwritten Qabalah within a 55 day silence only ingesting liquid fruit and vegetables and I can assure you that if you follow this ancient method closely like a warrior you will shoot across the veil and be ready to receive.

Initiations along the way can come in the form of dreams; if you are dreaming of when you were a child then this is something engraved upon your soul, but if you dream of something cosmic or celestial then you will for sure know about it and you are pretty much in the right place. Other self-initations I received were:

- After a big dream, I found a lizard right outside my pyramid with only its head cleanly skinned.
- After Pathworking on Path 24, I opened my eyes to see a scorpion running towards me.
- Lucid Dreams with the Temperance and High Priestess archetypes giving me clues.
- Waking up to crystal clear messages regarding the Qabalah, akin to another voice in the room, but happening within conscious awareness.
- Major eureka moments within the secrets of the Tree and how it relates to creation, the self, man, and nature.

I saw with the eyes of my soul, and from my experiences my views upon the I, the world, and what I actually was, changed significantly, along with aspirations and perceptions of reality.

Deep into solitude I meditated for some days upon the question, Who or What is the invisible? The following is not correct in Qabalistic terms, but it is something I wrote nonetheless:

"It is the life force in fire, in the wind, the space in the atom, the love between mother and baby. It is the energy that enables trees to grow, and that which makes a flower long for light and for ants to crave for survival. It is everywhere but it is nowhere. Many humans spend eighty years and never notice it. It is the warmth of the sun, the cold of the snow, the shared smiles, the inner knowing. It is the vision of the painter and sculptor. The all potential within all seeds.

It is in me, the authentic me.

The invisible wants to multiply, be it the cat wanting kittens, or the turtle laying eggs. The role of the invisible is to experience itself and to create. It knows not good or bad, it just is. It is invisible on the Tree as we need to strip off the layers of our visible to become in alignment with it. Only then can it be found and seen.

It is the umbilical cord to the bigger Tree. The bridge is a pure soul with fusion; the hermaphrodite with no stories, no desire, no attachments, and no opinions.

It is the little girls smile as she waits for her daddy, it is the moment before birth. It is the light from the sun, too bright to look at but we know it is there. It is the noise of a lonesome tree falling, it is the clouds, it is the moment just before a first kiss.

The invisible is not divisible, it is all one, but the illusion of separation creates more experience for the invisible.

But people crave and desire, and hang on to the visible; the spirit in dense manifestation creating the ultimate veil over the invisible."

To answer Who or What is the invisible one must make sense of it upon the Tree.

> "Ten is the number of the ineffable Sephiroth, ten and not nine, ten and not eleven. Understand this wisdom, and be wise by the perception. Search out concerning it, restore the Word to its creator, and replace Him who formed it upon his throne." The Sepher Yetzirah

Alchemy & The Philosophers' Stone

"Philosophy is an agent science."

Introduction

We can make a sideways step now and due to what we know from Hermetic Qabalah we are already a great way to understanding much of Hermetic Alchemy (though there is hazy separation and both are linked). All of the symbols of Alchemy emphasise the aspect of change; the transmutation of the base metals into Gold through a process of Solve et Coagula, Separatio et Coniunctio (disintegrate and unite, separate and join). Hermetic Alchemy should really be looked at as a sacred science of enlightenment, or the science of the soul.

It is the Great Work of nature that perfects matter through transmutation. It is a scientific formula that can be repeated and taught, and is essentially an expression of the fact that light is hidden in darkness.

During the middle ages the doctrines were written in confusing, contradicting allegory to hide the art from the Catholic Church, and to protect it from the profane. The 15th to 17th century doctrines were often a mix of mainstream science, poetry, and esotericism, so only the wise could see the hidden doctrine within. These doctrines took the guise of planetary, herbal, metal, elemental, mineral, and animal properties, and each were written in a way impossible to understand without meditation.

> *"If it really did dawn on the alchemists that their work was somehow connected with the human psyche and its functions, then it seems to me probable that the passage from the Rosarium is no mere misprint. It agrees too well with the statements of the other authors. They insist throughout upon careful study and meditation of the books."*
> Jung, C.G, Collected Works, Bollingen, 1968, volume 12

As a spiritual doctrine, alchemy differs from all other traditions because its poetic use of symbols and objects to convey spiritual and philosophical teachings is completely unique.

> *"That from which a thing has been made in a natural way, by that same thing it must return to a dissolved state into its own nature. Everything has to be dissolved and reduced into that form from which it arose."*
>
> Anton Joseph Kirchweger, 1728

The Process

Alchemy is essentially about retreat in solitude and pounding, putrefying, and purging the dense matter of the body, the false personality, and false I. The sacred marriage, the "coniunctio" or "coitus," refers to the union of our divine spirit with the soul, and finally with the body. In common man the spirit, soul and body are kind of separated from each other although they are working with each other. When the Great Work has been completed the divine spirit has been brought down to shine through the soul and body. What the alchemical proccess does is give an allegorical route map for this unification. Most Alchemical doctrines take us through the process that flowings down the order below:

Operation	Processes	Planet	Metals	Chemical Arcanum
Calcination	Roasting; Conflagration; Reduction; Trituration	Saturn	Lead	Sulfuric Acid (Vitriol)
Dissolution	Dissolving; Corrosion; Cibation; Bain Marie	Jupiter	Tin (Pewter)	Iron Oxide (rust: water on metal)
Separation	Sifting; Filtration; Fission; Cutting	Moon	Iron (Steel)	Sodium Carbonate (bubbling)
Conjunction	Fixation; Reunion; Amalgamation; Conglomeration	Mercury	Copper; (Bronze; Brass)	Sodium Nitrate (union with Life Force)
Fermentation	Digestion; Putrefaction; Congelation; Ceration	Mars	Mercury (Copper)	Liquor Hepatis (Balsam of the Soul)
Distillation	Potentising; Exaltation; Cohobation; Multiplication	Venus	Silver (Mercury; Antimony)	Black Pulvis Solaris
Coagulation	Sublimation; Projection; Fusion	Sun	Gold (Silver)	Red Pulvis Solaris

The first stage of the Great Work is the Nigredo, the stage of Blackness, disintegration, chaos, where the material (metal, the soul of Man, or what have you) is reduced to the "Prima Materia" or formless original stuff, before it can proceed to the second stage, the Albedo (whiteness), where the material may be unified once again. The Alchemical process is circular, alternating between Solve and

Coagula on its path towards perfection. The whole process is about manipulating physiology and consciousness, which is in essence a chemical formula of change, hence Alchemy. Let us look at this whole process a little more deeply.

Calcination

Chemically, the Calcination process involves heating a substance in a crucible or over an open flame until it is reduced to ashes. In the Arcanum Experiment, Calcination is represented by sulfuric acid, which the alchemists made from a naturally occurring substance called Vitriol. Sulfuric acid is a powerful corrosive that eats away flesh and reacts with all metals except gold.

Psychologically, this is the destruction of ego and our attachments to material possessions. Calcination is usually a natural humbling process as we are gradually assaulted and overcome by the trials and tribulations of life, though it can be a deliberate surrender of our inherent hubris gained through a variety of spiritual disciplines that ignite the fire of introspection and self-evaluation.

Physiologically, the Fire of Calcination can be experienced as the metabolic discipline or aerobic activity that tunes the body, burning off excesses from overindulgence and producing a lean, mean, fighting machine. Calcination begins in the Base Chakra.

Dissolution

Chemically, it is the dissolving of the ashes from Calcination in water. In the Arcanum Experiment, Dissolution is represented by iron oxide or rust, which illustrates the potentially corrosive powers of Water on even the hardest of metals. When processed, Vitriol breaks down into sulfuric acid and iron oxide, which are the first two arcana or secret ingredients. The Egyptians smelted Iron as far back as 1500BC and used iron compounds in tonics and as disinfectants.

Psychologically, this represents a further breaking down of the artificial structures of the psyche by total immersion in the unconscious, non-rational, feminine or rejected part of our minds. It is, for the most part, an unconscious process in which our conscious minds let go of control and allow the surfacing of buried material. It is an opening of the floodgates and generating of new energy from the waters held back. Dissolution can be experienced as "flow," the bliss of being well-used and actively engaged in creative acts without traditional prejudices, personal hang-ups, or established hierarchy getting in the way.

Physiologically, Dissolution is the continuance of the Kundalini experience, the opening-up of energy channels in the body to recharge and elevate every single cell. Dissolution takes place in the Sacral Chakra and involves the lungs and spleen.

Separation

Chemically, it is the isolation of the components of Dissolution by filtration and then the discarding any false or unworthy material. In the Arcanum Experiment, Separation is represented by the compound sodium carbonate, which separates out of water and appears as white soda ash on dry lakebeds. The oldest known deposits are in Egypt. The alchemists sometimes referred to this compound as Natron, which meant the common tendency in all salts to form solid bodies or precipitates.

Psychologically, this process is the rediscovery of our essence and the reclaiming of dream and visionary "gold" previously rejected by the masculine, rational part of our minds. It is, for the most part, a conscious process in which we review formerly hidden material and decide what to discard and what to reintegrate into our refined personality. Much of this shadowy material is things we are ashamed of or were taught to hide away by our parents, churches, and schooling. Separation is letting go of the self-inflicted restraints to our true nature, so we can shine through.

Physiologically, Separation is following and controlling the breath in the body as it works with the forces of Spirit and Soul to give birth to new energy and physical renewal. Separation begins at the Chakra located at the level of the solar plexus.

Conjunction

Chemically, it is the recombination of the saved elements from Separation into a new substance. In the Arcanum Experiment, Conjunction is symbolised by a nitrate compound known as cubic-saltpeter or potassium nitrate, which the alchemists called Natron or simply Salt. Blue-coloured Natron acid (aqua fortis) was made by mixing potassium nitrate with sulfuric acid and was used to separate silver from gold. The inert residue precipitated from the acid during the reaction like a child being born.

Psychologically, it is the empowerment of our true selves, the union of both the masculine and feminine sides of our personalities into a new belief system or an intuitive state of consciousness. The alchemists referred to it as the Lesser Stone, and after it is achieved, the adept is able to clearly discern what needs to be done to achieve lasting enlightenment, which is union with the overself. Often, synchronicities begin to occur that confirm the alchemist is on the right track.

Physiologically, Conjunction is using the body's sexual energies for personal transformation. Conjunction takes place in the body at the level of the Heart or Copper Chakra.

Fermentation

Chemically, Fermentation is the growth of a ferment (bacteria) in organic solutions, such as occurs in the fermenting of milk to produce curds and cheese or in the fermenting of grapes to make wine. In the Arcanum Experiment, the process of Fermentation is represented by a compound called Liquor Hepatis, which is an oily, reddish-brown mixture of ammonia and the rotten-egg-smelling compound hydrogen sulfide. Egyptian alchemists made ammonia by heating camel dung in sealed containers and thought of it as a kind of refined Mercury that embodied the life force. Liquor Hepatis means "Liquor of the Liver," which they believed was the seat of the Soul, and the colour they associated with the compound was green, the colour of bile. Surprisingly, Liquor Hepatis exudes a wonderful fragrance, and the alchemists made a perfume of it called "Balsam of the Soul."

Psychologically, the Fermentation process starts with the inspiration of spiritual power from Above that reanimates, energises, and enlightens the alchemist. Out of the blackness of his purification comes the yellow Ferment, which appears like a golden wax flowing out of the foul matter of the Soul. Its arrival is announced by a brilliant display of colours and meaningful visions called the

"Peacock's Tail." Fermentation can be achieved through various activities that include intense prayer, desire for mystical union, breakdown of the personality, transpersonal therapy, psychedelic drugs, and deep meditation. Fermentation is living inspiration from something totally beyond us.

Physiologically, Fermentation is the rousing of living energy (chi or Kundalini) in the body to heal and vivify. It is expressed as vibratory tones and spoken truths emerging from the Throat or Mercury Chakra.

Distillation

Chemically, it is the boiling and condensation of the fermented solution to increase its purity, such as takes place in the distilling of wine to make brandy. In the Arcanum Experiment, Distillation is represented by a compound known as Black Pulvis Solaris, which is made by mixing black antimony with purified sulfur. The two immediately clump together to make what the alchemists called a "bezoar," a kind of sublimated solid that forms in the intestines and brain.

Psychologically, Distillation is the agitation and sublimation of psychic forces and is necessary to ensure that no impurities from the inflated ego or deeply submerged id are incorporated into the next and final stage. Personal Distillation consists of a variety of introspective techniques that raise the content of the psyche to the highest level possible, free from sentimentality and emotions, cut off even from one's personal identity. Distillation is the purification of the unborn Self; all that we truly are and can be.

Physiologically, Distillation is raising the life force repeatedly from the lower regions in the cauldron of the body to the brain (what Oriental alchemists called the Circulation of the Light), where it eventually becomes a wondrous solidifying light full of power. Distillation is said to culminate in the Third Eye.

Coagulation

Chemically, Coagulation is the precipitation or sublimation of the purified Ferment from Distillation. In the Arcanum Experiment, Coagulation is represented by a compound called Red Pulvis Solaris, which is a reddish-orange powder of pure sulfur mixed with the therapeutic mercury compound, red mercuric oxide.

The name Pulvis Solaris means "Powder of the Sun" and the alchemists believed it could instantly perfect any substance to which it was added.

Psychologically, Coagulation is first sensed as a new confidence that is beyond all things, though many experience it as a Second Body of golden coalesced light, a permanent vehicle of consciousness that embodies the highest aspirations and evolution of mind. Coagulation incarnates and releases the Ultima Materia of the soul, the Astral Body.

Physiologically, this stage is marked by the release of the Elixir in the blood that rejuvenates the body into a perfect vessel of health. A brain ambrosia is said to be released through the interaction of light from the phallic-shaped pineal gland and matter from the vulva of the pituitary. This heavenly food or viaticum both nourishes and energises the cells without any waste products being produced. These physiological and psychological processes create the Second Body, a body of solid light that emerges through the crown chakra.

"Putrefaction is so effective that it destroys the old nature and form of the rotting bodies; it transmutes them into a new state of being to give them a totally new fruit. Everything that has life dies; everything that is dead putrefies and finds a new life."
Pernety, 1758

"The Alchemical process is a method for self knowledge that the soul undergoes far outside its realm of existence."
Marry Anne Atwood

"Man is unsatisfied because his desires are limitless. He has to unchain himself from his desires. By this purification of desires and dirt rebirth happens. Therefore an alchemist has to shy away from the masses, and start the process of meditation, self-reflection, in silence."

"To drink the interior life in a long draft is to see the higher life."
Michael Maier, Alchemy author

Alchemical Art

In the 16th and 17th centuries hundreds of alchemical paintings and artworks were created to help share and continue the art of The Great Work. Some of the artworks helped to display the process.

The Body is to be decomposed so one can shift one's awareness to the inner self. The planets are both stages of the process and energies in the body to be transmuted. The Saturn star is black as Saturn reigns over Nigredo (blackness). Sun and Moon are the opposites to be united, and fire and air are the elements stimulating the decomposition. The black crow is another symbol for Nigredo and the two birds coming out of the body are the soul and the spirit. The circle emphasizes the idea of union or unification.

V.I.T.R.I.O.L.U.M used in alchemical literature, is formed by the Latin expression "Visita Interiora Terrae Rectificando Invenies Occultum Lapidem Veram Medicinam", which means "Visit the interior of the earth, and by rectifying you will find the hidden stone which is the true medicine".

It is vain that the elixier of life and ambrosial wine be poured into a dirty or broken vessel.

The entire alchemical process is nothing but one continued action of warming and cooking. You can call it meditation, or clear awareness, but it needs to be done continuously. This is the only way purification of body and soul will result in uncovering the true divine nature of the practitioner.

One of the symbols of Nigredo is the "decapitation," and also the "raven's head" (caput corvi). Those symbols refer to the dying of the common man, the dying of his inner chaos and doubt because he is unable to find the truth in himself.

The egg is the Subject of the Art, which must be struck by the martial igneous agent wielding the double-edged sword of the Secret Fire. Mars thus comes to the help of Vulcan, and from the ensuing darkness of Putrefaction (Nigredo) the Hermetic chick will hatch.

The chaotic situation is emphasised by the emergence of the seven planets on the horizon, a symbol of universal disorder. As indicated by the sign of sulphur, the sinking island is set on fire by sulphurous flames from the hellish interior of the earth. Yet the alchemist's sinking island is supported by a sealed chest of drawers emerging from the sea and containing immense riches of silver and gold. Although the adept's world has become a sinking island, it has been simultaneously transformed into a treasure island."

Above, the alchemist performs the squaring of the circle, thereby turning the two sexes into one. The motto repeats a saying of the Rosarium, "Make a circle out of a man and woman, derive from it a square, and from the square a triangle: make a circle and you will have the philosopher's stone." As informed by the text, the triangle denotes the unity of body, soul and spirit. Of this operation Petrus Bonus says: "In this conjunction of resurrection, the body becomes wholly spiritual, like the soul herself, and they are made one as water is mixed with water, and henceforth they are not separated for ever, since there is no diversity in them, but unity and identity of all three, that is, spirit, soul and body, without separation forever."

The union of the Red King with the White Queen is symbolic of the union of male and female. In other words, when after having attained albedo (having discovered the divine light in oneself), the spirit must be fixated (the descending eagle), resulting in rubedo, the final stage and commensing of experiencing a different reality.

The Philosophers Stone

> "Between eternal birth, resurrection from the fall, and the distillation of The Philosophers Stone, there is no difference"
> Jacob Boehme, Shoemaker and Mystic, 1575-1627

At the pinnacle of all Hermetic Work is the use of the prepared Philosophers Stone. Also known as the Elixier of life, or the Quintessence, it is said to bring rejuvenation and immortality. Many have said it is a powder, or a liquid, or gold made from metals but I can tell you it is none of these things. The most famous myth is that of English scholar John Dee and his assistant Edward Kelley (who formed Enochian Magik). Kelley claimed that he had acquired in England small amounts of two powders, one white and one red, which had allegedly been found in Wales, in the raided tomb of a Bishop. From these two powders, Kelley would prepare a red "tincture", one drop of which could turn a larger quantity of heated mercury into gold. There are reports that he performed this feat several times, once even in the presence of Rudolf's court officials and the gold was later tested and found to be genuine. He is also reported as sending to Queen Elizabeth I of England a copper bed warmer which had been partly transmuted into gold.

The stone is created through a tangible and dense crystallisation or condensation of a subtle substance.

I am not going to say too much about the Stone as I am already stretching my karma credits with what has been shared in these sections. What I will say is that the Stone is already used by many people but they do not know they are using it. For if they knew they were using it and everyone knew the world would be very different within the hour. The Stone can only be with the pure, so therefore the stone is for all, but in few it shines.

The secret of the Stone can be first gleaned within the Unwritten Qabalah, for if one finds the Key upon the Tree of Life then this Key can for sure open the door to the Philosophers Stone.

Here is some choice Alchemical quotes and axioms that will help explain the process. Some are of unknown origin and others are written by myself.

> *"When you make the two into one, and when you make the inner like the outer and the outer like the inner, and the upper like the lower, and when you make male and female into a single one, so that the male will not be male nor the female be female, when you make eyes in place of an eye, a hand in place of a hand, a foot in place of a foot, an image in place of an image, then you will enter the Kingdom."*
> *Gospel of Thomas, 22*

> *"There is Wisdom, a light that is the breath of the divine energy. This Wisdom is a ray, brilliance, a mirror, and is the manifestation of the divine energies. It moves everything. It rules over and emanates Nature; it is invisible and a maintaining fire, an inscrutable power of the uncreated interior."*
> *Franciscus Kieser*

"It always has been a strong idea that there was some kind of liquid, or drink that could prolong the life span and give the body a (near) immortality. Unfortunately common man took this often literally and tried to create a physical liquid. This liquid, or water of life, is a symbolic term for what is present within man himself."

"Only when one had attained the highest state of perfection one could make the Philosopher's Stone. Therefore one must unify himself with the divine, resulting in a new birth or new state of consciousness."

"Once the inner light has been discovered it must be made into the only reality in our consciousness. After having descended into the unconscious, into the darkness, into the underworld, we found the Light, we found the volatile Spirit. Now the volatile Spirit, or quicksilver, has to be fixated or coagulated. This means that our conscious, or attention, must completely penetrate our unconscious, or soul, or everything that lies hidden in ourselves. By doing this we fixate (that is bring it into the conscious) the volatile and make it durable. When everything in ourselves has been purified and the Light appears, we have to fixate this Light and make it durable so it remains always present."

"There is a secret life principal within the actual nature of man."
Manly P Hall

"He is at our doors, deceiving our intellects with subtlety and flattering our hearts with beauty, we have no trust but in thee."
Rosa Alchemica

"Ascend above any height, descend further than any depth; receive all sensory impressions of the created: water, fire, dryness and wetness. Think that you are present everywhere: in the sea, on earth and in heaven; think that you were never born and that you are still in the embryonic state: young and old, dead and in the hereafter. Understand everything at the same time: time, place, things: quality and quantity."
Corpus Hermeticum

"When the soul and spirit are trapped together, then being becomes more spirit than material man. Then the door will open."

"Nature is a temple where living pillars sometimes let out confused words, man journeys through it as if across forests of symbols that observe him with friendly eyes."
Charles Baudelaine

"Nature. There is a boundless peace. Ones mind embodies all this. The owl, the bird singing, it's all the same. We shrink but also we are amplified by all this. Oneself and the whole, the opposites meet. A little melting in the absolute. a little bit of nature. That's enough. That's where the peace comes from."
Cristino de Vera

"Come to the edge he said, they said we are afraid. Come to the edge he said. They came. He pushed them. They flew."
Christopher Logue

"There is a way of manipulating matter n energy so as to create what modern science calls a force-field. This force field acts upon the observer and puts him in a privileged position in relation to the universe. From this privileged position, he has access to realities which are normally concealed from us by time and space, matter n energy. This is what is called the great work."
Fulcanelli, 1937

"When you make the two one, you shall become sons of Man, and when you say, "mountain be moved," it will be moved."
The Gospel of Thomas

Conclusion

It is the allegories within the art of Alchemy and the hunt for the Stone that spins up lots of mini eurekas around consciousness. This is particle physics and this is a vehicle and a core part of creating a Merkaba.

The Chemical or Alchemical Marriage could be seen as Netzach and Hod, or The Lovers Trump in the 777 system, and the creation of Gold as being the entry into Tipareth. There are many parallels to the Tree of Life and these are why most Alchemists also studied Qabalah, and vice versa.

Modern chemistry (which derived from Alchemy) has turned the art of Alchemy into a myth, but Alchemy carries far more weight than any of the new-age fads currently haunting and disorientating the spiritual seekers of today.

Two main messages come from The Great Work in Alchemy, one is that man is divine, and two is that man can overcome his fate, but to really delve into alchemy one needs at the very least 21 days in silent solitude. Many Alchemical doctrines talk of the 40 day furnace, this is regarding the time it takes to putrefy the dense matter, but it can be done in 21 days if one has few issues deep in the cave.

The Great Work can be found in its entirety in the Egyptian myth of Osiris. Osiris was a God-king who was locked up in a chest by his brother Seth. Seth is the symbol of the powers of decomposition, the fire that causes putrefaction. The chest is the alchemical "vas," or vessel. The chest was closed with nails and lead (lead is the metal of Nigredo, or blackness). Then, Seth threw the chest into the ocean. The ocean is the alchemical water, or the second stage of the Great Work, when the earth has been reduced to water. The ocean itself is a symbol of the Prima Materia to which the matter has been reduced. The chest eventually washed ashore under a tamarind tree. The tamarind is also a symbol of the second stage, Albedo or whiteness, because of its white blossom. Isis, the wife of Osiris finds the chest and brings it back to Egypt. This is the coagulation of condensation. By her magical powers she is able to receive the seed of Osiris and gives birth to Horus. Here the alchemical seed of matter has been found, and a new birth takes place, that of a pure consciousness. Horus is a sun God, thus the light has come through. When Set also finds the chest with the dead Osiris (Osiris is the symbol of the common man that has died) he cuts the body up in fourteen pieces and scatters them around. This again refers to the decomposition and sublimation that needs to happen again and again until everything is pure. Isis looks for all the pieces and buries each of them at the spot (the fixation). Only the phallus of Osiris she could not find because an oxyrhinchus fish had swallowed it. This could mean that the sexual power has been transformed into a higher energy and will nevermore express itself on a lower level. It is said that the lower expression of the sexual drive binds man to the physical world or the world of darkness. The phallus is no longer necessary because Horus has been conceived. Horus represents the reborn man. In his appearance as a child he is called Harpocrates, and corresponds with the boy Mercurius. Horus is also the resurrected Osiris. In Alchemical terms, the old King has died and the young King is born.

Osiris is also the universal principle of life. He is the seed, like the wheat berry. The Egyptian would sow wheat berries on mummies, so they would sprout, symbolising the resurrection of the dead. Osiris was also a God of fertility, and thus he had the name "the Great Green One." His skin colour was often painted green. The alchemists talk about the "green seed" in nature, that is the "prima materia," or "green dragon," the fertile energy of life that penetrates everything.

***

Symbolism regarding the Alchemical process is hidden from the uninitiated in many Catholic churches and Hollywood films, and the parallels with Shiva-Shakti symbolism in the east are plentiful.

The method of Hermetic Alchemy as a spiritual practice yields amazing results I can assure you, and this is why it has lasted millennia, and will last as long as the human race. Once the process is perfected, one can see projects, ideas, and the world from a completely new angle. It is little known that Newton, Galileo, Dee, Paracelsus, Bacon, and Kepler were all much more alchemists than scientists, astronomers, or philosophers.

"Flee the many, find the one."

Emerald Tablet Merkaba Ascension

"The only way of discovering the limits of the possible is to venture past them into the impossible."
Arthur C Clarke

Introduction

Hebrew letters that spell out the word Mer-ka-ba are Mem-Resh-Caph-Beth, from the root word, Resh-Caph-Beth, meaning to "ride". Mer-ka-ba is usually translated as "chariot", or sometimes as "wagon," but really they are equivalent to the English word "vehicle", or "conveyance", being something that transports you somewhere. We find the word in the Bible within the passages of Ezekiel when referring to the throne-chariot; the four-wheeled vehicle driven by four Cherubim (or sacred animals). Prophets Elijah and Elisha in the old-testament were assumed into "heaven" by a chariot too, and Elijah never died in the story, he just disappeared within a "whirlwind." There are also trails of the Merkaba process being practiced as far back as the 2nd century BC in the Tosefta, a Jewish doctrine from 200AD.

Merkaba mysticism can be traced to Jewish mystics at the time of the destruction of the second temple in Jerusalem in 70AD. The Ma'asei Merkabah movement left writings known as the Hekhalot (Palaces/Temples) literature. The main interests of all Hekhalot writings are accounts of mystical ascents into heaven, divine visions, and the summoning and control of angels, usually for the purpose of gaining insight into Torah.

In a little-known Kabbalistic text, the *Midrash Proverbs*, Rabbi Ishmael says, "If there comes before God one who is learned in the Talmud, the Holy One says to him: "My son, since you have studied the Talmud, why have you not also studied the Merkaba, to perceive my splendour? For none of the pleasure I have in my creation is equal to that which is given me when scholars look beyond the Torah and see and behold and meditate on: My throne, and the hashmal seen by Ezekiel, and the fiery streams under my throne, and the bridges that cross it, and the ofanim [a class of angels], and the gilgalim (another class of angels). And is this not my greatness, and My glory and My beauty: that my Children know My splendour by seeing all this?"

Merkaba mystics experienced ecstatic visions of the celestial hierarchies and the "throne of God," and many mystical literatures describe the ascent of the soul as a perilous journey through seven spheres, or heavenly dwellings manned by hostile angels. The visionary's goal was to behold the divine throne. Merkaba symbolism is abundant and hidden within much Christianity and Renaissance art.

The process *can* be dangerous; in Jewish tradition one must be over forty years old and know the old testament extremely well. It is not to be done out of curiosity alone, it is to be done for a reason, to bring something back. The Talmud, a doctrine of Jewish law and tradition has a tale of four men who engaged in Merkaba; one died, one went mad, one apostatised, and only Rabbi Akiba Ben Joseph had a true visionary experience.

In Egypt Merkaba was actually three words; Mer meant a kind of light that rotated within itself. Ka meant spirit, in this case referring to the human spirit, and Ba meant the human body. The entire word in ancient Egypt referred to rotating fields of light (wheels within wheels) that would transport the spirit/body from one dimension into another.

We must not get muddled with the new-age pranayama fad of the seventeen breath "Merkaba" meditation that comes from Drunvalo Melchizedek's Flower of Life workshop. I have done this workshop and the following practice, and this is nothing more than very good pranayama with visualising a star tetrahedron around oneself.

The true Merkaba is a process by way of creating a protective shell around consciousness and ascending up to a state of being where you travel to other dimensions and collate visions and messages.

Your physical body, emotions, thoughts and spirit are all made up of energy, blended in ways that make you unique in the universe. Due to all this being made up of energy it has a frequency and therefore we can change it, and as it increases you can see and perceive things not possible before. The Merkaba is a temporary shell of ultra fast spinning particles that allow you to attune to the nature and vibration of the universe, to awaken a deeper experience of the truth of the connectedness of all life.

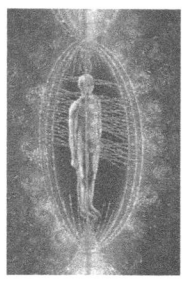

In Qabalistic terms we are ascending up to Tipareth to merge with our spirit, to a place where space, time, obstructions and limitations will peel away and warp. You can get to know who you are in terms of your carnations, what you are learning from each, and how each is a bold and daring mission through which the source learns more about itself.

The Merkaba process is only for warriors, and it will be needed to be performed during the coming changes by those who seriously want to help the flow of spirit through the species evolution.

The Emerald Tablet

Before we commence we need to look at The Emerald Tablet associated to Hermes Trismegistus. It is the core doctrine of all Hermetics and Alchemy, the arcane of arcanes, the ultimate formula, and it fits the Merkaba process like a glove. Along with the Corpus Hermeticum it is the root of all Hermetic thought and study.

The roots and history of the table are lost to antiquity, but there are very tangible traces through Arabia, Persia, Syria, Greece, Rome and then through Western Europe, with many stating that it comes from Hermes and the Egyptian priesthood. One legend states that Alexander the Great discovered the tablet in the great pyramid, but the true links to Hermes and the Egyptian priesthood have never been proved. Some scholars state it is a summary of Egypto-Alexandrian Hermetism but this cannot be known for sure.

It captured the imagination of mystics, scientists, magicians, and alchemists throughout the ages, and after the translation into Latin many interpretations of The Emerald Tablet appeared, from Isaac Newton to Fulcanelli, to Blavatski. We will view the translation that was passed to me.

1. It is indisputable, can't be doubted, without deceit, veritable, wholly truthful.
2. That which is Below is as which is Above, and that which is Above is as that which is Below, to accomplish the miracles of the One.
3. And a all things have come from One and through One, so all things are born from One by reproduction.
4. The Sun is his father, the Moon is his mother, the Wind has carried him in its womb, the Earth is his nurse and guardian.
5. His strength is whole if it is united to Earth. Power undivided.
6. You will separate the Earth from Fire, the subtle from the dense softly with great skill and care prudently with judgment.
7. He rises from earth to heaven, and returning he comes down to earth, by this he receives strength of the superior and inferior things.
8. It is the primordial force of all forces because it will overcome all subtle things and will penetrate all solid things. Light and darkness will fly away from you. Thus the world was created.
9. From it are born admirable adaptations of which the way here is given.
10. For this reason I have been called Hermes thrice great who processes the three parts of the wisdom of the whole world.
11. What I have said about the Suns work is accomplished and finished, the perfect seed ready for multiplication.

There are many commentaries of the table but it is in essence a meditative text, its secrets would mean little if told. The core meanings need to be found by the deep self during the process.

Prerequisites

We need an environment that gives every chance for a successful Merkaba, here we will look at the most important factors in planning the logistics and prerequisites of a Merkaba process.

- Location. The location should be in as much solitude as possible with as much natural surroundings as possible. The less manmade structures, and electronic waves the better.
- Culture is something we wear like clothes, our minds are at ease with culture, we gather the language of a given culture around us, but when a man goes into the wilderness and perturbs the mind with yoga, mysticism, and solitude, we then see the mind undressed away from language and convention.
- Silence. Language and words are a veil, and communication will affect the process like tying led to a balloon. Spoken language drowns out the spirit and a Merkaba cannot be created without silence; we need to get rid of man to find out about man.
- Diet. The delivery of organic fruit and vegetables once a week would be the ideal plan, a small greeting and thank you covering a few seconds won't harm the process but is better avoided. Going to a quiet outdoor market where you have an arrangement with one of the vendors could be done if you keep your consciousness focused away from the dynamics of "normal life." Don't use caffeine or many spices, nor use onions, garlic, mushrooms or peppers, as all of these are cleansers and will affect mediation. Some fasting is recommended, as are many soups and smoothies. It is better not to eat at all within six hours of going to sleep. This all sounds extreme but after a few days this routine will become easy, it is all in the mind. Some nutmeg would also be good for early morning astral and lucid dreaming techniques.
- Time. Rid yourself of all watches, clocks, and calendars. To align with nature one must be with as little man made conventions as possible. The twenty-four hour clock and the Gregorian calendar are both dogmatic, but the sun, the moon, light and darkness are of truth, and they will harmonise natural bio-rhythms.
- Care. It may be good to have someone check up on you every few days, this could be someone just knocking on the door and asking if

you are okay. The rules of this engagement need to be set clearly from the outset.
- Duration. One needs to set a plan for how long the process should be, I recommend 44 days with 6 days descending (explained soon), but 21 days with 3 days descending could be enough to fire up a Merkaba. It all depends on how much in the self one needs to clear to fire up the particles. I can now fire up a mini Merkaba in a handful of days but this is due to having done the process a few times. After a few days, thoughts and emotions will become amplified.
- Energy leakage. There is to be no masturbation during the process as this will leak life force energy and create desire for physical contact. After ten to fifteen days you will go through some erotic dreams and then this will flatline.
- Habits. Smoking and other habits are a waste of attention and will waste energy, kill them before the process starts.
- Caveats. It is possible that a big issue in the self may come and you will have to stop the process, it could be family or relationship orientated. If progress of vibration stops rising for over 7 days due to an issue, it is time to stop. Also it is wise to tell loved ones you are not contactable for the duration of the Merkaba process. Text messages and emails to the outside world are a big no unless strict rules are set up beforehand. Deep into the process one could be thinking about a single text message for hours, then the energy and thought constructs associated can dominate consciousness.

If nothing is sacrificed, nothing is obtained, and you need intense enthusiasm of being free from earthly desires and the auto-mechanics of man. It is only fifty days in over twenty thousand (if you live for over sixty years), it is nothing, and what you could gain could affect your soul for carnations to come.

It's the determined hunt for truth that makes one ready to receive. One cannot be in the land of tick tock and ask for answers and just get them, it's a process, and the Merkaba is the best vehicle. In this environment we can start to see life in archetypes and in a more subjective mode, this will allow new patterns to open up. The habit of talking is the most important thing to release, you become more alone, everything becomes more subtle, you feel more, become more sensitive, and other faculties then increase. The mind is a mechanical machine programmed by the outside world, and silence will rid you of background anxiety; the humdrum of survival and distractions.

You will soon realise that humans talk without thinking and that at least eighty percent of speech is of no purpose at all. The pleasure of paradise must be earned, and it is a pleasure one can keep, it is the opposite of the normal world where people look for pleasure in external things, this latter pleasure is not real and always falls away.

In eastern terms, we are leaving Maya (illusion) and invoking Shakti (primordial cosmic energy).

"If you do not fast as regards the world, you will not find the Kingdom. Blessed are the solitary and elect, for you will find the Kingdom. For you are from it, and to it you will return."
The Gospel of Thomas (Hidden by the Catholic Church)

"Conversation enriches the understanding, but solitude is the school of genius."
Sir Edward Gibbon

"Whosoever is delighted in solitude is either a wild beast or a God."
Aristotle

The Merkaba Motors

"A man may be born, but in order to be born he first must die, and in order to die he must first awake. Born here is to receive and start living in the new essence but to get to this he must die, detach from culture, people, attachments, personality, views, vices, ego, sufferings, habits. The I must die. Then he sees all these are not really his own, he then dies. He is in nothingness, but then unity comes, and here you see yourself and all as you really are."

So how does the Merkaba work, how do we spin it up?

The less mass something has, the faster it can go. Light photons are of no mass (at rest), hence they can travel at the speed of light (which is a border of what we can perceive as a human). According to relativity, as an object increases in velocity, the amount of energy it takes to accelerate it increases.

Bearing this in mind we can turn to consciousness. It has no mass or volume, and cannot be sampled, measured, analysed, or dissected. It is a field with no charge, polarity, or density. It is a state that cannot be observed, created or destroyed.

Knowing this we can take the laws of the universe onto consciousness and know that we can speed up the energy within consciousness as can be done with light.

What we are doing is a massive condensing of a carnation. Normally we need causal events and relationships to gain knowledge of the self, learn lessons, and implement self evolutionary tweaks.

This can even take multiple carnations if the plane of causality does not have the correct properties in the local environment, or if you have chosen incorrect paths against certain signs.

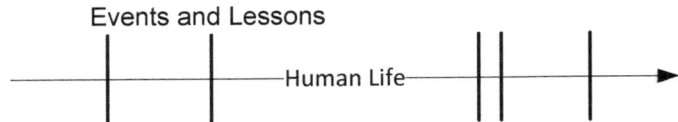

The Merkaba creates a gap within a carnation, and in this gap the soul rises up through a heightened vibration and can gain the knowledge, lessons, and evolution it needs in a small amount of time. It is an accelerated learning of dharma and karma in a condensed apparatus. We could think of it as rising from Malkuth up to Yesod and then beyond with a membrane around our consciousness keeping out individuality as not to dissolve in unity. A round trip with the goal being to grab some wisdom.

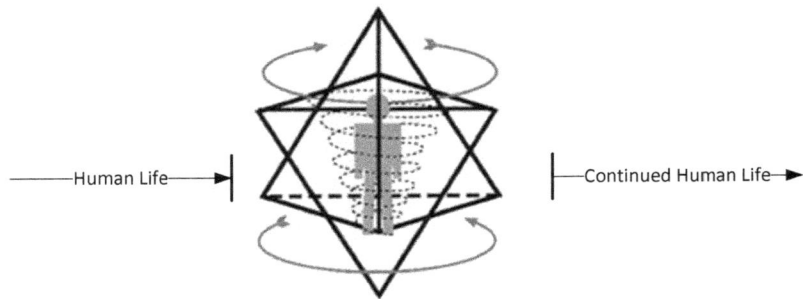

To do this we need to be in the force of Chokmah; inner creation, creating force, creating the buildup of eurekas. We need to stay away from Binah and absorbing information. In fact any more reading than two periods of five minutes a day will slow down the process. Saying this, reading short summary sentences, and creating and viewing of diagrams is advised. Even some writing can be done, as long as it comes from dreams, imagination, and intuition instead of intellect.

We also need to be raising our frequency and vibration of our body, mind, and soul; all three need to be worked on equally.

> "The level of awareness that decided to come here is different to that which experiences being here, but you can rise up to it."

Life Trajectory

We are looking for union with ones spirit, but we should elaborate on this a little. A linked intelligence exists in the invisible, a being in its own right, and it responds when called forth using the appropriate methods. Man is an exact image of the universe, and therefore the universe is represented within; man was created by the emanations through certain hierarchies, each contributed but also a part descended into the man upon formation.

Scholars call this union contact to the higher self, or the guardian angel, but for this book we will just call it our spirit. To merge with your spirit (to enter Tipareth) one needs to attract it, and create, calibrate, and understand your unique individual language of communicating with it. It is like riding a bike; you turn one peddle, your spirit turns the other, and the first peddles of effort are the hardest until momentum and velocity builds up.

So we have stopped our life effectively, and this our spirit knows for sure. The best way to start to attract the spirit in the first few days is to create a life trajectory thus far. This is a graph or diagram that shows key events in your life that have changed your physical, mental, or emotional self. These are the events that changed your look on life and the forks in the road that ended up having a bearing upon your core self and inner philosophy. One way of preparing this is to show

harmony and disruption too. You can create this anyway you wish and below is an example.

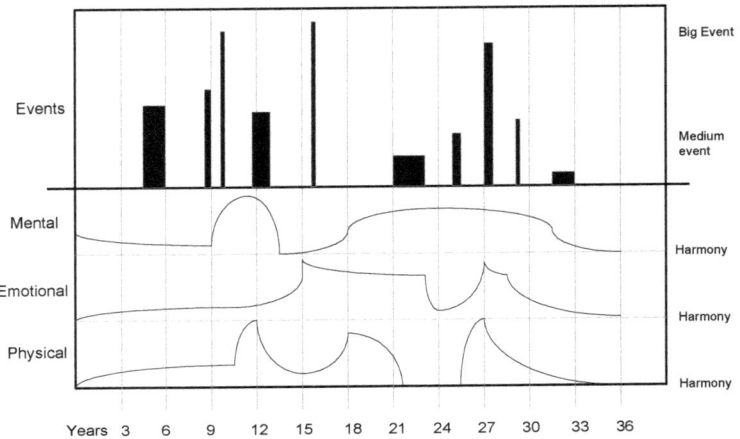

The top half of the example shows events and the bottom half shows the mental, emotional, and physical trends. Also we need to identify the series of events that took you be in isolation creating a Merkaba. The whole reason of this exercise is to try and find patterns of numbers and trends, it could be every 43 months something happened, or ever 4 years, or Phi or golden mean could be involved. It will take some searching and meditating to find the patterns but they are evident in almost everyone. It is as if our life design trajectory is held in Tipareth, and we are sailing in the plane of causality in the lower Sephiroth.

With stopping your life and analysing your life in numbers and geometry your spirit across the veil for sure starts to sit up and say "what is going on here, this could be interesting."

"I have seen many miracles and tried to explain them but it has bought me no real understanding. Yes, I'm empty, it's too late...perhaps it's not too late. If you feel with all your being that you really are empty, if you agree to one condition then I really can help you…..the condition is; die, consciously to the life you have led until now."

Gurdjieff with the Sufi Mystics in the film, 'Meetings with Remarkable Men.'

Self Alignment

"Look. This little finger covers the eye and prevents the whole world from being seen. In the same way this small mind covers the whole universe and prevents Reality from being seen."
Ramana Maharshi

To commence the Merkaba we will need to perform some inner shadow work to balance out, integrate, or purge what currently will inhibit the process. To explain this better we can place some of Tarot Cards upon the Tree of Life in a different way.

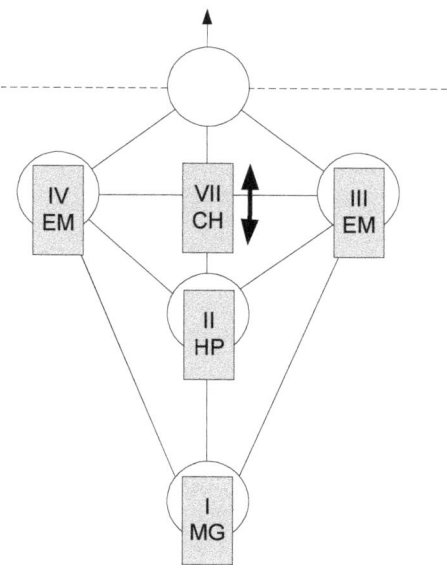

You are the Magician in Malkuth, earthed, and ready to start the process by learning. You need to get into the subconscious and dream world, and to ask questions, to find the hidden knowledge, and this could be seen as the High Priestess in Yesod. The Emperor and Empress represent Hod and Netzach and will need to be harmonised and brought in to alignment. If this is all done successfully, and your vibration is being raised daily using the force of Chokmah, the High Priestess will then allow the motors of the Chariot to start. How far this Chariot goes up the middle pillar is based on how strong the Merkaba force is and how you overcome any perils, puzzles, and tests along the way.

We are looking for the Magician to push buttons so that Yesod reflects more from Tipareth, and then when Hod and Netzach are aligned, you are to control all three forces from Yesod. The normal patterns of life, those of Malkuth, Hod, and Netzach have all ceased, so we need to merge them into Yesod. This is not easy as we are all carrying issues, energy blocks, traits, opinions, pain, and belief systems, from family, pain caused, relationships, experiences, and pain lived through. These clouds attached to the being will be attached to Malkuth, Hod, or Netzach, and with gratitude and grace, we need to harmonise, integrate, putrify, pound, purge, and purify.

Due to being in silent isolation, many of these issues will surface automatically because our core being is being amplified due to having no external distractions. Some internal Hod and Netzach issues will surface that you will already be aware of, but often there are issues deep down that are surprising. The work is to pinpoint all of these, and you can think of it as going fishing deep into the sea of the self.

Shadow work means peering into dark corners of our minds where secret shames lie hidden and violent voices are silent. Doing Shadow work means asking ourselves to examine closely and honestly what it is about a particular individual that irritates us or repels us; what it is about a belief system or reality tunnel that horrifies or captivates us; and what it is about a lover that charms us and leads us to idealise him or her. You will reject the shadow, then project it outside yourself, but then face it and become it.

When you have pinpointed something you need to process, realign, let go of, integrate, or putrify, we need to face it head on. Revel in all of the feelings, opinions, and fears. Focus on the issue until serenity in the soul is found, and make sure this is all written down. It could be as easy as going to a place of acceptance and sending love, or integrating and knowing your shadow instead of hiding and denying it.

This process will also bring up character traits in the self that do not serve you, to help with these you can create a soul mirror with the elements from earlier on.

You start to see that all your experiences and beliefs are not you and they start to collapse, you enter the dark night of the soul. If I am not these things then what am I? Darker parts of the psyche will come and need to be faced, balanced, accepted, and integrated.

At this point you should be able to see the self as others see you, not the illusion of how you see yourself. We are dividing the real from the invented. There is a real need to separate from this false self as much as possible, to look at life from afar with neutral eyes, as though through someone else.

You need to be sponged out, to be made nothing. It is the going in reverse, the no adding, the dissolving of who you are. This takes courage, but it is the only way.

> "Your pain is the breaking of the shell that encloses your understanding."

Cease to be a body carrying the mind, or vice versa, unite these because both of these all dissolve at the end of life anyway. Then go behind these.

This initiatory formula as it relates to our exploration is as thus; first, crisis and the plunge into the "sub-conscious," then self exploration, and ultimately self knowledge or mastery. The nature of the crisis differs from individual to individual, however the first two steps of this process are easiest to express as the ancient Greek aphorism, "know thyself."

> "If you bring forth what is within you, what you bring forth will save you. if you do not bring forth what is within you, what you do not bring forth will destroy you."
> Gospel of Thomas, Verse 70

> "Seek not abroad, turn into thyself, for in the inner man dwells the truth."
> Augustine

> "Knowing you own darkness is the best method for dealing with the darkness of other people."
> Carl Jung

Around this point you will be in no-mans-land, miles from who you thought you were and still a distance from the veil. You will be in inner chaos and may even want to go back the way you came. If you feel fear and think about going back, just remember what the great Nietzsche once said.

> "I tell you: one must have chaos in one to give birth to a dancing star."
> Frederich Nietzsche

The reason for the self-alignment work is to balance Hod and Netzach in perfect equilibrium. Only then can we begin to rise up to Yesod.

Dreams and Yesod

To fire up the Merkaba you need to concentrate on the main border of the human existence, the dreamworld. With your vibration rising from solitude and the daily work you will be doing (see the next section) the dreamworld is going to take on a whole new feel.

We need to be working day and night, and look at the dreamworld as a sort of laboratory for our daily work, or as the daytime as the laboratory for the night work. In the daytimes spend at least an hour recording dreams because dream patterns will form, and tests and messages will come and be presented over a string of dreams.

It is a good idea to record all of your main life memories on a wall as then the subconscious and your spirit can use the related images from your memory in your dreams. Record lovers, hobbies, locations, events, pretty much the information from your life trajectory, but include more memories that are poignant.

When remembering your dreams record the following:

Feelings, ambiance, what happened, sudden changes, objectives, people, colours, known and unknown locations, speed and mode of travel, numbers, lucidity, and elements.

What memories or feelings does the dream stoke up in you?

What soul, life, or Qabalistic message is deep within?

How does the dream relate to other dreams?

Most important when recording the dream is to draw the dream, this is hard at first but will give you much better results when referring back in days to come. Create a bridge between meditation and dreams too, and when dream images appear in meditation, don't add; let it flow like a river and float down the river with it. See what comes because what comes in this mode is usually from the astral plane.

Dreams are the main way to find the language of your Spirit because Tipareth is reflected in Yesod.

Dreams may become very scary at times, and will seem more real than real life. You will wake with your heart pounding and the room you're in will feel less real than what you've just experienced. Don't be a coward, accept the fear, and take the lessons and messages. Many tests are attempts to scare you, to see how much far you are willing to go. If one dream leaves you a little jilted, have a cold shower, go into nature, and perform grounding techniques. The "scary" dreams come from the same place as the wonderful dreams, the source, and love is the source, and love and light are greater than any fear or darkness.

Be a warrior and use the flaming pentagrams to banish if need be (check the previous flaming pentagrams section).

Be prepared for up to ten dreams a night, the ones in the early morning usually will become the most significant due to REM science.

You need to send questions to your dreams (the Magician in Malkuth to the High Priestess in Yesod), and chase down the reflected signs. Ask the questions in different ways, use the Qabalah, the Tarot archetypes, and your imagination. The answers will be twisted and contorted at first and hard to understand, but keep working on the dreams. Sometimes these answers will come in the daytime, they are always there but normal life gets in the way.

The most important thing with looking at dreams is to separate each dream. When recording a dream separate which part came from Malkuth (images and events from your physical day), what part came from Hod (thought constructs in your mind), and what part came from Netzach (feelings and emotions you have). It is like having three basketball hoops; throw each part of the dream into one of these hoops, and if it doesn't fit then leave it, only throw what is "definite" for now. You can use different coloured pens to help separate out the dream when working on dreams in the day.

Every seven days the dreams will increase in momentum and force, an octave jump so to speak. After twenty-one days there will be a large increase of a fractal nature, the dreams will be faster and encompass much more information from the big dreams experienced during the first twenty-one days.

Parts of dreams will repeat; numbers, images, or feelings, and you need to work out the message. What did you do to make a dream appear? What buttons were pushed to create the dream? See where the answers come from.

Upon waking ask yourself what is going on, be passive, what is coming into consciousness? I woke up with songs in my head and soon realised there was always a double letter in the songs sentence. So I set up a container for these letters, if it is A give me this letter, if it is B give me this letter. In this you are calibrating the language between you and your spirit. In devising your own language you need to be receiving clear feedback.

In the process of focusing heavily upon dreams it is highly probable you will have dreams of sacred temples, geometry, or ancient symbols. This is a sign you are on the right path, and these can be from past lives, information stored on your DNA, from the akasha, or your spirit. Focus upon these dreams in the daytime with more intensity and they should reappear with an associated story.

The whole reason to focus upon the dreamworld so much is to elevate the whole core being up into the realm of Yesod.

Vivid dreams of the past will appear as though they are the now. There will be more recollection in these dreams than your conscious mind can recall. This lends weight to the theory that time is not linear, and that all is recorded in a non-local plane or dimension.

On one occasion I was dreaming I was awake and then I woke up and found myself asleep.

"There is an old Chinese story of man who dreamed he was a butterfly and upon waking wondered if he is a butterfly dreaming he is a man."

Daytime Work

Each day there is much to do to keep your vibration rising steadily. We have a treasure-box of toys to help; Tarot, Unwritten Qabalah, Genesis and Revelations in the Bible, Gematria, The Emerald Tablet, third eye techniques, work with the elements, and the study of nature.

It is good to have a rough plan for the day, but mix this up every few days, and sometimes just spend a whole day in nature. If one sticks to a too rigid "routine" then stagnation will creep in.

Here is an example of a routine:

- Night time; record keywords to help remember dreams.
- Pre-sunrise; lucid dream techniques.
- Watch the sunrise, feel its essence.
- Astral travel techniques.
- Yoga asanas, then pranayama.
- Fruit, then cold shower.
- Meditation.
- Time in nature.
- Dream recollection, recording, and interpretation.
- Concentration and visualisation meditation.
- Emerald Table, Qabalah work, and *your* project or work.
- Candle meditation.
- Eat (before dark).
- Watch Sunset

- Meditation. After 30 minutes enter into pathworking, followed by Mantras.
- Tarot.
- Programme the coming nights dreams. Push the buttons.
- Candle meditation.
- Pore breathing as falling asleep.

Having an order in the day with stubborn techniques and exercises will help to kill the self. It allows little choice for the individual and the being is then working solely to constantly raise vibration.

Nietzsche said this "slave mentality" was a necessary discipline to unregenerate human nature; proud of its own ignorance and conceit. In this you will need patience, gratitude, and commitment. It is imperative you are grateful for this period in your life, hard work will come for sure but frustration will set you back. Gratitude and innocence will help you. You need joy along the path to witness joy at the summit.

With the concentration techniques it is intensity you are looking for; quality and not quantity. With your will forbidding certain thoughts for the duration of the process, it will enable conscious control over

the physical and mental constructs. This leads to a powerful current of will, and the previously troublesome ego lacking in concentration should become a caged hamster.

Another way to increase the will is every few days just stop what you are doing, stop. Hold your position, enforce the fact that the will is in command. The body will want comfort and the mind will want to think, but the new master of will is to be in control.

A programme like the above will lead to the fusing of conscious and subconscious minds, and you will subject this fused ball of intelligent energy to pure will. Push the boundaries, do not do only what is required; hold an asana for 2 minutes longer, hold the candle in the third eye for another 3 minutes, push it!

As you are building up eurekas, and realisations, don't let them come to fruition, build them up and then start to build another. This is a vital key.

It is hopeful that you are using the Merkaba process to gain insight into something that interests you. What do you want to see? What do you wish to gain? What are you doing to create vibrational and energetic foundations towards this?

It is wise to mix up the routine completely coming up to a full moon, planetary alignment, equinox, or solstice. This is because energy is much higher and we can align with it. A 3 to 5 day fast before a full moon will give your vibration a massive lift, especially if you expend physical energy while fasting (note: make sure you are hydrated with electrolytes or similar).

Near the end of the process you can perform some days "out of time," this is where you cease all of the routines and techniques and just be. If this is for you, you will know when the time comes. I performed five days out of time after 35 days, this included no yoga, eating, or anything that made me attached to the human vessel in any way.

Merkaba Rising

Welcome to the love filled Yesodic dreamworld.

Yesod has become your reality, your state, and Hod and Netzach have melted and dissolved with complete harmony into Yesod. You now have the capacity to watch the self because you are now in Yesod above Malkuth.

Just due to the process itself you will start to rise up the planes as your vibration increases. You will notice the auto-mechanics of the brain; the impulses, automatically going to get a drink, or going to toilet. See this, feel this, what is the source of these auto-mechanics? Behind this is a core essence and when you feel this, then cling to it, stroke it, and really be inside it.

You must keep resigning from the self, stop thinking and feeling from self-hood, and when the nervous system has adapted to the physiological changes, mystical experiences will come.

By now the layers of the self will have peeled away, and you can see them for what they were and how they were given energy. The personality is now passive, and the essence will become active. Consciousness will be more expanded and the range of frequencies you can tap into will be increasing.

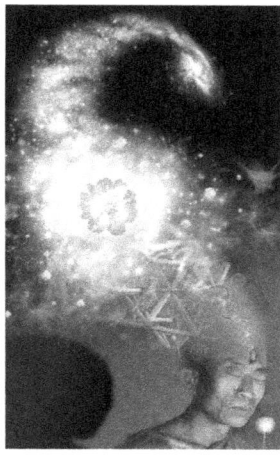

The world looks different and IS different and consciousness goes up the rungs. A different moral stance and self identity will soon come when you realise you have perceived the world through a broken hazy window.

By now words, language, and orthodox communication will have melted from your consciousness. It will maybe feel like there is no way back to what you were, you will be in "no man's land" and the only way to progress now is to use the forces, energies, and handles from the Sephiroth and Paths. The motivation to keep going is tohav4e a strong desire to find out just what that core essence within your life force and consciousness actually *is*, and what resides there.

You cannot go from an acorn to a forest in one hit, you have to go slowly and correctly from an acorn to an oak to feel the oneness of the forest. The stages are so important.

In the separating of dreams, sooner or later something will come from somewhere else, something poignant. This something is not from Malkuth, Netzach, or Hod. It will be subtle at first but it will be the sign that something is coming from Tipareth (your spirit). Think of this as a thread you have to pull, and soon this will become string, and then a rope. It is important to study this part of the dream and to push buttons to keep getting information and images from Tipareth repeating from this moment onwards.

It is a tightrope of sorts, we have our core being in Yesod, but we are climbing up towards Tipareth. We need to spin the wheel in the daytime, and make the correct foundations for Tipareth to spin the wheel too during the night time, this wheel needs to be spun faster and faster. The messages from Tipareth may also start to come in the daytime, and in a way of tests, and less information will come to you from Hod and Netzach.

So now you are at Yesod and starting to climb up to Tipareth by concentrating your consciousness upon messages, experiences, and tests coming from Tipareth. At this point you may not feel too much difference between day and night realities, it will start to merge and this is an important sign you are on the right track.

At this point perceive the daytime reality as a movie that consciousness perceives, and look at the dreamworld as a movie that consciousness perceives. View the only real truth as being that which is behind these; that core essence, the realm of pure spirit.

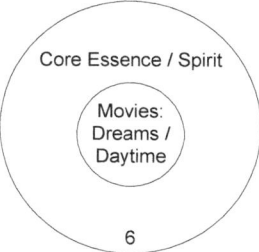

In effect, you have balanced and dissolved Hod and Netzach into Yesod, and then moved your being into Yesod. Then you have merged Malkuth into Yesod and started to step behind and above this "ball of energy" into Tipareth. From here you view this merged energy as illusory movies from the truth that exists in Tipareth.

At this time many synchronicities will start to come, even Carl Jung once said that "when one observes dreams over a long period of time, one sees outward events link. Both worlds coincide."

It may appear a little crazy as you start to merge with your spirit and enter Tipareth, but remember the Hanged Man in the 777 system and how it works. Just observe, be a warrior, and keep raising your vibration.

> "But I don't want to go among mad people," Alice remarked. "Oh, you can't help that," said the Cat, "We're all mad here. I'm mad. You're mad." "How do you know I'm mad?" said Alice. "You must be," said the Cat, "or you wouldn't have come here."

At this point you should have some near eurekas built up, and you will feel these as a force like a shield of spinning chaos all around your core being. This is the force of Chokmah, and The Emerald Tablet mentions this force too. This energy is strong and you will want to tap into it, but don't force it. Keep the clutch in and let it build for as much as you can. This is hard to explain but those in the zone will know what I mean, this is the Merkaba vehicle being prepared.

> "The middle name of chaos is opportunity."
> Terrence McKenna

The faster and more energy you build at this time the higher you will go. Think of it as an archer taking time over his aim as he pulls his bow more taught.

You do not want to project or force yourself over the veil, you wish to glide with serenity and mastery. Keep building the energy and seeking to align with it. Seek advice and signs in meditation and from the Tarot too.

What is being discussed here has links to a painting by the French James Tissot (1836-1902).

Following the deprivations in the wilderness, Jesus receives the care of angels who restore his strength. Rejecting art-historical traditions in which Jesus takes material sustenance in the form of dates and pomegranates, Tissot insists on otherworldly agency. Here blue-hued, flame-haired angels extend their fingers to touch the prostrate form of the spent Jesus, who appears to assume a cross-like position.

***

How much energy can you build, sustain, and manage?

You need to be the warrior; still, strategic, waiting patiently and knowingly. You need to be the magician: will with imagination, attached to the "out there" reality, with knowledge that Malkuth is empty of inanimate matter. You need to push the buttons to make things happen using universal laws, consciousness, and vibration.

The essence pouring into the being is sacred, and you need to have a sacred respect for it or you will not climb any higher. This essence is the spirit, your spirit, connected to all spirit, that which is rushing through humanity like water through a river.

When this essence is found and merged, memory and imagination are penetrated and inspired with the superb radiance of another superior nature. Inspiration will meet the aspiration.

When we see someone we love, we see things others can't see, the alchemist who has gone through this transformation has made a conscious decision to see the world this way. The adept sees how the world really works and this is hidden from the profane.

If the dweller upon the veil of Paroketh makes an appearance as it is prone too, you will need to accept the fear and to stand up knowing and declaring that "I AM." Realise it is only there to show you that you are not ready to pass yet. The following axioms; To Dare, To Know, To Will, and To Be Silent, can also bring you the command "To Go." I say no more on this matter as it is your quest alone to achieve.

The tightrope is getting thinner and thinner, and around this time you will pierce through the veil; you will know it, you will feel it, and words can do no justice to this experience.

"It is easier for a camel to pass through the eye of a needle, than for a rich man to enter into the kingdom of God."
The Gospel of Mark 10:25

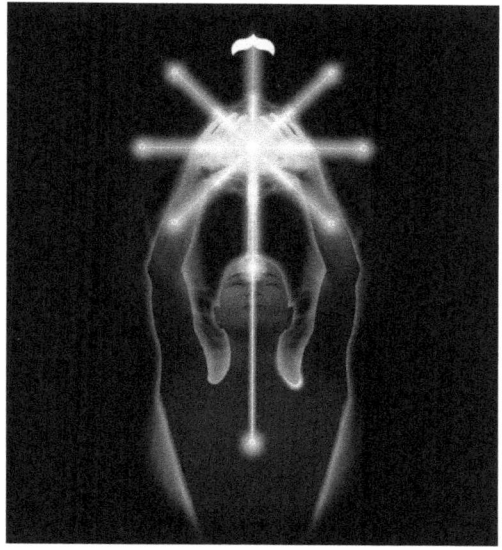

Risen

"As we go up the spheres, we get markers or stop signs, there are no short cuts. One rung at a time. The art takes man, strips him of all internal non-essentials and then penetrates into the soul...then the soul is cleaned and purified then the climb begins until it finds its sovereign lord, or union with the divine. Man, though still in a body, is lifted and elevated beyond the heavens entering a spiritual congress with the forces of the universe."

"The power of the macrocosm has manifest in the microcosm."

What was subtle at the start of the process has now become the dense, and just like water that has boiled you have now become the vapour. Dormant brain cells and DNA have now activated, and the Merkaba has risen. How far it goes is only up to the pilot.

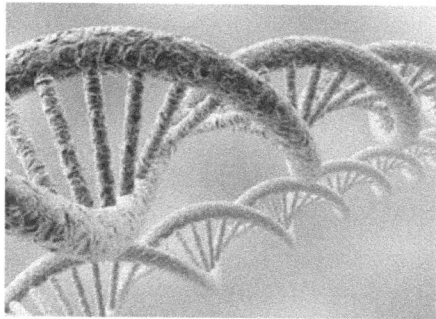

The Adeptus Minor ritual of the Hermetic Order of the Golden Dawn has an apt quote for this experience, "I have entered the invisible, I have passed through the gates of darkness to the light, I am a dweller of the invisible, let the white brilliance of the divine spirit descend."

You will feel linked to everything and melted into the essence of each life force. A flower, a thought, a sunrise, a meditation, each will pour into you with energy, and no longer will the realm of words and concepts be the focal part of your reality.

You have fallen in love with your spirit, merged via the chemical marriage, and you are in a love that you cannot experience with any person. This is a love amplified, a flower or tree or sunrise will stoke more love than any lover has, and this love in your essence is the love in each part of every life form. Your notions of male, female, top, bottom, inside, outside, heaven, earth, and back and front will have melted and vanished.

You are in your natural state, and though you can see it and touch your body, you will feel like pure energy with no edges. You will taste a divine nectar in your throat that runs down your spine, and a move of just a finger will feel like energy that can has the potential to create universes.

This illumination is when you don't just know but you really *feel* duality is an illusion and that the soul is infinite. Jubilation comes to the heart, as does lightness to the brain, and now the night is not the oblivion of sleep but one continuous flow of soul consciousness.

If invoking you will notice that though still human, through arcane symbols you are invested with the sacred forms from archetypal deity.

Time may warp and bend so much that you could suffer a bout of synaesthesia, this is a spatial perception of time. Also your vibration will be so high that you may not sleep for nights on end close to a full moon or celestial alignment. Vision and perception will be a rapture; an ecstasy which is beyond all human conception and speech. The soul is lifted up on high and senses things not lawful to tell, and you can see the true nature of life from a seed that is buried deep within each man. This seed now burns bright.

> *"My tongue lacks words, and what happens in me my spirit sees clearly but does not explain. It sees the invisible, that emptiness of all forms, simple throughout, not complex, and in extent infinite. For it sees no beginning, and it sees no end. It is entirely unconscious of the meanings, and does not know what to call that which it sees. Something complete appears, it seems to me, not indeed through the being itself, but through a participation. For you enkindle fire from fire, and you receive the whole fire; but this remains undiminished and undivided, as before. Similarly, that which is divided separates itself from the first; and like something corporeal spreads itself into several lights. This, the path of the visible Gods will appear through the sun, the God my father. It is not separated when it becomes many, but remains undivided, and it is in me, and rises in my poor heart like a sun or circular disk of the sun, like light, for it is light."*
> Symeon, the New Theologian (970-1040)

The love force in here is so massive and so strong that most of your philosophies will dissolve and melt, and you see Qabalah only as the guiding vehicle for bringing you here. Revel in it, feel it, experiment, but don't get lost blissing out for you need to use this state you have worked so hard to get to. Start to look at the big picture; philosophise, record, look at flow trajectories, study eurekas, channel information, and glimpse your destiny. You cannot stop the flow of the species trajectory but you may find out where to place a few rocks to help the flow.

All great initiates can see spirits plans for humanity and help the flow, and the door is now open to a higher knowledge of the world; the species, and your place within the story. Chase this information down by using Tipareth, by invoking your favorable archetypes, and via the Yesodic dream reality.

Depending on how purified you have become, and how much karmic baggage you have evaporated or transcended, the books of knowledge may be opened to you.

You may need to prove yourself worthy once more if you have any fight left in you, and my only advice if you get this far is to place your being within sacredness, gratitude, and innocence. The sacred books may be glimpsed upon, and the help of those from the higher planes may also have messages for you. Use this time.

"When the Spirit of truth comes, he will guide you into all truth. He will not speak on his own but will tell you what he has heard. He will tell you about the future."
The Gospel of John 16:13

You are more in the spirit world than that of the human design.

"The word of God is living and active and sharper than any two-edged sword, and cuts so deeply it divides the soul from the spirit."
Hebrews 4:12

I will share some of my experience in this state, but each human will experience it differently. I felt pure union, but the word union was not in my consciousness because it was further than that. The word conjures a few conceptions and perceptions, but in this state I *was* union. The word was non-existent. For instance, the essence in all life was not separate from what I actually was, and the essence of everything was not separate either, and all was born from love and painted with a sublime sacredness.

I really knew who and what I was, and I saw and understood all of the events in my lifxe with crystal clarity and humor; but I no longer made myself the centre of the stories sphere because I did not exist. All things were alike as shadows sweeping across the still surface of a lake, their images had no meaning for the water, no power to stir its silence.

Thought streams and reality dynamics would spin into beautiful fractals within my being, and I would float and glide amongst these.

These fractals and waves of electromagnetic energy would only subside when a eureka or realisation would jump through my being as though the force of a universe creating a singularity was within it.

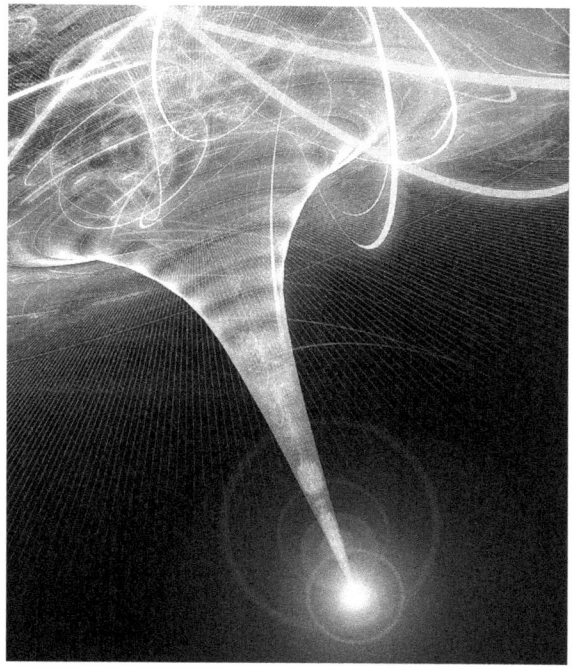

Everything was communicative via energy, electromagnetics, geometry, mind, and the Qabalah Tree of Life. At one point I thought there may be no way back to the human design state I had spent 32 years in before, but I did not care, I had so much energy, clarity, vision and flow, that thoughts of what was normal or socially accepted just did not matter.

I tuned into an individual rhythm of sleep, dreams, urges, feelings, and I surfed the flow. Thoughts were living beings whose carnations, durations, and causes were all under my guile. They would spark into life and weave in and around me in an ancient sense of wonder. I could project to other people and feel their energy and thoughts. I could feel nature as though it was inside me; it's sacred relentless request for expression, growth, survival, and multiplication was immense and in the energy everywhere. This moment is summed up well in 'The Vigil of St Hubert' in Crowley's *Book of Lies*:

In the forest God met the Stag-beetle. "Hold! Worship me!" quoth God. "For I am All-Great, All-Good, All Wise....The stars are but sparks from the forges of My smiths...." "Yea, verily and Amen," said the Stag-beetle, "all this do I believe, and that devoutly." "Then why do you not worship Me?" "Because I am real and your are only imaginary." But the leaves of the forest rustled with the laughter of the wind. Said Wind and Wood: "They neither of them know anything!"

I was ingesting only liquefied fruit and vegetables, and at one point I could still here a voice from within saying "I want a larger orange, how much longer before the next vegetable juice drink?" This last voice of desire had to be killed, so I placed myself on a water diet mixed with Grade B syrup and cayenne pepper. This pushed my vibration even higher as this removed all hunger from the vessel.

I could feel the solar system grinding and spinning, all of it. I could feel the moon in motion, its position relative to the sun, and for sunrise and sunset I could feel the earth spinning and the energy of light. The celestial energies were open to me, or I could say that my energy was open to them. Words just cannot describe.

The ecstasy of this silence is deafening as one returns to the source of it all. Every day I would lie down on the earth and feel and bind with the sun passing at the highest point in the sky.

I would feel this from my soul and connect to our nearest star in a way that made me understand all of the Sun Gods throughout the millennia. The Hymns to Aten from ancient Egypt could only have been written and truly felt in this state of consciousness.

Reality was bending, I was seeing visions and having dreams that were more real than real life; I was in ceremonies in the astral dreamworld where I was being initiated and taught.

Some days I felt like I had taken ayahuasca, I would have memories from the past come that were so present it was untrue, and I was receiving so much humor from my spirit it made me cry on more than one occasion.

I felt a soft warm control over the elements and I was able to harness energy from the sun, stars, planets, and weather.

Then one day the person who guided me into this state came to me. He would come every few days and shout from a few metres away to inquire into my wellbeing. This day was different. I didn't want any contact, I was flying, I was in bliss, I was collecting more information than an office workers computer during a lunchtime download spree.

"Mark, today you are going to the city." I shook my head in surprise and sent the energy to him that said "no way Mr, with love but no way." In the state I was inm a City would be dangerous to my vibration, and the whole process. What was he on?

"Treat it as a dream" he said. "No way"...but two more hours of convincing me I was in the back of a car, placing my feet through the floor of Tipareth to slip back into Yesod. I had completely forgotten about the ego, falsity, and the folly of a city on our planet, and the state I was currently in was far from conducive. I placed my consciousness into dreamworld mode, and my guide gave me handles, caveats, and techniques to help me through this one hour visit.

His knowing smile parted as he said, "Just wait and see." His eyes shone pure light and wonder, and I said to myself "this really is going a bit too far," but I have always like to push it and my curiosity pushed me onwards.

For the duration of the one hour journey I was to keep my eyes closed and meditate.

The agreement was that I would sit on a bench alone in the centre of Antigua in Guatemala for one hour, and then he would walk up to me and take me back up the volcano. It was dicey, in his previous five merkaba processes he had done the city experience only three times, but each time with amazing results. I felt like I was going on a mission to earth as an alien guinea pig. I felt great though and I was more excited than a four year old at Christmas. Bear in mind I had not left the volcanic shack area in over sixty odd days.

I sat on the bench in the city, opened my eyes, and tuned into the present moment. I could feel everything, it was information overload but in smooth waves. I couldn't so much see people as a human normally does, I saw waves, streams, and currents of electromagnetic. I could see auras and feel them. It was a thick beautiful syrupy soup of energy and my aura and being was expanding out for about fifty metres in each direction. I concentrated to find my centre.

In the harmonious play of "normal life" I could see and feel all of the attraction, retraction, pull, push, play, that arose from all of the individual energy centres (humans). I was awe struck, it was so colourful. I could read a whole person, the story, mood, quest, truth, and letups. Everything.

I got brave and after twenty minutes I decided to go for a walk. All of the people were gliding upon a layer of harmonic geometrical mathematics. I started to feel people stray a little bit out of my way, whether this was really happening physically or just on an energetic level I cannot recall. I remember seeing people's eyes meet, and I felt their souls connect and trade information so that the collective electromagnetic soup was fueled and creation could progress and deepen.

The chaos and rhythm was beautiful, I saw synchronisities burst open like the meeting of universes, these were synchronisities that would of appeared so small or even nonexistent to those scurrying the streets in "normal" mode, but I could see them, feel them, and watch them.

I felt in this colossal scurry the auric eggs hunting for money, value, survival, self worth, respect, and the receiving of love. Running pretty far in the wrong directions with no traces of gratitude or devotion. I turned a corner and on someones T-shirt was a whole message that I dreamed about the night before, the missing part. I just smiled and carried on walking, trying to walk, trying to breath, trying not to keel over or fly away.

I sat back down and someone who I had never met came to me and showed me a movie on his mobile that had massive links to some dream work I had been doing. I had not told anyone about this dream construct and this was purely my spirit at play, showing me how things can manifest in our reality. I walked again and gained a smile from of an attractive female, this felt like the whole of Binah coming into my Chokmah chaos and some sort of holy trinity meeting in a divine ecstatic rapture. Wow, this brought new images to my mind, they darted in with the I being passive. It was the hard coding on my DNA being used; the coding linked to reproduction, the same as the plants and flowers looking to multiply.

I really cannot intellectualise this hour of my life, all I can really say is that the divination in the perfection of it all shone forth, and this is the virtue of Tipareth. All was unified energy and light. This is all at play ALL of the time but we are cut off from it due to the veil, the norms, and the vibration of society in 2010.

I went back to the volcano and processed my hour in the city just as I was processing my dreams. It fitted into my dreams as though it was a dream, and to my mind it actually was a dream. In the state I was in both Malkuth and Yesod were a single merged ball of energy on the horizon as I looked from Tipareth.

For the rest of my process I worked on turning myself into a Qabalistic precognitive to gain a glimpse of the trajectory of the species. During this time all I could feel and know was that I was an infinite soul in a beautiful sacred creation placed so we can express, love, learn and evolve. I am in truth an eternal spark of oneness within the cosmic mind.

***

"We live in illusion and the appearance of things. There is a reality. We are that reality. When you understand this, you see that you are nothing, and being nothing, you are everything. That is all."
Buddhist Quote

"In him is an illimitable abyss of glory, and from it there goeth forth in one little spark which maketh all the glory of the sun, and of the moon, and of the stars. Mortal! Behold how little I know of God; Seek not to know more of Him, for this is far beyond thy comprehension, however wise thou art; as for us, who are His ministers, how small a part are we of Him!"
Pat Zalewski Quoting an ancient oracle, Kabbalah of the Golden Dawn

"But your holy place shall be untouched throughout the centuries: though with fire and sword it be burned down and shattered, yet an invisible house there standeth, and shall stand until the fall of the great equinox."
Liber Al Vel Legis. The Book of the Law.

In this state you must use this time, this may be your only chance within lifetimes so use it. What can you glean from being a human being in this state? If you need even more fuel to rise you being, work on the following in meditation:

How does consciousness function? What is the absolute? Why does oneness have such diverse variations? Moments of time come out of the future and then move into the present and then into the past, how? What is a place? Where are places? What is open space?

You need to overcome the fascination with your consciousness being so different, don't lose too much time blissing out with the fractals, geometry, and reality bending. Work hard, this is a rare place to be.

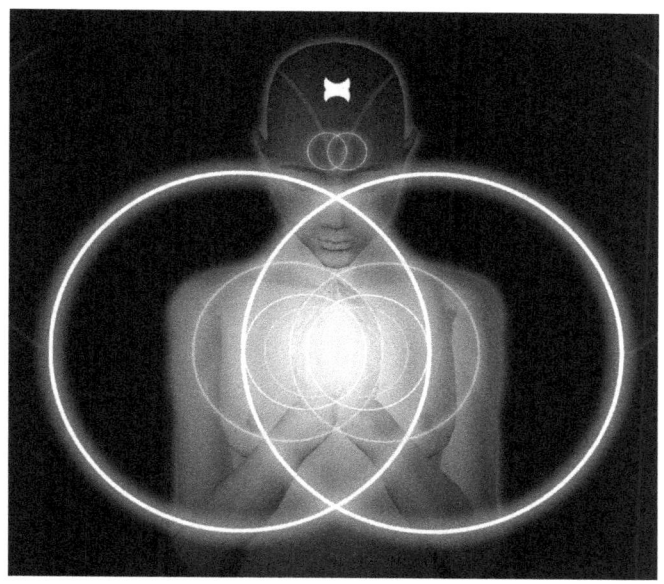

"To see a world in a grain of sand, and a heaven in a wild flower, hold infinity in the palm of your hand, and eternity in an hour."
Blake

"And following it my spirit demanded to embrace the splendor beheld, but it found it not as creature and did not succeed incoming out from among created beings, so that it might embrace that uncreated and uncomprehended splendor. Nevertheless it wandered everywhere, and strove to behold It. Penetrated the air, it wandered over the Heavens, it crossed over the abysses, it searched, as it seemed to it, the ends of the world." But in all of that it found nothing, for all was created. And I lamented and was sorrowful, and my breast burned, and I lived as one distraught in mind. But it came, as it would, and descending like a luminous mystic cloud, it seemed to envelop my whole head so that dismayed I cried out. But flying away again it left me alone. And when I, troubled, sought for it, I realized suddenly that it was in me, myself, and in the midst of my heart it appeared as the light of a spherical sun!"
Symeon the Theologian in a letter to H. Schar.

Descent

You may not want to, you may fight for reasons to stay, but you will need to come back. Why? Because here is where the work is, and you need to switch your mindset and desire to descend.

Zen Buddhism has a saying, "before enlightenment, mountains are mountains and rivers and rivers. With enlightenment, mountains are no longer mountains and rivers are no longer rivers. After enlightenment, mountains are once again mountains and rivers are once again rivers."

It is best to allow a few days for descent as this time is very delicate. How you descend can affect your energy for months, or even years to come. The best way is to move your core-being slowly from Chokmah chaos to Binah, therefore you need to start absorbing information; reading, talking, and ingesting light information is like lead weight to your balloon. Stop processing dreams, and spend time near other energies. Enter into very light communication with those who have some sort of understanding towards what you have just gone through. Write, reflect, but clamber down from the signs, visions, and messages, and focus consciousness behind each of the five sense receivers. Eat heavier food and also eat before sleep.

Most importantly wrap up all loose ends from your process, there will be some, but some of these you are to carry forth with you. Some of the information you received in this process you will not understand now, but I can assure you there will be times in your future when the jigsaw piece will fit. Wrap these items up into a small box; write them down and close them out into summary form so that your consciousness can "move on." As life goes on you will sometimes get dreams that you will know are related to this process, or have come from your spirit, this is such a gift that you have now earned.

Slowly venture out of your space, move your vessel into the world, speak to friends and do some logistical things, things humans "normally" do - this will help you descend smoothly and quickly. Do not divulge too many of your sacred or profound experiences as you will disipate energy faster than you can believe. If you keep what you found sacred within you, it will hold all of the glory for the rest of your days. Remember Corinthians 2:14; "The man without the Spirit does not accept the things that come from the Spirit of God, for they are foolishness to him, and he cannot understand them, because they are spiritually discerned."

You will feel like an essence in a human vessel space suit, and awe for how you can change reality by using free will to focus energy towards certain events, people, expressions, and dynamics. It all seems so amazing....because it is! What a gift!

You need to come back balanced and earthed upon the earth, but also able to connect to the stars. You will never fully descend for the rest of this carnation but you will be 'longer' so to speak; more grounded and more tuned in to subtle energies.

When you go to places you have been to before, especially those from your childhood, it may feel like a past life. You will feel the residual energy and stoked memory constructs, but you will be more the observer and feel the surrounding stories so much more. It will be more impartial.

When I went to my first major city after my descent I could still notice synchronicities and energy, and this still continues to this day. Now though I can control to an extent the level of the input I collect from this energy. In this city I could feel the energy behind the corporate advertising attempting to throw grenades into my subconscious, I could feel the unnatural light of the indoors, and feel the energy of the masses scurrying after money and survival whilst ingesting toxic energy in a myriad of forms. Humanity was living in a narrow percentage construct of what it could actually live like. I was shocked.

This is not the way humanity is supposed to live I felt.

I looked into the window of a Pizza fast food restaurant, I saw plastic furniture amidst ghastly painful lighting, sharp lines, edges and corners, people in uniforms only there for money, a large flat screen television on the wall showing a movie with violence, and small groups thinking they are having a treat by entering this environment and eating the poor unhealthy food. I could feel the wrongness of it all, the profit, the subconscious lies to get people to enter. I felt sick, but I laughed and remembered that it is here in Malkuth where the work is, and where the changes are soon to come.

***

So what did I take away from my process?

The knowledge that we actually live in Yesod all of the time and that Malkuth is an illusion. That we come into this electromagnetic field as karmic energy, an iron filing, and we are a consequence of that which we are, from actions and reactions.

Events are connected to everything, nothing is in isolation, and it is our minds that divide, and create separate events. All is a part of the whole totality, the natural flow, but we only see the fragment so don't understand the flow. We don't actually need to "do," we just need to let the light and life force flow through us and adjust with subtlety and grace, for we are all a unique expression of the all.

I have long stopped living under the irrational untrue laws of accidents, luck, and coincidences, and have become centered in the flows within flows. In here there are no hindrances, but plenty of markers and signs to feel, and all became simpler. For instance if you keep bumping into someone or repeating an event or pattern then there is something there to learn and evolve from.

I realised that all the negativity that I project onto another human being, or any given situation, is nothing other than my own psychology mirrored back at me. Truly understanding this has made me realise that there is nothing to be gained from criticising anyone or anything, and if I do want to live my life as I believe it should be lived, conscious negative focus has to come to an end.

Some of us have more free will than others as some have a stronger set trajectory, but for all of us the illusion of separation is a mirror so we can evolve; 3D reality is free feedback for what we are putting out and where we are in our stage in evolution.

All we can do is merge with our full potential archetype and create positivity and growth in this theatrical stage, and never take anything too seriously.

Every thought, plan, action, and reaction is recorded, and every tiny aspect in your life from a near accident, a fly on your cup, to a chance encounter is for a reason based upon harmonious electromagnetic flow. Everything we do stirs up a corresponding energy in other realms of reality. Actions, words, and thoughts set up reverberations in the universe.

> "Everything you have seen, every flower, every bird, every rock will pass away and turn to dust, but that you have seen them will not pass away".

Recently researchers proved that over ninety percent of DNA's function is not in protein synthesis but in the realm of bioelectric signaling, and that the heart generates the strongest rhythmic electromagnetic field in the body. We are an electromagnetic expression of our highest cognitive function.

***

I realised that life is *how* we look at things, and not *what* we are looking at, *how* you connect with things and not *what* you are connected to. Appearances are very deceptive in all things and it is the effects the perceived object has on *you* that matters and not the *appearance* of the object. The truth is that it is mental imagery that modifies your world, especially when these images are expressed in sound vibrations (known as words and speech to most).

Integral alignment is important for the whole being to function too, congruent alignment between your heart, soul, thoughts, words, feelings, decisions, and actions. Just one of these out of sync with the others creates disharmony within the electromagnetic field.

I remember sitting on a rock for two days staring at a tree and its surroundings after a 6 day silence with the Sefer Yetzirah. I felt that the tree cared not for observers. It just wanted to be the best tree it could possibly be. It was humble and beautiful and was aligned with its purpose and potential tremendously.

I remember overhearing some people chatting and I had a massive realisation that it is nonsensical to speak unless it improves upon the silence. For silence is not no-thing, communication is always occurring, people attract through energy; it is how one feels when one is close to or within another's aura. Attraction and union occurs in nature all of the time with no noise, it is the same for all living things.

Emotions remind us of the beauty of being human, when emotions run high this is where we feel we are alive more than other times. To be a master of emotions and to still feel them with all you can is one of the best goals within life.

The moment I develop any sort of belief system I leave the moment, the place where wisdom exists. Therefore to remain outside the hypnosis state I must not become emotionally connected to the thoughts intellectually implanted within, or build a belief structure. There's no need for a belief structure as wisdom knows all things. As we watch and wait, we reconnect to this unlimited knowing, and in watching and waiting, we can reclaim our eternal paradise state.

"You have merged the many into the naught, then when you are again in the many, you know it is just the naught acting as the many. You will see man in his folly and allow."

"Compassions sees the one as the many, wisdom sees the many as one."

It really was a rebirthing experience, and I can still tune into the astral plane on occasion and glimpse energies and information. I will now always be conscious that other life exists in dreams and after death, and I completely understand one may need to go there and feel it to believe it.

After my descent I forever feel nature as the crispy and solid, and the cities are now as spongy floppy cartoons of falsehood.

I now strongly feel that we are only here to evolve the soul and only once this is achieved do we stop coming back and transcend to a higher frequency. This planet is such a gift though because due to its density and separation the karmic history of the soul can be rebalanced.

Every human being can easily purify, intensify, control, and then set to work the love-force in their being. Then the comments from the Gospel of Thomas start to ring true, "The Father's kingdom is spread out upon the earth and people don't see it."

I am so grateful that I tore myself away from the safe comfort of certainties to seek truth, for truth rewarded me. For me there are only two mistakes one can make along the road to truth; not going all the way, and not starting.

"There is no more "I think I am" or "I think I can," there is only I am, I can, this is what I see, this is what I feel, this is how I know."

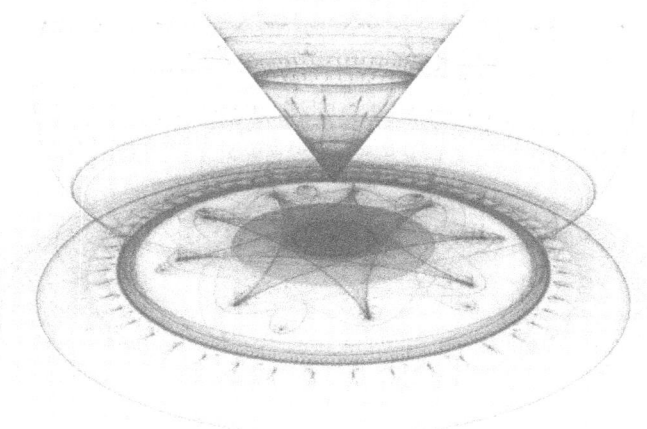

Evolution & Change – Part II

In the fifty days theory before commencing my Merkaba I had an idea based upon tests done with ESP (extra sensory perception). Tests from people watching films have shown that people laugh or are shocked a split second before the catalyst actually happens. I found that ESP exists and is very real.

During the theory days I placed my consciousness within centuries by studying history, timelines, large events, and epochs. The idea was that when the Merkaba was raised I could grab a "split second" glimpse of time to come, but as a fractal this would be "years" because this was where my consciousness was placed. I theorised that to know the future one needed to know past, and if today is a consequence of yesterday then tomorrow is a consequence of today. Therefore, if one knew the past hundreds and thousands of years of humanity very well, then one could use the Merkaba to project a glimpse into the future.

It was worth a shot.

Deep in my mode of being a "Qabalistic Precognitive" within my Merkaba much information was given to me. Early on I had a dream that was more real that the reality we "normally" live in where a shaman gave me a potion and then as I watched fractal geometry he told me that my information would come in my dreams. I awoke with my heart pounding and my core being vibrating like crazy.

Soon my Merkaba was spinning, and from hereon in I had many reoccurring dreams and vision shown to me in Tipareth whilst my vessel was asleep, or in sleep paralysis. They were repeated and shown to me many different ways so I fully "got the message." The most vivid of these were:

- Tsunamis, floods, and sea level rises.
- The end of money.
- The end of the Internet.
- The end of TV and celebrity,
- The end of commercial air travel.
- Social panic, bit needed chaos before clam serenity.
- People scrambling to get to places in a "last chance."
- High up and floating communities.

In all of this there was no fear or sadness because of the way these were presented to me. All was with so much love and humour and those who have taken ayahuasca will understand this humour.

I felt a massive sense of ease and impartialness, a very real nurtured feeling of a natural flow and that everything is naturally unfolding. Whether these visions were an allegorical representations is open to interpretation, but one should take into account the solar, earthquake and volcanic activity at present maybe.

This much is certain, the water bearer of Aquarius is ready to pour.

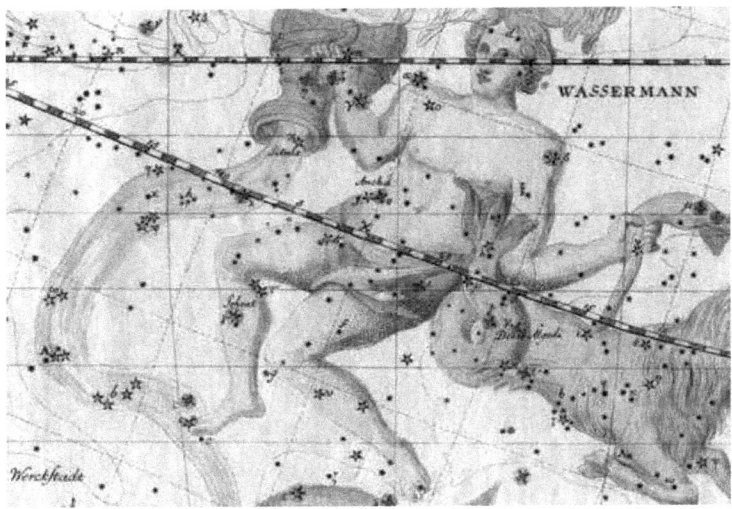

On my last day of the Merkaba I wrote the following, it includes some allegory for those with the eyes and ears.

The pendulum is about to swing back according to law five, earth cannot and will not take it much longer....the way humans live is just not sustainable. It seems humanity will get another chance as the saving grace is that all humans deep down love love, this gives us hope.

The ancients around the world point to this time as a time of change, but the worldwide disease of believing THIS lifetime is the only one with no looking forward or back ensures the majority see prophets as a nonsense, and profits as THE REALITY.

Four white dragons from a larger brotherhood are here, they have been for a long time, they hear and feel every thought, action and reaction from our species, their time is soon. When they manifest; one brown, one green, one blue and one red, they will show little mercy, and the green dragon will show the most Ferocity and soar the highest. All four will hunt those worshiping the pinnacle of false idols.

Those closest to the land will rise the highest and prepare to rain down the seeds for another cycle of life.

The flow of our species is akin to a tree, but there are new branches growing, and the dead wood at the top is about to be cut; Chokmah is issuing a new pulse and Kamiel is ready with his sword.

Rejoice, don't be alarmed, wave to the dragons, hail them, we are lucky enough to be here to witness the catalyst for the change, we don't need to posses SO surrender.

Fear is normal but courage is a choice, pain is normal and IS TO be FELT with an untroubled mind. For those cut off from loved ones, use the new email....hold them in mind and send love.

Find your kin, find your tribe, collect wisdom, refrain from dense populous and be a rock, a beacon admist the chaos and confusion coming.

Events could occur sooner than later due to the two spheres seen between aleph and beth, but look to our life giving sun as it hurtles through the outer rim of our galaxy, smile, breath, feel, and THEN you will know deep in your soul it is the way it needs to be, and geometrical perfection is leading our path.

Since my Merkaba process (a year ago now) I still get some strong messages within dreams; I have seen two earthquakes in locations that came to pass only a few days later, and seen Australia near the north pole and the sun rising in the west.

***

The only way forward is if man overcomes his current ills and realigns with natural harmonics of the planet, this is not going to happen with the current status quo, so the earth and the divine are stepping in.

Confusion is coming, noise is coming, the world is on the precipice of some very large changes and it is so important that we are able to maintain silence and stillness within to become beacons to help smooth the coming times.

Many would deem these times coming as chaotic, but it is essentially a time to rejoice. The world will come sustainable again and no more will man be robbed of his wealth, health, freedom, and energy. The sad, centralised, globalised, monopolised and privatised money system will become a tragic relic of history. We can embrace a new paradigm where not only three percent of the population benefit. We are divine beings and divine beings need nobody to rule them. It is only matrix programming that will jump in and say that cannot be possible.

Many will perish from these changes but in truth this will all part of the natural harmonious flow. It's okay, it's progressive, embrace the fact that the earth will become sustainable for the human species once more. It's just a cycle and akin to a diseased ant hill being washed away where many innocent perish. We are infinity and there is no end times for infinite beings. During the changes float like an angel but keep your being rooted deep in the earth, this type of solidity will be called upon greatly.

> *"You just have to love the eye of the tornado... not care too much about the chaotic wind... just love from within the calm heart."*
> Eric Gauthier, friend and author.

The cutting down of forests for profit and 'owning' parts of the earth based upon a rulers conquests centuries before will be looked upon as nonsense. It will be a time for celebration.

Before the changes we will see the last throws of the dice by the elite. Toxic controlled food, the manipulated media, and the controlling central banks will tighten their grip in a childish panic. How strong is your determination? Can you endure the night while you wait for the dawn?

In the mean time what can one do? Don't try and heal a broken system, walk away and help to create a healthy system. Let the last throws of the dice play out for the falling globalisation monster. Take no interest in the beast and act and operate outside the box, because the box is collapsing.

If you are fighting symptoms of the beast by "weed pruning" then ask yourself if it more productive to help create the conditions for new beautiful new flowers to grow. Weeds die on their own if they are not watered and don't have the right soil. To keep trying to mend at the symptom level is like trying to catch all the drops from the waterfall. Is it better to help a starving orphan or to awaken a hundred students about to enter into centralized banking? I know my answer.

It is during the coming changes that the Merkaba process can help to settle the times humanity will be living in. This is ultimately why this book was written.

***

We are evolving, time is evolving, reality is evolving and when it all coalesces the fireworks are sure to be magnificent.

Post the changes the initiation of young men will return, living in harmony with the abundance of the earth will return, and children will learn more naturally and never stop learning. This planet will be seen as a university for creators in training.

It will not be about searching for, or finding love, but merely releasing and peeling away the barriers within ourselves that we have built up against love, the future will can then only be a paradise. Love is an energy we can just tap into at a moments notice.

It is above the personal love which loves a person, it is a higher manifestation of love which itself is love and loves no person or thing but is a state of consciousness in which all is embraced.

Congruence in feeling, thought, word and action is the only thing that creates human integrity.

Be a positive force in the immediate environment.

Light doesn't flee from darkness; it dispels it.

Here's to the crazy ones. The misfits. Rebels. Troublemakers. Round heads in square holes. Ones who see things differently. Not fond of rules, they have no respect for status-quo. You can quote them, disagree, glorify, or vilify them. But you can't ignore them. They change things. Some see them as the crazy ones, we see ...genius. Because people crazy enough to think they can change the world, are the ones who do.

> *"What we now want is closer contact and better understanding between individuals and communities all over the earth, and the elimination of egoism and pride.....peace can only come as a natural consequence of universal enlightenment."*
> *Nikola Tesla 1919*

If only a few people throughout the world find themselves and enter into a hallowed communion with the very source of life, then they because of their illumination become the wick of humanity and cast a respondent and glorious aurole of gold over the universe. In those individuals who constitute a minute, almost microscopic minority of the populace of this globe, willing and eager to devote themselves to a spiritual integral, and truthful cause, lies the only hope for the ultimate redemption of mankind.

Our reality is only a virtual reality to evolve the soul.

For all of the now moments experienced by humanity on this planet within this reality, forever will it be that Truth, Philosophy, and Hermetic Alchemical Qabalah make up **The Trinity of Wisdom**.

Bibliography

A Brief History of Everything - Ken Wilber
A Depth of Beginning - Colin Lowe
A Little Book of Coincidence: in the Solar System - John Martineau
A Practical Guide to Qabalistic Symbolism Vol1 & Vol2 - Gareth Knight
Alchemical Allegories - Bill Harran
Alchemy: Ancient and Modern - Stuart Nettleton
Alchemy: The Science of Enlightenment - Arion Love
An introduction to the Study of the Kaballah - Wynn Westcott
Anatomy of the spirit - Caroline Myss
Astral Dynamics - Robert Bruce
Astrology, Psychology, and the Four Elements - Stephen Arroyo
Corpus Hermetica - Various Translations
Desire Came Upon That One in the Beginning - Barbara Mikolajewska
Developmental Theories - Sigmund Freud
Elements of the Qabalah - Eliphas Levi
Emanation and Ascent in Hermetic Kabbalah - Colin Lowe
Formation of the Tree of Life - Patrick Mulcahy
Golden Dawn Hermetic Timeline
Hermeticism: Rise and Fall of an Esoteric System - John Nash
IlluminatiMATRTIX
In Search of the Miraculous - P.D. Ouspensky
Infinite Self - Stuart Wilde
Initiation into Hermetics - Franz Bardon
Kaballah of the Golden Dawn - Pat Zalewski
Kundalini Tantra - Swami Satyananda Saraswati
Kundalini Yoga - Sri Swami Sivananda
Liber 500 - Aleistair Crowley
Liber 777 - Aleistair Crowley
Liber LVIII - Aleistair Crowley
Numbers, Their Occult Power and Mystic Virtues - Wynn Westcott
Origins of Christian Kabbalah - John Nash
Out of Body Experiences - Robert Peterson
Power Versus Force: The Hidden Determinants of Human Behavior - David Hawkins

Prometheus Rising - Robert Anthony Wilson
Psychology and Alchemy Vol12 - Carl Jung
Qabalistic Tarot - Robert Wang
Rosa Alchemica - W.B. Yeats
Rosicrucian and Masonic Origins - Manly P Hall
Sacred Path of the Warrior - Chogyam Trungpa
Secrets of the Exodus, Did the Pharaohs Write the Bible? Messod and Roger Sabbah
Sefer Yetzirah - Various Translations
Serpent in the Sky - John Anthony West
Seven Hermetic Letters - Dr. Georg Lomer
Skrying on the Tree of Life - Chic Cicero, Sandra Tabatha Cicero
Symbolism - Manly P Hall
The 7 Laws of Spiritual Success - Deepak Chopra
The Alchemy Key - Stuart Nettleton
The Art and Meaning of Magic - Israel Regardie
The Atlantis Blueprint – Colin Wilson and Rand Flem-Ath
The Aurora of the Philosophers - Paracelsus
The Bible - King James Version
The Book of Lies - Aleistair Crowley
The Book of the Secrets of Enoch - Unknown
The Dead Sea Scrolls Deception - Michael Baigent and Richard Leigh
The Emerald Tablet - Various Translations
The Equinox - Various - Aleistair Crowley
The Four Agreements - Don Miguel Ruiz
The Golden Chain of Homer - Anton Josef Kirchweger
The Golden Section: Nature's Greatest Secret - Scott Olsen
The Golden Tractate of Hermes Trismegistus - Unknown
The Great Art - Antoine-Joseph Pernety
The Hermetic Arcanum - Translated by Elias Ashmole
The Hermetic Museum - Arthur Waite
The Jesuit Enigma - E. Boyd Barett
The Kaballah Unveiled - McGregor Mathers
The Key of the Mysteries - Eliphas Levi
The Kybalion - The Three Initiates
The Magical Mason - Wynn Westcott
The Mirror of Alchemy - Roger Bacon

The Mystical Qabala - Dion Fortune
The New Hermetics - Jason Augustus Newcomb
The Origins of the Mithraic Mysteries -David Ulansey
The Paradoxes of the Highest Science - Eliphas Levi
The Philosophers Stone – Israel Regardie
The Pictorial Symbols of Alchemy - Arthur Waite
The Prophecies of Paracelsus - Translated by J.K.
The Rosicrucian Manifestos - Unknown
The Rosie Crucian Secrets - John Dee
The Secret Book of Artephius
The Secret History of the World - Jonathan Black
The Secret Teachings of All Ages - Manly P Hall
The Secret Terrorists and the unmasked enemy - Bill Hughes
The Secret Wisdom of the Qabalah - J.F.C. Fuller
The Six Keys of Eudoxus
The Stone of the Philosophers - Edward Kelly
The Training and Work of an Initiate - Dion Fortune
The Tree of Life - Israel Regardie
The Universe in a Nutshell - Stephen Hawkin
The Way of the Superior Man - David Deida
The Yoga of Jesus - Paramahansa Yogananda
Twelve Keys - Basil Valentine
With Mystics and Magicians in Tibet - Alexandra David-Neel

***

Image Credits:

Page 11, Bruno Gori
Page 66, agyaatdarshan.wordpress.com
Page 73, www.tashimannox.com
Page 88, grinagog @ deviantart
Page 93, teakster @ deviantart
Page 100, www.mondolithic.com
Page 101, Collin Cunningham
Page 103, Gary B. Meisner, www.goldennumber.net
Page 129, Roger von Oech, www.creativethink.com

Page 167, www.mahavajra.be, www.hermeticsoft.com
Page 268, M. Schoenman
Page 309, The Great Temple, under copyright of Andre Surya
Page 317, www.staffordstone.com
Page 318, Alexander Dunton @ http://pathworking.deviantart.com/
Page 319, The late Johfra Bosschart
Page 323, www.mondolithic.com
Page 329, Alexander Dunton @ http://pathworking.deviantart.com/
Page 330, Mattijn Franssen
Page 334, xmandypandy @ deviantart.com
Page 336, Sean Davey, www.seandavey.com

Lightning Source UK Ltd.
Milton Keynes UK
UKHW040744060519
342177UK00003B/1240/P